THE GREATEST DECISIONS ...EVER!

HISTORY'S BIGGEST IDEAS

AND THE PEOPLE WHO MADE THEM

METRO BOOKS
New York

An Imprint of Sterling Publishing Co., Inc.
1166 Avenue of the Americas
New York, NY 10036

ISBN 978-1-4351-6465-9

For information about custom editions, special sales, and premium and corporate
purchases, please contact Sterling Special Sales at 800-805-5489
or specialsales@sterlingpublishing.com.

Manufactured in China

2 4 6 8 10 9 7 5 3 1

www.sterlingpublishing.com

Editorial & Design by Tall Tree

[THE GREATEST DECISIONS ...EVER!

HISTORY'S BIGGEST IDEAS
AND THE PEOPLE WHO MADE THEM

BILL PRICE

METRO BOOKS
New York

CONTENTS

INTRODUCTION

In another book in this series, *The Worst Decisions Ever*, Stephen Weir took us on a journey through his selection of the worst decisions made in history, a catalogue of errors of judgment and acts of sheer stupidity of the sort that most of us are probably capable of making given the chance. This book, *The Greatest Decisions Ever* could be regarded as a companion piece to Stephen's work because it looks at the opposite side of the coin in an effort to establish that, at least on a few occasions, there have been people who, when faced with difficult circumstances or apparently impossible choices, were capable of making a big decision and getting it right. So here we have fifty of these decisions, set out in chronological order and spanning the entire length of our experience, beginning in the far distant past with one of our earliest ancestors, who, in making a stone tool about 2.6 million years ago, demonstrated the mental ability not only to make a decision, but also to act on that decision. In the process, this exhibited one of the defining characteristics of human beings: rational thought.

FROM PREHISTORY TO THE RENAISSANCE

From that starting point, we then move on through some other examples from prehistory, such as the beginning of farming, when the decisions made by our ancestors had enormous consequences for humanity, until we arrive at the invention of writing by Sumerian scribes in the ancient Mesopotamian city of Uruk. From this moment, prehistory gradually becomes history and we can start to put names to those people who made the decisions, beginning in the Egypt of Ramesses II and then moving on to classical antiquity to look at decisions made by the likes of Julius Caesar and Constantine the Great. From there, we continue to the Medieval period to look at the birth of the Magna Carta and then on to the Renaissance—that remarkable period in history when, it could be argued, the modern world was invented.

MAKING THE MODERN WORLD

The opening up of the New World to European colonization by Christopher Columbus and his successors provides us with another strand of historical decisions—those involved in the creation and expansion of the United States of America, described in chapters on the Declaration of Independence and the Monroe Doctrine. We then reach the nineteenth century to look at Charles Darwin's decision to sail around the world on a journey of scientific inquiry and Lincoln issuing the Emancipation Proclamation during the American Civil War. Then we move on to the twentieth century, characterized by technological advances, world wars, and the civil rights and independence movements. This brings us up to the modern world and the invention of the World Wide Web by Tim Berners-Lee as well as, in the final chapter, the end of the Troubles in Northern Ireland marked by the signing of the Good Friday Agreement, part of a peace process that continues today.

WRIGHT FLYER
The *Wright Model A*, a two-seater version of the *Wright Flyer III* and the first airplane to be commercially produced.

DEFINING "GREATEST"

When I first began to consider writing about great decisions, I must admit that I was initially at something of a loss to think of any examples at all. After doing some research, however, I began to get my eye in, so to speak, and discovered a great many more examples than I had been expecting to find, making the process of settling on the final fifty an exercise in the decision-making process in itself.

In compiling my list, I have made a few assumptions about the type of decisions included. One is that peace is better than war, although sometimes war is inevitable when it becomes a question of making the right military decision.

It could be argued that none have been so important as Eisenhower giving the order to go on D-Day in World War II, despite the weather. Other assumptions are that democracy is better than tyranny, equality is better than the oppression of minorities, and that innovations and breakthroughs in science and culture are better than everything remaining the same.

I hope the decisions that I have come to through this method are a reasonable interpretation of the book's title, but in the end, it can only be a subjective process. We all make decisions every day of our lives and, while most of those may not have too many long-term consequences, a few people have made decisions that have affected many millions of others and may still affect us all today. Here is my selection of those big decisions, which are, in my opinion at least, the greatest made in the history of humanity.

MAKING THE FIRST STONE TOOLS

ca. 2.6 million years ago

Circumstances: The changing environment and climate of East Africa

Protagonists: *Homo habilis* or another species of early humans

Consequences: The evolution of our ability to make decisions

The oldest artifact on display in the British Museum is a piece of dark gray volcanic rock small enough to fit comfortably into the palm of the hand. It is, at first sight, a little less than impressive and for anybody too lazy to read the accompanying label it could easily be taken for a lump of coal that has somehow found its way into its own display case in the museum. There is, however, rather more to it than that. It is a stone tool, found in 1931 in the Olduvai Gorge of northern Tanzania by the archaeologist Louis Leakey and it was made about 1.8 million years ago by one of our very distant ancestors. With that in mind, it quickly becomes apparent that the sharp edges on the rock have not been formed by natural processes, but have been intentionally fashioned to produce a cutting or chopping blade. Somebody held this stone in their hand all that time ago and made the decision to alter its shape, most likely by hitting it with a harder stone to make it into a more useful tool. In doing so, they demonstrated the sort of mental abilities and thought processes—the cognition, as it is known by scientists—that marked them out as being different from other animals. The person who made that stone tool was a human being and inadvertently demonstrated that to us, not just by showing that they could make the stone tool, but by having the intelligence to decide to make the tool in the first place.

OLDUWAN TOOLS

The Olduvai Gorge cuts across the Serengeti Plain in the Great Rift Valley in East Africa. It holds a central place in the study of human evolution because so many archaeological discoveries relating to our ancient ancestors have been made there, leading to it becoming known as the "Cradle of Mankind." Excavations

"Every animal leaves traces of what it was; man alone leaves traces of what he created."

—Jacob Bronowski, *The Ascent of Man*, 1973

in the layers of sediment at the bottom of the gorge have uncovered many indications of early human life, including fossilized remains of different species as well as a variety of stone tools. The tool in the British Museum was found in the bottom layers of sediment, indicating that it is the earliest type to be found at the site.

These tools are named Olduwan by archaeologists, after the gorge where they were first described, and are also sometimes known as pebble tools. They represent the earliest known style of stone tools from prehistory and, since those first ones were excavated at Olduvai, even older examples have been found in other parts of East Africa. Currently, the earliest known finds are those from Gona in Ethiopia, which have been dated to 2.6 million years ago.

CRADLE OF MANKIND
The tools in the British Museum, along with many other finds relating to early humans, were found in the Olduvai Gorge, in the Great Rift Valley of East Africa.

DRIER CLIMATE
The date of these earliest tools is significant because it coincides with a major change in the environmental conditions in East Africa, known in scientific terms as the transition from the geological epoch of the Pliocene to the Pleistocene. The climate became much drier, causing the tropical forests formerly in the region to retreat toward the south to be replaced by the more open grassland of the savannah. This change is thought to be one of the main driving forces behind the evolution of early humans, who adapted to these

different conditions by becoming more upright in stance. As well as allowing early humans to walk and run on two legs, this also meant that their hands were free to be used for other purposes, such as making tools.

THE FIRST TOOL MAKER

The fossil record from this period is fragmentary and no remains from human skeletons have yet been found near the tools, so it has not been possible to establish for certain which of the various species of early human were the first to make use of them. A likely candidate is *Homo habilis*, one of the earliest members of the genus *Homo*, with a name that literally means "man the maker." The problem with this, however, is that the oldest known fossils of *H. habilis* date to about 2.3 million years ago (and the

BIGGER BRAINS

The reason why early humans had larger brains is a matter of dispute. According to one theory, it may be a result of early humans living in larger groups on the savannah (their predecessors lived in smaller groups in forests). The most successful members of these larger groups, so the theory goes, were the ones who had the greatest social intelligence, the ability to understand and deal with others in complex and ever-changing situations. Humans with better social intelligence would be likely to have more young (the next generation), which gave them an evolutionary advantage.

The date of these earliest tools is significant because it coincides with a major change in the environmental conditions in East Africa.

oldest known tools have been dated to 2.6 million years ago). This had led some evolutionary biologists to propose that one of the earlier australopithecine species, such as *Australopithecus gahri* or *Paranthropus boisei*, could have first learned how to make tools, which was then taken up by later *Homo* species. This has become a controversial subject in human evolution, because it is so difficult to pinpoint any new fossil discoveries with a particular species. There is also the possibility that an entirely different species, one that has either not survived in the fossil record or has yet to be discovered, was the first tool maker. Whatever the truth, the debate looks set to continue until more definitive evidence has been discovered.

GENERAL INTELLIGENCE

One argument in favor of *Homo habilis* as the first tool maker is that these early humans had brains that were 50 percent larger than those of the australopithecines, giving them the greater mental ability required for the task. A larger brain leads to greater social intelligence (the ability to deal with other humans) as well as better general intelligence, which gives *Homo habilis* an evolutionary advantage. Evidence of these great changes in our ancestors comes in the form of the first emergence of stone tools simply because these are the artifacts that have survived from this period. If people were capable of making tools out of stone, then they

must have used other materials as well, such as wood, bone, and leather, but these have rotted away over time.

The tools that have survived, like the one in the British Museum, are really important because they provide us with evidence, literally carved in stone, of the cognitive abilities of early humans, and it is this that makes us different from other animals. Looked at in this way, this seemingly insignificant object is not only the oldest in the British Museum, but one of the most remarkable as well.

FLEETING GLIMPSE

Most of the events discussed in this book concern either an individual or a small group of people who, when faced with a particular problem, have come to a decision about how best to deal with it. Here, we are concerned with a much more general aspect of the decision-making process: of when it first evolved in our distant ancestors and why it was a vital part of our development.

The combination of intelligence and manual dexterity, which enabled early humans to make tools, represents one of the qualities that defined them as human and that continues to define us today. That lump of rock in the British Museum, then, not only tells us about where we came from, but also offers us a fleeting glimpse into the mind of one of our earliest ancestors, allowing us to get a better appreciation of ourselves and of what it is that makes us human.

If people were capable of making tools out of stone, then they must have used other materials as well, such as wood, bone, and leather.

THE MIGRATION OUT OF AFRICA

ca. 70,000 ago

Circumstances: People looking across a stretch of water wondering what the land on the other side was like

Protagonists: A small band of early modern humans in East Africa

Consequences: The spread of human beings around the world

I n *The Descent of Man*, published in 1871, Charles Darwin proposed that human beings first evolved in Africa. He based this theory on the presence of gorillas and chimpanzees, observing that, in many places around the world, living species of mammals were closely related to similar extinct species from the same region. He went on to say that he expected examples of extinct species of apes to be found in Africa. It was a controversial theory at the time and remains so today, at least to those who deny the whole idea of evolution (how living organisms develop and diversify) in the first place. Over the years, evidence has accumulated to support Darwin, including the discovery of fossils of our early ancestors and, as we saw in the previous chapter, evidence of their cognitive abilities in the form of stone tools. So, if we accept that human beings originally

> **Difficult decisions must have been made for people to leave behind their homeland and head out into the unknown.**

evolved in Africa, then people must have migrated out of the continent at some point because we now live in almost every available habitable place on Earth. In order for this migration to take place, difficult decisions must have been made for people to leave behind their homeland and head out into the unknown.

OUT OF AFRICA

The most widely accepted theory of human migration is known as the Out of Africa theory, which suggests that modern humans evolved in East Africa about two hundred thousand years ago before spreading out across the continent and then migrating farther afield. Fossil evidence of modern human bones found in Israel dating to 125,000 BCE indicates an early migration took place from what is now Egypt and across the Sinai, the peninsula of land separating the Mediterranean Sea from the Red Sea. Yet signs of habitation only continue here for about ten thousand years, so this is usually taken as a false start.

The earliest date supported by good evidence for a continuous migration out of Africa is at about 70,000 BCE, when people crossed the relatively narrow Bab el Mandeb Strait at the southern end of the Red Sea, which separates the African state of Djibouti from Yemen on the Arabian Peninsula. At present, the strait is about 12 miles (20 km) wide, but seventy thousand years ago the sea level was 250 feet (80 m) lower as a result of the Ice Age, which made the crossing at the time almost half the distance. Today the coast of the Arabian Peninsula is mostly barren desert, but at the time of the migration it consisted of a low-lying plain, now underwater, where numerous freshwater springs created a band of green vegetation. Presumably this lush plain would have been visible across the narrow strait and must have looked very inviting to those people on the much drier African coast.

OUT OF AFRICA
Modern humans most likely first migrated out of Africa across the narrow Bab el Mandeb Strait but could also have crossed the Sinai Desert.

IN THE GENES
The interior of the Arabian Peninsula in about 70,000 BCE was an arid and inhospitable desert, as it still is today, so the people who first made the decision to cross over the strait probably stayed in the coastal region. As the climate began to warm at the end of the Ice Age, about twelve thousand years ago, sea levels rose and covered any signs they may have left behind, preventing the discovery of any material evidence to support the Out of Africa theory. Since the late 1980s, however, advances in the field of genetics have meant that the theory has been verified by research into genetic markers known to have first arisen in Africa in various populations of people from other parts of the world. So far, a good deal of this research has been concentrated on investigating mitochondrial DNA—strands of genetic material in the mitochondria (organelles involved in respiration and energy production) of cells that are passed down

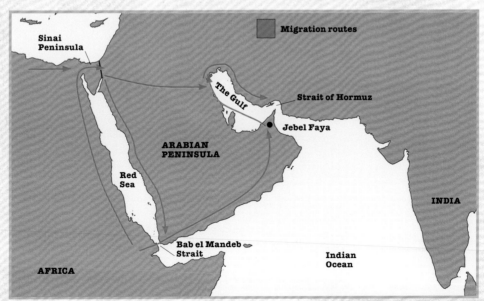

Migration routes

Sinai Peninsula

The Gulf

Strait of Hormuz

Jebel Faya

ARABIAN PENINSULA

Red Sea

INDIA

Bab el Mandeb Strait

AFRICA

Indian Ocean

CHARLES DARWIN
Natural historian and geologist Charles Darwin first came up with the theory that humans evolved in Africa and then migrated out from there.

exclusively through the female line of inheritance. Mitochondrial DNA is relatively stable compared to the DNA found in the cell nucleus, which mutates and changes as the cell divides so can vary much more over time. This relative lack of change makes it possible to track sections of mitochondrial DNA, known as haplogroups, back over long periods of time, allowing geneticists to unravel the route specific haplogroups have taken as people have moved around the world.

One of these haplogroups, known as L3, arose in East Africa, making it possible to differentiate between people from this region and those from the south and west of the continent, who most commonly have the L1 and L2 haplogroups rather than L3. Everybody else in the world outside of Africa has a haplogroup derived from L3, indicating that they are all descended from people of East African origin rather than from anywhere else on the continent. The relatively high level of genetic conformity between people who are not African in origin compared to the much greater differences between those from different parts of Africa also suggests that a small number of people left the continent in the first migration, perhaps as low as two hundred but more likely a few thousand, and that everybody who is not African is descended from this small genetic pool. As mitochondrial DNA does vary over time, if only slightly, it has been possible to date this first migration to approximately seventy thousand years ago based on the amount of variation that has occurred. Going further back still, this slight variation in mitochondrial DNA has also been used to propose the theoretical existence of a single woman, known as Mitochondrial Eve, who was the common ancestor to all of us and lived about two hundred thousand years ago somewhere in East Africa.

OTHER THEORIES
The Out of Africa theory may be the most widely accepted theory, particularly

> **The Out of Africa theory suggests that everyone who is not African is descended from a small genetic pool, possibly as small as two hundred people.**

since it has been backed up with genetic evidence, but it is not supported by everybody working in the field of human evolution. A competing idea, known as the Multiregional theory, suggests that modern humans evolved in separate parts of the world as a result of a much earlier migration out of Africa, occurring at around 1.5 million years ago, by an older species of human known as *Homo erectus*. According to the theory, *H. erectus* was effectively the same species as modern humans and, after migrating out of Africa, it adapted to the different conditions it encountered in various parts of the world, thereby giving rise to the diverse populations of people we have today. The relative conformity of DNA

LAKE TOBA

The volcanic winter resulting from an eruption in Sumatra, Indonesia, in about 72,000 BCE resulted in a drastic reduction in human populations.

found in people who are not of African origin does not support this theory because it indicates that they are descended from a small group who migrated much more recently. Supporters of the theory have attempted to account for this by suggesting that migrations occurring after that of *H. erectus* have had the effect of mixing genes from different populations so that, while they show local adaptations, their genetic makeup has remained very similar.

THE AMERICAS

It is thought that modern humans colonized the Americas long after they had colonized the rest of the world, some time between twenty thousand and fifteen thousand years ago. They crossed a land bridge between Russia and Alaska at a time when ocean levels were lower, exposing a wide stretch of the sea floor. The bridge is now a body of water that connects the Pacific and Arctic Oceans known as the Bering Straits.

Recent research, published in the journal *Science* in 2011, also challenges the Out of Africa theory as it stands at the moment. Stone tools found in the United Arab Emirates have been dated to 120,000 BCE and are consistent with those being used in Africa at this time by modern humans, suggesting a much earlier date for the first migration into the Arabian Peninsula than previously thought. No fossil remains have been found, which would convincingly prove the case, and this might be another instance, like the finds from Israel, of people existing outside Africa for a limited period rather than going on to migrate around the rest of the world. One possible explanation for this is the Toba event, one of the largest ever volcanic eruptions, which occurred on the Indonesian island of Sumatra in about 72,000 BCE. It would have caused a major reduction in the human population as a consequence of a prolonged volcanic winter, in which dust and ash in the atmosphere caused a significant drop in temperature and a corresponding fall in the available food resources. Any people who had migrated out of Africa before this, it has been speculated, either did not survive or, if they did, remained in such small numbers that they have left few traces behind them.

THE BEACHCOMBER MODEL

Whatever the truth of the matter, genetic research has shown that people certainly began to spread out across the world seventy thousand years ago, most likely by moving along the coasts in what is sometimes known as the beachcomber model of human migration. The coastal routes would have been where most resources were available, but this has made archaeological research difficult because of the rising sea levels at the end of the Ice Age. What we can say is that people appear to have moved along this coastal route quickly, getting to India just a few thousand years after leaving Africa and continuing to spread through Southeast Asia before arriving in Australia by about 50,000 BCE. This rapid expansion eastward is in sharp contrast to a much slower migration to the north. Modern humans only began to enter Europe about forty thousand years ago, perhaps as a consequence of the colder

Insatiable curiosity, together with a desire for a better future and, perhaps, our general dissatisfaction with our given lot, has been the driving force behind many decisions made in human history.

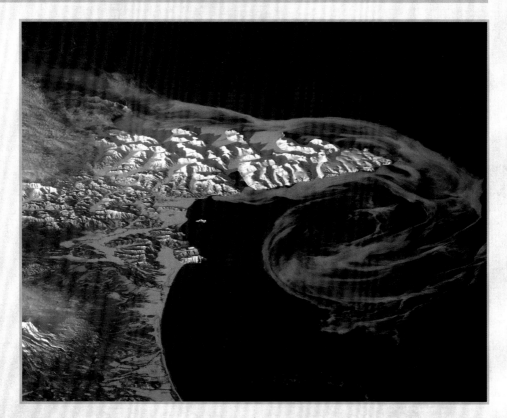

climate in this region or perhaps because the territory was already occupied by a now extinct species of human, the Neanderthals (*Homo neanderthalis*).

FILLING IN THE GAPS
We still have a long way to go before we fully understand the nature of human migration around the world, but over the past few decades advances in technology, particularly in DNA analysis, have begun to fill in many of the gaps. As the body of knowledge increases, the more it tends to confirm Darwin's theory of an African origin of modern humans, who then migrated out from there, first across the Red Sea into the Arabian Peninsula and then on into Asia and the rest of the world.

BERING STRAITS
An image of the Bering Straits taken from the International Space Station in 2016. It is believed that modern humans crossed from Asia into America at this point across a land bridge that is now covered with water.

DRIVING FORCE
It is, of course, impossible to know now exactly what motivated those first migrants to embark on such a dangerous adventure. They could have been forced from their land by drought or famine. It is not, however, hard to imagine people looking across the Bab el Mandeb Strait at the lush green vegetation opposite and simply wondering what the land on the other side was like.

HUNTER-GATHERERS SETTLE DOWN AND START FARMING

ca. 10,000 BCE

Circumstances: The right environmental conditions for the first adoption of farming

Protagonists: Hunter-gatherers and farmers in the Fertile Crescent

Consequences: The greatest social change in the history of humanity

It may be hard to envisage for most of us, but almost everybody living in the world today is part of a society fundamentally based on agriculture. In the more developed countries, less than 1 percent of the population is directly involved in farming, so it is hardly surprising if the vast majority of people give little thought to the role it continues to play in the modern world.

NEOLITHIC TRANSITION

When it comes to the overall history of humanity, agriculture is actually a recent development, going back for only about twelve thousand of the two hundred thousand years since human beings first evolved as a separate species. For most of that time, we have existed as hunters and gatherers, as a very small number of people still do, finding sustenance from the natural world. The change from this foraging way of life to one based on farming has been described as the greatest social upheaval human beings have ever been through. It is known to archaeologists as the Neolithic transition, after the period in which it occurred, when the adoption of farming was accompanied by a whole array of related changes. People began to live in more settled communities, use more advanced stone tools, and develop methods of making pottery. As the transition began thousands of years before the invention of writing, we can only get an idea about how these momentous changes happened by looking at the archaeological record. It's impossible to know for certain what was going through the minds of people during this critical turning point in human history. But the decisions made during this process had a huge impact at the time and continue to be relevant today, making them among the most important in all of human history.

THE FERTILE CRESCENT

Agriculture has arisen independently on a number of occasions around the world, but was first practiced in the region known as the Fertile Crescent. An arc of land straddling an arid interior, it began in the foothills of the Zagros Mountains in modern-day Iran and extended across Iraq and Syria, and into southern Turkey along the valleys of the rivers Tigris and Euphrates, before continuing southward

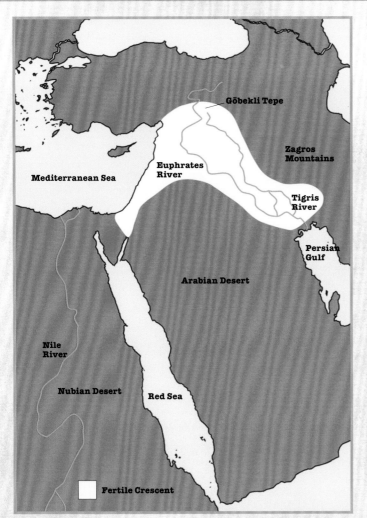

Göbekli Tepe

Zagros
Mountains

Euphrates
River

Mediterranean Sea

Tigris
River

Persian
Gulf

Arabian Desert

Nile
River

Nubian Desert

Red Sea

Fertile Crescent

FERTILE CRESCENT
Farming first began in the crescent-shaped region between the deserts and mountains of what is now the Middle East.

have their origins in wild species from the slopes of the Taurus Mountains.

The reason why farming first took hold in the Fertile Crescent, as opposed to anywhere else, has been a hotly debated subject. Numerous theories have been put forward to explain it. One of the most widely supported theories suggests that climate change at the end of the last Ice Age, beginning about fifteen thousand years ago, was instrumental in bringing about the adoption of farming. The warming climate created favorable conditions in the Fertile Crescent for those species of animals and plants used by hunter-gatherers, leading to a rise in their population. There was then a sudden cold snap, beginning in about 10,800 BCE, which returned the region to the climatic conditions of the Ice Age. This change appears to have happened very rapidly, perhaps in the space of only a few years, and it lasted for more than a thousand,

through the Levantine Corridor of Lebanon, Israel, and Jordan. Many of the cereal crops that are still farmed around the world today, including wheat, barley, and rye, were first grown here, as were a number of other important food crops, such as various varieties of peas, beans, and lentils. A similar story can be told for livestock; cattle were first domesticated from aurochs, their wild and now extinct ancestors, while both sheep and goats during which time there would be far less food available for hunter-gatherers. Farming may have been adopted as a response to these changing conditions because it provided a more reliable source of food than could be obtained solely from hunting and gathering. The decision to farm may, therefore, have been made out of necessity.

IN ONE PLACE

The French archaeologist Jacques Cauvin came up with an alternative theory for the adoption of agriculture. He observed that human beings are rarely forced into a course of action entirely by circumstances outside of their control. This led him to propose that the domestication of livestock and crops was a conscious choice made as a consequence

A BETTER LIFE?

Research has found that hunter-gatherers were healthier than farmers, living to an older age and suffering from fewer diseases. Farmers were exposed to more disease from their livestock and more likely to develop health problems, like back pain or arthritis. Studies have also shown that hunter-gatherers spend less time providing food for themselves than farmers. All of this supports the theory that people only started farming because climate change forced them into it. Why would anyone choose long hours of back-breaking work unless they had no other choice?

Ritual feasting and beer drinking may even have led to the development of agriculture as this was the only way to ensure there was enough food and beer for a feast.

of "sedentism," the phenomenon of people settling down to live permanently in one place. Sedentism, according to Cauvin, was accompanied by a shift in religious belief from the veneration of animals and places characteristic of nomadic hunter-gatherers to the worship of the ancestors and sky gods commonly found in more settled communities.

The Natufian culture of the Levantine Corridor, which existed from about 12,000 BCE to 8,000 BCE, spanned the transition from hunter-gathering to farming, and provides some support for Cauvin's theory. At the beginning of the Natufian, some hunter-gatherers were living in permanent villages of about two- to three-hundred people, while others on the edge of the desert continued to move from place to place. Archaeologists have found stone sickles and grinding stones, used in the harvest and processing of wild cereals, in Natufian villages, showing that the technology needed for farming was already present before cultivation began. This implies that the transition to agriculture could well have been quite smooth, taking place over a relatively long period of time rather than in one revolutionary moment.

GÖBEKLI TEPE

This process of sedentism is further supported by a current excavation at Göbekli Tepe, a site in southeastern Turkey considered to be one of the most

FARMING TODAY
A valley in the Fertile Crescent of eastern Turkey, where agriculture has been practiced for thousands of years.

important archaeological discoveries made in recent times. Excavations so far reveal that it contains the oldest religious buildings discovered anywhere in the world. The lowest layers have been dated to 10,000 BCE and are thought to have been used entirely for ritual purposes. Twenty circular enclosures contain twelve standing stones, most decorated with carvings of animals and some with human arms and clothing, which suggest they are symbolic of ancestors or gods. Large numbers of animal bones and cereal grains found there, all from wild species rather than domesticated ones, suggest the site was constructed and used by hunter-gatherers rather than farmers. Both the symbolic art and the social organization required to build such monumental structures are remarkable and unparalleled from a site of such an early date.

The picture emerging from ongoing excavations is of a highly organized and complex society experiencing a fundamental transition. While climate change and population growth must have played a role, the main driving force appears to have been the people themselves and the decisions they were making. It is impossible to point to a single key decision that led directly to the adoption of farming; more likely, it was a long process involving many choices. But it is no coincidence that the region where farming originated was also the one where people first began to live together in towns and cities, because such societies relied on farming to provide a sufficient supply of food. And, as far removed from farming as most of us have now become, much the same remains the case today.

THE SUMERIANS BEGIN TO WRITE

ca. 3400 BCE

Circumstances: The need for a method of keeping track of an increasing amount of information in an expanding city

Protagonists: The scribes of the Sumerian city of Uruk

Consequences: The first use of true writing

Writing was developed independently in a number of different parts of the world, but it is generally agreed to have first been used in Uruk, the largest city-state of Sumer, which had developed in southern Mesopotamia during the fourth millennium BCE (Mesopotamia was an ancient region based largely in present-day Iraq). Technically speaking, this was the moment at which prehistory becomes history, and yet we still have to rely on archaeological findings to get an idea of how this major advance in human culture occurred.

Writing was initially used as a means of record-keeping in the administration of the city. The first written documents were made by those professional scribes in Uruk who were employed to keep track of the quantities and movements of agricultural produce and manufactured goods. They appear to have hit upon a way of simplifying their method of record-keeping by using what is known in linguistics (language) as phonetic symbols. The decision to adopt these symbols—made by a small number of scribes or perhaps even just a single individual—would lead to what might be described as true writing. But before going on to consider the decisions made by these Sumerian scribes and the wider consequences, perhaps it would be a good idea to pause briefly to look at what constitutes true writing.

WHAT IS TRUE WRITING?

In linguistics, true writing involves the use of phonetic symbols, such as the letters of the alphabet, to stand for spoken sounds that, when put together, make up the words of a particular language. Before this, people were using simpler methods of recording information, beginning with pictograms, which were straightforward drawings of an object. Pictograms evolved into logograms—more abstract symbols representing entire words—so that, as

> **The first written documents were made by professional scribes in Uruk who were employed to keep track of the quantities and movements of goods.**

introduce phonetic symbols, indicating particular sounds rather than complete words, into the writing system they were already using. While this cannot be classed as true writing, which technically must consist of a complete phonetic system of both vowels and consonants, it is reasonable to say that it was the beginning of the process that would eventually lead to true writing.

long as people knew what each symbol meant, more complicated pieces of information could be written down. The disadvantage of this method is that spoken languages are made up of thousands of words, so thousands of symbols are required to represent them, making the process of learning to read and write long and complicated.

Splitting words up into their main sounds greatly reduces the number of symbols required, making the learning process and the use of grammar much easier. The innovation achieved by the Sumerian scribes of Uruk was to

URUK IN SUMER

At its height, around 2900 BCE, Uruk had a population in excess of fifty thousand people, making it by far the largest city in the world at that time and allowing it to dominate the whole of the Mesopotamian region. The administration of such a large city was the driving force behind the innovations in record-keeping, which were initially made by using a pointed wooden stylus, or rod, to make marks on a wet clay tablet. Once these tablets had dried in the sun, or had been baked in an oven, they proved to be much more durable

CLAY DISKS

The system of clay tablets used in Uruk may well have developed alongside an accounting system that used clay cylinders. Small disks of clay, each impressed with logographic symbols to represent a certain quantity of goods, say a number of sheep or a certain quantity of cloth, were placed in a cylinder, which was then sealed with wet clay. A separate record of the transaction was then made on a flat piece of clay. However, it gradually dawned on everyone that the cylinders and tokens were not actually needed so long as everyone recognized what had been written on the clay tablet.

than later writing done on paper or prepared animal hides (parchment and vellum, which was originally made from calf skin). Today, huge archives, some containing thousands of tablets, have been found during archaeological excavations of many of the ancient cities in Mesopotamia and beyond.

WRITING EVOLVES

At Uruk, the earliest clay tablets date to about 3400 BCE. Used to record a system of accounting, the symbols marked on the tablets, representing sheep, cloth, or whatever else was being traded, were gradually simplified so that, rather than drawing a sheep every time a deal was struck, a scribe could make a mark indicating a sheep with a few marks of the stylus. Over time, the symbols became more abstract, and easier to

write, establishing a logographic system of writing in which only these stylized symbols were in use. The leap from this simple system to using abstract symbols to represent sounds rather than complete words might have been accomplished first by using the same symbols for homophones—words that are pronounced in a similar way but mean different things (such as "deer" and "dear" in English)—and then putting a number of these together to make a completely different word. This established the principle that a symbol stands for a sound rather than an object. In this way, a phonetic writing system began to emerge, even if in Uruk words constructed in this way were used alongside logographic symbols rather than replacing them completely.

CUNEIFORM

By about 3000 BCE, the influence of Uruk was beginning to diminish in Mesopotamia, but by that time the writing system first developed there had spread to other city-states in the region. By about 2500 BCE, documents were being written on clay tablets in a number of different languages in what is known as the cuneiform script, including the Akkadian language used in the region immediately to the north of Sumer. Akkadian was more closely related to other Mesopotamian languages than Sumerian and so became much more widely used because it could be readily understood by a larger number of people. The method of writing also changed; documents were written by impressing the end of a piece of reed into the clay to make a wedge-shaped mark. Known as cuneiform, it was in use for the next fifteen hundred years and, despite retaining some logographic symbols as well as phonetic ones throughout this period, it is widely regarded as being the earliest example of a true writing system.

Cuneiform was gradually replaced by the much simpler Phoenician alphabet from about 1000 BCE, which consisted of only about twenty symbols and was fully phonetic, even if it did not originally contain any vowels. The seafaring Phoenicians, who were from what is now the coast of Lebanon, developed extensive trading links around the Mediterranean and their writing system was widely adopted throughout much of this region. The Ancient Greeks used the Phoenician alphabet and added vowels to it, which greatly increased the capacity of the written language to reproduce the same sounds that existed in the spoken language. From Greece, the alphabet would eventually spread to Rome, where it was adapted into the form that many of us use today.

The development of writing, then, was by no means a straightforward process that can be traced by a direct line from Sumer through to the Phoenicians and then on to the Greeks and Romans. But the decisions made by those Sumerian scribes in Uruk more than four thousand years ago to simplify their accounting method so that they could deal with an increasing amount of information can be seen as the point when writing first began to develop in the direction that would eventually lead to true writing. Some experts have argued that the

Phoenician alphabet arose out of Egyptian hieroglyphics via a script known as proto-Sinaitic and had nothing to do with the cuneiform script at all. If this were the case, then the path toward fully phonetic writing had nothing to do with the Sumerians. Nevertheless, even if cuneiform was an evolutionary dead end in the history of writing, it takes little away from the decisions made by those Sumerian scribes all those many years ago, which demonstrated that necessity is a great motivating force for innovation and change.

HIEROGLYPHICS

Some academics consider that Egyptian hieroglyphics are at least as old as Sumerian writing, and a debate continues among them as to whether hieroglyphics arose independently or were the result of contact and cultural diffusion between Egypt and Mesopotamia.

Decisions made by Sumerian scribes in Uruk more than four thousand years ago to simplify their accounting method can be seen as the point when writing first began to develop.

THE EGYPTIAN AND HITTITE PEACE TREATY

ca. 1259 BCE

Circumstances: Warring empires' attempt at peacefully settling their differences

Protagonists: The Egyptian Pharaoh Ramesses II and the Hittite king Hattusili III

Consequences: A mutually beneficial peace treaty

The United Nations Security Council attempts to maintain peace and security in its member states through dialogue and diplomacy. If that approach fails, it has the power to authorize further measures of intervention in conflicts through the use of sanctions (usually restrictions in trade between countries), peacekeeping forces, or direct military action.

Immediately outside the chamber where the council meets in the UN Headquarters in New York, there is a copy of a clay tablet hanging on the wall. It contains the text, written in the cuneiform script, of a peace treaty negotiated in about 1259 BCE between the representatives of the ancient Egyptian Pharaoh Ramesses II and those of the Hittite king Hattusili III. The original was found in 1906 during archaeological excavations of Hattusha, the capital city of the Hittites in central Turkey, and, taken together with the corresponding inscription on the wall of an Egyptian temple, it is the earliest known example of a peace treaty that has survived into the modern age. The copy of the clay tablet was given to the UN by the Turkish government in 1970 and, by hanging it in such a prominent position, the intention was presumably to inspire modern diplomats as they entered the Security Council chamber and show them that negotiating peace between warring states has had a very long history. It might also suggest that, if the Egyptians and Hittites could decide to sort out their differences in such a sensible manner more than three thousand years ago, then surely it is not beyond us to do the same today.

COMPETING EMPIRES

Little was known about the Hittites before the discovery of their capital city Hattusha, where monumental building work and huge city walls were uncovered by archaeological excavators. Here they found an extensive archive of over ten thousand clay tablets that contained details of many aspects of Hittite society and included a library of diplomatic documents and letters concerning relations with their neighboring states.

RAMESSES II
The massive rock temples at Abu Simbel, Egypt were built by Ramesses II as a lasting monument to himself and to commemorate the Battle of Kadesh.

By about 1500 BCE, the Hittites had expanded beyond their original homeland in central Anatolia to occupy territories in northern Mesopotamia and the Levantine region of what is now Syria, Lebanon, and northern Israel. Some of this territory in the Levant had formally been under Egyptian control, leading to a long-running conflict between the Hittites and the Egyptians that came to a head in about 1274 BCE at the Battle of Kadesh. Ramesses II had come to the throne in Egypt five years previously and, in an effort to regain the territory lost to the Hittites by his ancestors, personally led his army against the forces controlled by the Hittite king Muwatalli II, the elder brother of Hattusili III. Ramesses declared the ensuing encounter as a great Egyptian victory although in reality the battle reached a stalemate.

Over the following fifteen years, numerous other smaller military encounters between Egyptian and Hittite forces occurred in this disputed region, without either being able to gain a decisive advantage. It is against this background of constant low-level warfare that the two sides would eventually negotiate a settlement that would put an end to hostilities between them.

If the Egyptians and Hittites could sort out their differences over three thousand years ago, then surely it is not beyond us to do the same today.

TOWARD A TREATY

Hattusili III came to power in Hattusha in about 1267 BCE after deposing his nephew Mursili III, the son and heir of Muwatalli II. Wanting to legitimize his position as king of the Hittites at home and abroad, he tried to establish good diplomatic relations with neighboring states. The Hittite archive contained numerous examples of correspondence between Hattusili and other rulers from all over the region, but, as much as he proclaimed his right to be king, not all of his subjects accepted him. He was also facing the rising power of the Assyrian Empire on the eastern borders of his empire, so the last thing he needed was more trouble with the Egyptians on his southern border.

Circumstances in Egypt were a little different. Ramesses II was certainly not

CHARIOT BATTLE

The Battle of Kadesh, fought between the Hittites and Egyptians, is thought to have been the largest chariot battle ever fought, with as many as six thousand chariots taking part. It was proclaimed afterward by Ramesses as a great victory for the Egyptians, with the details inscribed on the walls of a number of Egyptian temples. It appears, however, that Ramesses may well have been exaggerating the success of his forces in which the Egyptians had been unable to capture the strategically important city of Kadesh, but had nevertheless prevented any further raids by the Hittites into Egyptian territory.

facing any challenge to his authority at home; he was widely regarded at the time as being one of the greatest of all the Pharaohs. In line with the traditional practice of Egyptian Pharaohs, he had embarked on a huge and expensive program of monumental building projects to further enhance his reputation and ensure that he would be remembered in the future. But the constant state of war with the Hittites had placed a great strain on his resources and he was well aware of the potential threat posed by the rising power of the Assyrians in the Levant, so he may well have been more open to the idea of a peace treaty than first impressions might indicate. The stumbling block was that he had boasted about winning a great victory over the Hittites at Kadesh, so Ramesses could hardly approach them fifteen years later to propose a peace settlement without having to admit that the battle had not gone quite as well as he had claimed.

MUTUAL BENEFITS

We don't know exactly how the peace treaty came about, but it appears likely that Hattusili made the first move. The resulting treaty was written in the usual diplomatic language of the period, stressing the sort of ideals of brotherhood and eternal peace that are a feature of international agreements today. There can be little doubt that what led to the settlement were pragmatic decisions that had mutual benefits for both sides. As well as all the flowery language, the treaty contained provisions ensuring that neither side would invade the territory of the other and would come to each other's aid if either was attacked by a third party, which, without actually saying it, meant the Assyrians. The wording of the

PEACE TREATY
The original Hittite version of the Egyptian–Hittite peace treaty, found in Turkey in 1906. It now resides in Istanbul's Archaeological Museum.

treaty allowed both sides to present it as a significant victory at home; Ramesses could claim that the Hittites had come to him asking for peace, while Hattusili could say he had dealt on equal terms with the great Pharaoh, the most powerful man in the world at the time.

CORDIAL RELATIONS
Relations between the Egyptians and Hittites remained cordial, if not particularly friendly, for a long period after the treaty came into force, enabling both states to pursue their own agendas without interference from the other.

Contact was maintained by a regular correspondence, and, thirteen years later, Hattusili sent one of his daughters to Egypt where she was married to Ramesses, becoming one of his many wives and given the title of Great Royal Wife. After Hattusili died, in about 1237 BCE, peace was maintained, but the power of the Hittite Empire began to decline as it faced challenges from the Assyrians and from raiders collectively known as the Sea Peoples. It would not be long before the terms of the treaty carried little meaning because the Hittites had ceased to present a threat to the Egyptians. In about 1200 BCE, Hattusha was abandoned and the Hittites disappeared from history completely until their capital city was rediscovered in the early twentieth century. The Egyptians were faced with similar threats from the Assyrians and Sea Peoples and, even though their empire persisted for much longer, they also entered a period of decline and would never regain the power and prestige that Ramesses II had enjoyed during his reign.

If the diplomats of today take the time to contemplate the clay tablet hanging on the UN wall, perhaps they can see that it is possible to negotiate a peace settlement between opposing states no matter how long or acrimonious the dispute. To be effective, however, it has to be mutually beneficial. With so many conflicts across the globe today, it might be worth pointing toward those decisions made by the Egyptians and Hittites as an example of a way forward.

The Egyptians and Hittites may not have liked each other very much, but, in the end, at least they found a way of living together in peace.

THE ATHENIANS CHOOSE DEMOCRACY

508 BCE

Circumstances: Athens emerges from a period of tyranny

Protagonists: The citizens of Athens

Consequences: The first attempt at a democratic system of government

In the Gettysburg Address, Abraham Lincoln clearly set out his vision of a democratic government, which, he said, should be "of the people, by the people, for the people." He openly referred to the Founding Fathers of America who signed the Declaration of Independence in 1776 and may have also made a more subtle reference to ancient Athens, widely considered to have been the first democratic state. The historian Garry Wills has pointed out the parallels between Lincoln's speech at Gettysburg and a speech at a funeral given by the Athenian statesman Pericles (495–429 BCE) during the Peloponnesian War, fought between Athens and Sparta. There is no way of knowing if Lincoln really drew inspiration from this source—and some reports of the occasion suggest he composed the speech while traveling on the train from Washington to Gettysburg,

writing it out on the back of an envelope. If he had, then it would have been entirely fitting to have evoked the beginnings of democracy at a moment when he was looking forward to the period after the end of the Civil War, to a renewal of America and what he called a "new birth of freedom." Whatever the truth of the matter, Lincoln's words stand as a powerful and eloquent reminder of the importance of a system of government in which citizens are free to make their own decisions, either directly on particular issues, as they did in Athens, or by holding elections to appoint specific individuals as representatives, as most democracies do today.

PEOPLE POWER
The roots of the word "democracy" are in the Greek words *demos* and *kratos*, which, taken together, literally mean "people power."

> "Fourscore and seven years ago our fathers brought forth upon this continent a new nation, conceived in liberty, and dedicated to the proposition that all men are created equal."
>
> —Abraham Lincoln at Gettysburg, November 19, 1863

It is generally agreed that the first truly democratic system of governance was established in Athens by Cleisthenes in 508 BCE, making this the date usually given for the beginning of democracy. The reforms introduced by Cleisthenes appear to have been based on a previous attempt at introducing democracy in about 594 BCE by the Athenian statesman Solon, who rarely gets the credit for his actions because the system he introduced lasted for only a few years before being overthrown by Peisistratus, a member of one of the noble families of Athens, who went on to rule as a tyrant. The democracy established by Cleisthenes, on the other hand, lasted for almost two hundred years, up until the period of Alexander the Great, and encompassed the golden age of classical Athens, considered by many to be the birthplace of Western civilization.

The democracy introduced by Cleisthenes involved a fundamental reform of Athenian society, from the city being divided into four tribes led by members of noble families to a more egalitarian, representative system based on the division of the city and the surrounding countryside into ten areas. These were known as demes, which are comparable to modern electoral constituencies. The idea was to reduce the influence of the nobility, who had been responsible for instituting tyranny, by encouraging Athenian citizens to be loyal to their deme rather than to a particular

CLEISTHENES

A modern bust of the father of democracy by Anna Christoforidis. No ancient likeness of him is known to exist.

individual within a tribe. Democracy was exercised through three bodies: the assembly, at which every adult male citizen was entitled to attend and vote; the council of five hundred citizens, selected by lot and consisting of fifty citizens from each deme; and the courts, which presided over legal cases and were made up of jurors numbering in the

CHURCHILL SPEECH

"Many forms of government have been tried, and will be tried in this world of sin and woe. No one pretends that democracy is perfect or all-wise. Indeed, it has been said that democracy is the worst form of government except all those other forms that have been tried from time to time; but there is a broad feeling in our country that the people should rule, continuously rule, and that public opinion, expressed by all constitutional means, should shape, guide, and control the actions of ministers who are their servants and not their masters."

—**Sir Winston Churchill at the British House of Commons, November 11, 1947**

hundreds who were also selected by lot from among the demes.

The important issues, such as those involving war and peace, were dealt with through the assembly, which met once a month in a large flat area on the Pynx, a hill overlooking Athens, which could accommodate an estimated six thousand people. Any citizen had the right to speak at the assembly and decisions were reached by a show of hands, making it very democratic, even if not all of the thirty thousand citizens of Athens could have attended an assembly meeting at the same time. Setting the agenda for the assembly was one of the responsibilities of the council, which also dealt with the more routine decisions required for the day-to-day administration of the city. Selection by lot for both the council and the courts was adopted because it was thought that elections would favor the wealthy and powerful families of Athens, who could exert influence over others by appealing to their loyalty or by bribery. Drawing lots was obviously random and would ensure people from all sections of society were represented, although the positions were unpaid up until the system was reformed by Pericles in about 457 BCE, so it favored those who could afford the time to take part.

A LIMITED DEMOCRACY

At first sight, this system of direct democracy in which all eligible citizens could take part in the decision-making process may appear to be as close to being perfect as possible, and it certainly led to a long period of stability in Athens that allowed the city to flourish. But the truth is that only 20 percent of the population of Athens were considered to be citizens, leaving all the rest, including women and people who were not born in the city, without any rights at all. The prosperity of the city was also based on slavery and, of course, slaves had no rights either. Rather, they were the ones who did all the work, allowing citizens, at least those wealthy enough to own slaves in the first place, the freedom to spend their time attending meetings and

The roots of the word "democracy" are in the Greek words *demos* and *kratos*, which, taken together, literally mean "people power."

exercising their democratic rights. The idea of equality, then, may have been central to the Athenian system, but it only applied to those who were, in George Orwell's words, "more equal than others."

It is, perhaps, too harsh to judge the Athenian experiment in democracy by comparing it with the liberal democracies of today, in which the right to vote and universal suffrage normally form a core part of the constitution. Before dismissing what the Athenians achieved, it is also worth remembering that universal suffrage only became law in Britain in 1928, when women were given the vote.

ATHENS
A view across the city from the Pynx, the hill where Athenian citizens met to exercise their democratic rights.

It had to wait until 1965 in America, at which point civil rights legislation guaranteeing the right to vote for everybody, including racial minorities, became enshrined in the Constitution. And there are, of course, plenty of countries around the world today where democracy either doesn't exist at all or has been hijacked in an attempt to justify despotic rule. So, if we can assume that democracy is a good thing, then it is not unreasonable to regard the Athenian version as the first step in a very long and ongoing process that continues today. It might not have been perfect, and the democracy that some of us enjoy today might not be perfect either, but at least the citizens of Athens could make their own decisions, so that, if it all went wrong, they had nobody else to blame but themselves.

SIDDHARTHA GOES IN SEARCH OF ENLIGHTENMENT

ca. sixth century BCE

Circumstances: A young man leaves his family to search for enlightenment

Protagonist: Siddhartha Gotama, aka the Buddha

Consequences: The beginnings of the Buddhist faith

The earliest accounts of the life of Siddhartha Gotama were written down in the first century CE, more than four hundred years after he is thought to have lived. So, even though these accounts may well be based on much earlier stories preserved in the oral tradition of the region of northern India where he lived, it is difficult to know if they were really intended to be an accurate portrayal of the man who became known as the Buddha, a title meaning "the awakened one." It is equally likely that these accounts were presenting a mythologized version of the Buddha's life, a story adapted over generations to place an emphasis on those important spiritual events that would give shape to the emerging Buddhist faith.

One of these key spiritual events, recounted in all the stories, is how, as a young man of twenty-nine, Siddhartha made the decision to leave his comfortable home and become a mendicant, a wandering monk who relied on the charity of others to support him. It was a decision that would determine the entire course of his future life, setting him out on the path toward enlightenment (spiritual knowledge) and, through his subsequent teaching, would lead to the establishment of the central tenets of Buddhism.

> *"Firm in his resolve and leaving behind without hesitation his father who turned ever toward him, and his young son, his affectionate people, and his unparalleled magnificence, he then went forth out of his father's city."*
>
> **—From the epic poem *Buddhacharita*, one of the earliest known accounts of Siddhartha Gotama, composed in the first century CE by the Sanskrit poet Asvaghosa**

SIDDHARTHA LEAVES HOME

Siddhartha was, we are told, born in the town of Lumbini in the foothills of the Himalayas of what is now southern Nepal. In some accounts of his life, his father is described as being the king of the Sakya people, making him a prince. However, there is little evidence to show that Sakya society actually included a royal family and it has become more usual to suggest that Siddhartha's family was in fact aristocratic and wealthy

STANDING BUDDHA

A first century CE statue of the Buddha from Gandhara in northern Pakistan, now in the Tokyo National Museum.

Siddhartha encountered for the first time in his life, people who were sick and dying, and was suddenly confronted by the reality of human suffering.

rather than royal. He grew up in the family home in Kapilavatthu, near where he was born, and lived a very comfortable early life, sheltered from the outside world by his father and protected from any signs of human suffering. This easy life continued until he was twenty-nine, when he began to take trips away from his home on his own. He encountered for the first time people who were sick and dying, and was suddenly confronted by the reality of human suffering.

The realization that the world is filled with pain and suffering appears to have had a profound effect on Siddhartha. He became intensely dissatisfied with his comfortable life and could find no pleasure in the birth of his first son, seeing only the inevitability of all the people he loved living in sorrow before eventually growing old and dying. On his next trip away from home, Siddhartha met one of the many mendicants traveling the roads and pathways of northern India at that time. He decided there and then to become one of them and to search for a solution to the suffering he had seen at the heart of humanity. That same night, at least according to some accounts of his life, he is said to have taken one last look at his sleeping wife and their newborn son, knowing that if he lingered he would not be able to leave his family and everything else that was tying him to the life he could no longer bear to live.

FOUR NOBLE TRUTHS

In her 2004 book simply entitled *Buddha*, the religious scholar and writer Karen Armstrong explains the Four Noble Truths in a straightforward way:

"The first of these verities was the noble truth of suffering (dukkha) that informs the whole of human life. The second truth was that the cause of this suffering was desire (tanha). In the third noble truth, Gotama asserted that Nibbana (Nirvana) existed as a way out of this predicament, and finally, he claimed that he had discovered the path that leads from suffering and pain to its ending in the state of Nibbana."

ENLIGHTENMENT

Over the course of the next six years, Siddhartha lived an austere and self-disciplined life, denying himself worldly pleasures and traveling extensively around northern India to study under a number of different religious teachers. He became skilled in the techniques of meditation, but this still did not lead him toward the awakening he was seeking. So, in apparent desperation, he tried to live an even more austere life by hardly eating anything at all. After almost dying of starvation, he realized that this was not the right path either, but he was not prepared to give up his search. He recalled a moment from his childhood when his father had taken him to see the ceremonial first plowing of the fields before a crop was planted in the spring. He realized that, when he had been left alone and was sitting under a tree, he had unconsciously entered into a meditative state in which he had been completely calm and happy but, at the same time, had retained complete awareness and was capable of deep reflection. He resolved to find a suitable tree where he could meditate in solitude using this new "middle way" he had discovered within himself, which took a path between lavish self-indulgence and extreme austerity, and, once he had found the right place, remain there until he had achieved enlightenment.

Siddhartha found the secluded spot he had been seeking under a bodhi tree—a variety of sacred fig—near what is now the town of Bodh Gaya in the Indian state of Bihar. During the first night of meditating, he achieved enlightenment by gaining a full insight into the causes of human suffering and the way in which it could be overcome. Bodh Gaya has since become the most important pilgrimage site in Buddhism, and the bodhi tree that grows there today is believed to be a direct descendant of the original one. The Buddha, as he can now be called, spent the following seven weeks at the bodhi tree thinking over what he would do next. He decided to teach what he called the Four Noble

Siddhartha resolved to find a suitable tree where he could meditate in solitude using this new "middle way" he had discovered within himself.

BODHI TREE
Young Tibetan Buddhists at Bodh Gaha, near the sacred fig tree where Siddhartha is said to have found enlightenment.

Truths, which he described to his first pupils in a talk known in English as *The Setting in Motion of the Wheels of Dharma*. These truths (see panel) form the fundamental teachings at the center of the Buddhist faith, and the Buddha would spend the remaining forty-five years of his life discussing, explaining, and elaborating on them as he continued to travel around northern India.

A DIFFICULT PATH
From a modern perspective, Siddhartha's original decision to give up his former life, to abandon his wife and newborn child to go in search of an entirely personal enlightenment, might seem very self-indulgent. Needless to say, none of the accounts of his life mention what his wife thought about his decision, but perhaps we shouldn't take the biographical details of his life too literally. When faced with having to decide between continuing to live comfortably with his family or leaving that life behind in order to search for a way of ending the pain and suffering of the human condition, Siddhartha chose the more difficult and uncertain path.

This tells us that such an undertaking will not be an easy journey for anybody else seeking to emulate the Buddha and that personal sacrifices will have to be made in order to achieve enlightenment. But, in making his great decision, the Buddha not only transformed his own life, but initiated a system of belief that would transform the lives of many millions of other people as well.

ASHOKA THE GREAT RENOUNCES WAR

ca. 262 BCE

Circumstances: The man who started a war of conquest becomes disgusted by its terrible consequences

Protagonists: Ashoka the Great and the people of the Mauryan Empire

Consequences: Empire ruled on the principles of nonviolence and tolerance, the spread of the Buddhist faith

At its height during the reign of the emperor Ashoka the Great in about 304–232 BCE, the Mauryan Empire extended over almost all of the Indian subcontinent and beyond into modern-day Afghanistan and eastern Iran. On ascending to the throne in about 274 BCE, Ashoka at first continued the military campaigns and empire-building of his predecessors, either occupying new territories by force or by the threat of force.

After eight years, he appears to have made the momentous decision not to continue with his campaigns of conquest and colonization and, instead, renounced the use of any further acts of war. From that time onward, he began to support the Buddhist way of nonviolence and

Ashoka the Great's empire was the largest ever to exist in the region, and nothing approaching its size would be seen again until the establishment of the British Raj more than two thousand years later.

tolerance, becoming what we might now call a missionary by promoting the Buddhist faith within his empire.

To achieve this, he sent representatives to those states that he may formerly have considered invading to spread the knowledge of Buddhism by entirely peaceful means. Much of what we know about Ashoka and his transformation from a warrior into a man of peace derives from Buddhist texts written centuries after his death, but there are also some primary sources, created during his lifetime and scattered around his empire that are still in existence today. These are known as the Edicts of Ashoka and mostly take the form of inscriptions carved into stone pillars and rock faces. Many deal with the concept of *dharma*, the Buddhist teachings of natural and moral law, covering such concerns as how to live a good life and, in Ashoka's case, how to run an empire in accordance with the principles of Buddhism. But some of the texts also provide us with insights into the reasons why Ashoka made what was, at the time, a radical and unprecedented decision to adopt the principle of nonviolence, one that, at least among kings and emperors, has few parallels in history.

THE MAURYAN DYNASTY

The dynasty was founded by Ashoka's grandfather, Chandragupta Maurya, who rose from obscurity to become a military leader and, in about 322 BCE, launched a successful plot to depose the king of the Nanda Empire in Magadha, formerly a kingdom in the east of India. As soon as he had taken control of the empire, Chandragupta began to mount aggressive campaigns against the states to the west of Magadha, taking advantage of a power vacuum that had developed after Alexander the Great withdrew his Greek and Persian armies from the region and left them under the control of his subordinates. Alexander's death in 323 BCE led to a period of turmoil in these regions, giving Chandragupta the opportunity to take possession of them and extend his own empire westward, right up to the Persian border. Chandragupta's son and heir Bindusara succeeded to the throne in about 298 BCE and continued the expansionist policies of his father, capturing territory to the south and adding much of peninsular India to the Mauryan Empire.

According to the Buddhist sources, Bindusara had many wives, who together bore him one hundred sons. Ashoka— born in Pataliputra, the capital of the empire (now the city of Patna in the Indian state of Bihar)—was one of the younger ones, born to a junior wife, and as such by no means the most obvious candidate to succeed his father. But from a young age, he gained a reputation as an intelligent and talented military commander, and was sent by his father to put down rebellions in parts of the empire while still in his teens. Bindusara died in 272 BCE, when Ashoka was twenty-two years old, and, with Shushima, the oldest son and heir apparent, absent from Pataliputra,

A ROCK EDICT
An impression of the first rock Edict of Ashoka from Girnar in Gujarat, written in the Brahmi script.

he seized the opportunity to claim the throne for himself. Shushima, we are told, was killed on his return to the capital. Once Ashoka became emperor, he had all of his other brothers killed as well, except for the youngest one, who was his full brother and had become a monk, so presumably did not pose any threat.

ASHOKA THE CRUEL

At the start of his reign, Ashoka proved to be ruthless and brutal, repressing any opposition and further expanding his empire by conquest, leading to him becoming known as Ashoka the Cruel. After eight years, he decided to invade Kalinga, a coastal region in the east of India. One of the best known edicts, known as the Rock Edict No. 13 and quoted here from the version given in Charles Allen's book, *Ashoka: The Search for India's Lost Emperor*, describes what happened:

> *Beloved-of-the-Gods, King Piyadasi [the titles and name adopted by Ashoka], conquered the Kalingas eight years after his coronation. One hundred and fifty thousand were deported, one hundred thousand were killed, and many more died from other causes. After the Kalingas had been conquered, Beloved-of-the-Gods came to feel a strong inclination toward the Dharma, a love for the Dharma, and for the instruction of the Dharma. Now Beloved-of-the-Gods feels deep remorse for having conquered the Kalingas.*

Buddhism spread so widely during Ashoka's reign that some people regard him as the second most important person in the history of the faith after the Buddha himself.

LION CAPITAL
A thirteenth-century replica of one of the Pillars of Ashoka from Sarnath with the Ashoka Chakra on top of four lions.

The remorse shown by Ashoka after the mass slaughter and deportation of so many people in Kalinga appears to have been genuine. For the remainder of his forty-year reign as emperor, he refrained from any further military campaigns, despite having by far the most powerful forces in the region. He could easily have overpowered the last remaining region of the subcontinent that he had not already conquered, the tip of the Indian peninsula in what is now Kerala and Tamil Nadu, but he appears to have shown no inclination to do so.

WHEEL OF LIFE

The wheel at the center of the Indian flag is the Ashoka Chakra, a symbol representing the eternal wheel of life that was inscribed alongside many of the Edicts of Ashoka. It can be seen on the base of the Lion Capital of Ashoka, a sculpture of four lions that originally stood on top of a pillar in Sarnath, near the city of Varanasi where the Buddha first began to teach the *dharma*. In 1950, a depiction of the Lion Capital was chosen as the emblem of the newly independent Republic of India and it has since appeared on currency, stamps, passports, government buildings, and just about every other official symbol of India.

A NEW APPROACH

The exact moment when Ashoka converted to Buddhism is unclear, but from that point onward he committed himself to following the teachings of the *dharma*. As well as ruling his people with tolerance and benevolence, he stopped hunting animals and became a vegetarian, extending his newfound compassion to all living things. It was the beginning of an attitude that still exists in many parts of the Indian subcontinent today and also one that would be recognized by anybody who follows the Buddhist faith.

This new approach may have been nonviolent, but it was by no means passive and, while Ashoka did not use force or intimidation to spread Buddhism, he did everything else he could to promote it within the empire and in regions beyond its borders. He sent his eldest son, Mahinda, to Sri Lanka where, according to the Buddhist chronicles, he converted the king and queen and then established the faith more widely among the people of the island. Missionaries were sent out elsewhere to perform similar tasks, spreading Buddhism far beyond the region of northern India and leading some people to describe Ashoka as being the second most important person in the history of the faith after the Buddha himself.

KEY BUDDHIST FIGURE

Ashoka died in 232 BCE at the age of seventy-two and was succeeded by his grandson Dasaratha. In decline by the time of Ashoka's death, the empire gradually unraveled until, fifty years later, its last emperor was assassinated and it fell apart completely. The achievements of Ashoka disappeared into obscurity, where they would largely remain for the next two thousand years, until new research into the era began in the nineteenth century. The major breakthrough was made by James Prinsep (1799–1840), a British scholar and employee of the East India Company, who deciphered the Brahmi script in which the edicts had been written. This allowed researchers to read the text written on pillars and rock faces during Ashoka's reign and compare the information uncovered with the Buddhist text that described the exploits of what had previously been thought to be a mythological king. But even after the man himself had been forgotten, he left a tangible legacy in the adoption of Buddhism and the teaching of the *dharma*, along with the observance of the principles of nonviolence and tolerance.

JULIUS CAESAR CROSSES THE RUBICON

49 BCE

Circumstances: Julius Caesar, standing on the banks of a river, thinks about what to do next

Protagonists: Caesar, Pompey, and the citizens of the Roman Republic

Consequences: The Roman Empire replaces the Roman Republic

To cross the Rubicon is, as the proverb goes, to decide on a course of action from which there can be no going back. By doing so, you may, to employ a few more expressions, pass the point of no return or burn your bridges. The Rubicon itself does not present much of an obstacle. It is a minor river in Italy, flowing eastward out of the Apennine Mountains to the coast between Rimini and Cesena, and it is no more difficult to cross today than it was on January 10, 49 BCE, when Julius Caesar stood on its northern bank with the soldiers of one of his legions, apparently hesitating while he decided what to do next.

The decision he faced had nothing to do with how to get to the other side—he was standing right next to a bridge; it was what the river represented that was giving him pause for thought. It marked the boundary between the Roman province of Cisalpine Gaul, then under his own governorship, and Italia, the region surrounding Rome itself and directly governed from the city. Military commanders were expressly forbidden by Roman law from entering Italia at the head of an army, as Caesar was about to do, and he was well aware of the consequences of his actions. To cross the river was a capital offense for both himself and for anybody who accompanied him, so, if he crossed with his legion, he would either have to seize control of the city by defeating the forces loyal to Rome commanded by his former ally and now bitter rival Gnaeus Pompeius Magnus, better known as Pompey, or face the death penalty. After taking a moment to reflect on the enormity of the decision he faced, Caesar crossed the Rubicon, and in the process ignited a civil war.

PATH TO THE RIVER

Gaius Julius Caesar, to give him his full name, was born in 100 BCE into an old aristocratic family of a class that had lost much of its former wealth and power. From an early age, Caesar appears to have set himself the target of regaining his family's past glory by distinguishing himself as a military commander. By 60 BCE, he had made his reputation as an

JULIUS CAESAR
A portrait of the Roman general, consul, and dictator who crossed the Rubicon and began the sequence of events leading to the establishment of the Roman Empire.

outstanding general in the Roman army and his achievements had propelled him into the political spotlight. To further his ambitions, he entered into an agreement of mutual understanding with two other successful military commanders who had also crossed over into politics, Pompey and Marcus Licinius Crassus. This alliance would become known as the First Triumvirate.

As a direct result of this alliance with the two men who would otherwise have been his biggest rivals, Caesar was elected as Consul of Rome, the highest elected political office in the republic. Bribery and corruption had been rife during the election, and suspicions about his conduct during his one-year term of office also circulated. While in office,

Caesar had been immune from prosecution and, again with the help of Pompey and Crassus, as his term was drawing to a close, he was awarded the governorship of three provinces: Cisalpine Gaul and Transalpine Gaul in the south of France, and Illyricum on the eastern coast of the Adriatic. Provincial governors were given immunity as well as the consul, allowing Caesar to continue to avoid the prosecutions his political opponents were intending to bring against him.

The governorships came with the command of four legions, which Caesar used over the course of the next ten years to complete the conquest of the remainder of Gaul—a victory that made him both very wealthy and very popular with the citizens of Rome. When Crassus died in 53 BCE, Pompey seized his chance to outmaneuver Caesar, who was still in Gaul, by forming alliances with his former opponents in the Senate, a group known as the Optimates. He was also well aware of Caesar's popularity as the conqueror of Gaul so, together with the Optimates, he pushed for an order to be issued by the Senate to recall Caesar to Rome to face the prosecutions he had managed to avoid. Caesar had expected to return in triumph after his victory and to be appointed as Consul again to ensure he would still not face any charges, but in 50 BCE the Senate did what Pompey wanted and summoned him back to Rome. Had Caesar followed the order, he could

On crossing the Rubicon, Caesar either had to seize Rome and fight on or lose his army and power, and face the death penalty.

have been charged with the capital crime of treason, thereby risking not only his political career but also his life.

DECISION TO CROSS

The Senate had effectively backed Caesar into a corner; he could either submit to the law of Rome, give up his army and political ambitions, and be put on trial for his life, or he could fight it out while he still had the command and loyalty of his legions. This was the apparent dilemma he faced as he was standing on the banks of the Rubicon; although, as he had one of his legions with him, it would appear likely that he had already made the decision to fight. In his own account, *The Civil War*, Caesar doesn't even mention crossing the river. All he records is that, because of the

HEAD OF POMPEY

When Caesar arrived in Egypt in pursuit of Pompey, the young Egyptian Pharaoh Ptolemy (who was only around fourteen years old) presented him with Pompey's severed head. Ptolemy was fighting against his sister Cleopatra for overall control of Egypt, and appears to have thought that murdering Pompey would please Caesar, making him a powerful ally against Cleopatra. Caesar instead was enraged that a consul of Rome could be assassinated and the body disrespected in such a manner. So, rather than allying himself with Ptolemy, he famously forged an alliance with Cleopatra.

injustices he had suffered at the hands of Pompey and the Senate, he marched the 13th Legion from Ravenna in Cisalpine Gaul to Rimini in Italia, a route that required him to cross the border between the two at the river. By omitting an account of crossing the Rubicon, he may have been attempting to avoid acknowledging that, by entering Italia at the head of a legion, he was breaking Roman law, even if this would have been obvious to his contemporaries. Caesar's account, in truth, is more an exercise in self-justification than an attempt to establish an accurate portrait of events, in which he presents himself not so much as leading a rebellion against Rome, but as freeing the city from the dictatorial rule of Pompey.

As Caesar's single legion, a force of six thousand men, advanced toward Rome, Pompey decided to abandon the city and retreat to the south of Italy, despite having a much larger army. Caesar pursued him and again Pompey refused to fight, this time escaping to Greece. Before going after him, Caesar marched to Spain, where Pompey had additional forces stationed, leaving Mark Antony, his closest ally, in command in Rome. After defeating Pompey's forces in Spain, Caesar took his legions to Greece and engaged Pompey in a number of battles before decisively defeating him in 48 BCE at the Battle of Pharsalus. Pompey fled to Egypt, with Caesar not far behind, and was assassinated there on the orders of the young Pharaoh Ptolemy XIII.

TRIUMPHANT ENTRY

The death of Pompey all but ended the civil war. Caesar quickly dealt with the few supporters of Pompey who refused to submit to him and pardoned those

CAESAR'S ANGER
The Head of Pompey Presented to Caesar by the Venetian artist Giovanni Antonio Pellegrini (1675-1741).

death in the Senate by numerous members of the conspiracy, including Brutus. If he spoke any last words, they were not recorded at the time and those most often attributed to him, "Et tu Brute?", were coined by Shakespeare.

Caesar left his estate to his eighteen-year-old great-nephew and adopted son Octavian who would prove to be ruthless and calculating in the civil wars that erupted after Caesar's death. Octavian eventually came out on top, defeating Mark Antony, his main rival, at the battle of Actium in 31 BCE and became the first emperor of Rome under the name of Augustus Caesar.

It is impossible to know if Julius Caesar had intended to become the supreme leader of Rome when he crossed the Rubicon. On defeating Pompey, he certainly became very powerful, but did not resolve the dilemma of how best to exercise that power. The only thing we can be sure of is that, by crossing the river, Julius Caesar began a sequence of events that culminated in the establishment of the Roman Empire, which would survive in one form or another for fifteen hundred years.

who did. In 46 BCE he returned to Rome and this time celebrated in proper style with a triumphal entry into the city. He became dictator of Rome for a period of ten years, an unprecedented term for a role previously only thought necessary in times of crisis. With this newfound power, he introduced widespread reforms in the administration of the city and empire. At the beginning of 44 BCE he was made dictator for life, becoming a king in everything but name.

STABBED TO DEATH

A group of sixty senators, including Caesar's friend Marcus Junius Brutus, opposed the idea of one man having so much power and began to plot a conspiracy to kill him. On the Ides of March (the 15th), he was stabbed to

PAUL CONVERTS ON THE WAY TO DAMASCUS

32–36 CE

Circumstances: A man sets out on a journey from Jerusalem to Damascus

Protagonists: St. Paul and the early Christians

Consequences: The development of Christianity into a major religion

What we know today of the life of St. Paul comes solely from the Acts of the Apostles and the Epistles in the New Testament of the Bible. These were letters written by Paul himself to the churches he had founded in various places around the Mediterranean. In the Epistles, Paul only writes about details in his life that have some relevance to the theological point he is making, so we have not been left with anything like a full biography from this source. The Acts are traditionally said to have been written by Luke, the author of the third Gospel, who apparently knew Paul personally and has provided us with more information about him. However, some of what Luke says does not exactly match the version given in the Epistles and we are still left with some large gaps. But Paul's conversion to Christianity on the road to Damascus, in which he saw a vision of the risen Christ, is described on a total of five occasions, twice in the Epistles and three times in Acts, indicating that it was regarded by both Paul and Luke as being a key moment in his life.

The event itself is described in both sources as being a miraculous occurrence and, if we accept these versions of the story, then Paul did not make a decision to convert to Christianity; rather, he was being directed by Christ to do so. Regardless of how the conversion occurred, Paul's subsequent decision about what to do afterward had profound consequences because it laid the foundation for the transformation of Christianity from being a minor sect into a major religion in its own right.

SAUL OF TARSUS

If we accept the nuggets of information we are given about Paul's life in the Epistles and Acts as being accurate, which not all religious scholars do, it is possible to get at least some idea of Paul's early life. He was born in the first or second year after the birth of Christ and came from a wealthy Jewish family in Tarsus, a Greek city within the Roman Empire in what is now southern Turkey. He was most probably known by the Jewish name of Saul. His father was a tent maker, a trade for which Tarsus was

CARAVAGGIO'S PAUL
The Conversion of Saint Paul by
Caravaggio (1571–1610) shows the
moment of St. Paul's revelation on the
road to Damascus.

well known, and it is reasonable to
assume that he followed his father into
that business. Tarsus was also known as
a center of learning and Paul, who both
spoke and wrote in Greek, appears to
have received a good education in the
city. As a young man, before going
to Jerusalem, he possibly studied Jewish
law under the eminent scholar Gamaliel,
a leading authority in the discipline at
that time.

Paul tells us that before his
conversion he had been a Pharisee, a
member of a Jewish sect committed to
maintaining a strict interpretation of the
Law of Moses. At that time, the Jewish
faith was coming under increasing
pressure to change thanks to radical new
ideas, particularly those articulated by
Jesus, who was seen as a heretic (not
believing in the established faith) in the
eyes of the Pharisees. Paul says that he
did not actually meet Jesus, although he
may have been in Jerusalem at the time
of the Crucifixion. As a Pharisee himself,
he may also have been involved in the
persecution of Christians, including being
present at the stoning of St. Stephen, one
of the earliest Christian martyrs. It was
in this context, as a persecutor of
Christians, that he decided to travel from
Jerusalem to Damascus, intending, he
tells us, to arrest any Christians he found
there who had fled to the city to avoid
persecution and bring them back to
Jerusalem in chains.

ON THE ROAD

While traveling to Damascus, Paul was
subjected to a sudden flash of light that
blinded him and caused him to fall to
the ground. At the same moment, a
vision of the risen Christ was revealed
to him, causing him to instantly convert
to Christianity. In the vision, Jesus
asked Paul why he had been persecuting
Christians and said that he would be
told what to do next in Damascus.
Once there, he was approached by a
follower of Jesus called Ananias, who
had also experienced a vision telling him
that Paul had been chosen to spread
the name of the Lord. Despite Paul's
reputation as a persecutor of Christians,
Ananias cured Paul of his blindness and,
after instructing him in the faith, he
baptized him as a Christian.

> **On the road to Damascus, a vision
> of Christ was revealed to Paul,
> causing him to instantly convert
> to Christianity.**

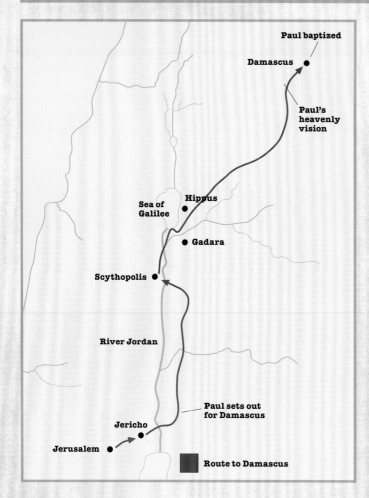

Paul baptized

Damascus

Paul's heavenly vision

Hippus

Sea of Galilee

Gadara

Scythopolis

River Jordan

Paul sets out for Damascus

Jericho

Jerusalem

Route to Damascus

ROAD TO DAMASCUS
The probable route taken by St. Paul on his journey from Jerusalem to Damascus showing the approximate location of the conversion.

SPREADING THE WORD
Paul reappears in about 45 CE at the beginning of his missionary work, which included traveling extensively around the Roman Empire to convert people to Christianity and to establish churches. He records how he was involved in three shipwrecks on his missionary journeys and was also imprisoned on a number of occasions because of his beliefs. Paul was preaching the New Covenant, a theology based on the belief that the route to salvation was to be found in Jesus's death on the Cross and the Resurrection rather than through the Law of Moses. He had been involved in long debates with other figures in the early church, most notably with Peter at what became known as the Incident at Antioch, in which he argued that Gentiles (non-Jews) should be permitted to join the Church as well as Jews and that the Jewish law relating to the circumcision of boys and the proscribing

LOST YEARS
In truth, we don't know a great deal about what Paul did over the next ten years. He appears to have spent time traveling in Arabia and also went to Jerusalem, where he met Peter, the apostle who would also have a huge influence on the development of the early Church. He also met James, who would go on to become the leader of the Christian Church in Jerusalem. Other than these fleeting glimpses from Paul's so-called "lost years," we can only assume that he was studying the faith.

of certain foods should be relaxed to make the faith more inclusive.

Written in about 50 CE, the Epistles were composed in response to inquiries from some of the churches Paul had established. As well as being the earliest Christian documents in existence, the Epistles formed the foundation stones of Christian theology. In them, Paul developed the principle of universality, in which all churches held to the same core beliefs, thereby preventing early Christianity from splitting into obscure sects. So, as well as spreading the Word around the Roman Empire and opening up the faith to Gentiles, Paul greatly influenced the direction of early Christianity, separating it from Judaism and establishing it as a religion in its own right, one based on faith and inclusion rather than law and exclusivity.

PAPAL BASILICA

The interior of Saint Paul Outside the Walls in Rome, founded on the site where Paul's remains are thought to rest.

VISION OF CHRIST

Over the years, many attempts have been made to explain Paul's vision and conversion to Christianity in a rational way. It has been suggested that he had some kind of seizure or an epileptic fit. Others have theorized that he had become disillusioned with his role as a persecutor and, perhaps as a consequence of feeling guilt over the death of the Christian martyr Stephen, was seeking a way of making amends for his actions. Whether it was a miracle or not, once he had converted, Paul threw all his energy into his new faith.

A WORLD RELIGION

The scriptures say nothing about Paul's death, which later traditions claim occurred in Rome in about 65 CE. Even though Paul may have died in obscurity, the influence he had on the early Christian Church, both in its organization and its doctrine, was enormous. Whether his conversion was a miracle or not, his devotion to the Christian Church and his subsequent actions rank among the greatest decisions ever made. It is impossible to know for sure, but without his energy and devotion, the Church may never have developed into the major world religion it is today.

According to some stories, St. Paul was martyred during the persecutions of Christians by the Roman emperor Nero.

CONSTANTINE BECOMES A CHRISTIAN

306–337 CE

Circumstances: The early history of the Christian Church

Protagonists: Constantine, his mother, and the Christians of the Roman Empire

Consequences: Christianity became the official religion of the empire

For much of its early history, Christianity was very much a minority religion in the Roman Empire and Christians were the subject of state-sponsored persecution. The fortunes of the Church changed completely under the rule of the emperor Constantine the Great (ca. 272–337 CE), when the religion not only became officially tolerated under the Edict of Milan, issued in 313, but would become the predominant religion throughout the empire over the following decades. The driving force behind this change is thought to have been the conversion of Constantine to Christianity. If this is the case, then it was one of the greatest individual decisions in the history of the religion because it created the conditions under which Christianity could grow into the major world religion it is today.

CONVERTING TO THE FAITH

The circumstances of the conversion are far from clear; Constantine himself later claimed that he converted during the Battle of the Milvian Bridge in 312 when, at least according to one version of the story, soldiers under his command reported seeing the sign of the Cross in the sky and, after painting crosses on their shields, went on to win the battle. No specifically Christian symbols or images were included on the Arch of Constantine—the monument erected to celebrate the victory, which still stands near the Colosseum in Rome—leading some to doubt this version of events. Constantine was not actually baptized until 337, twenty-five years after the battle, suggesting that, whenever he converted, it was perhaps not politically advisable to publicize the fact at the time or he was not as committed to the Christian faith during his life as was made out after he died. An alternative theory proposes that he was introduced to the Church at an early age by his mother, Helena, who is thought to have

By legalizing Christianity, the Edict of Milan kickstarted the biggest religious revolution in the history of the Roman Empire.

been a Christian at the time of his birth. This would mean there was no great conversion event in his life at all because he was already a Christian, but had kept his beliefs to himself until he became emperor because of the discrimination he would have otherwise experienced.

POWER STRUGGLE

Constantine was born in Naissus in the Roman province of Dardania, now Niš in Serbia. His father, Constantius, was a military commander in the Roman army who rose to prominence under the emperor Diocletian. In 293 CE, Constantius became part of the so-called Tetrarchy, a system of governance that

split the empire into eastern and western parts, each ruled by two men: a senior emperor to whom the title of Augustus was given; and a junior emperor who became known as Caesar. Constantius, who had been appointed as Caesar by Diocletian, governed the western empire, which included Gaul, Britain, and Spain. When he died in 306, Constantine was proclaimed as the new Caesar. By this time, Diocletian had retired and a power struggle was developing between senior army officers.

Constantine's main opponent in the west was Maxentius and their dispute reached a head at the Milvian Bridge, a crossing over the Tiber just to the north of Rome. In the ensuing battle, Maxentius drowned in the river, leaving Constantine as Augustus of the whole of the Western Roman Empire, with Licinius—the Augustus in the east—his only remaining rival for the position of

VICTORY ARCH

The Arch of Constantine was erected in Rome to celebrate victory in the Battle of Milvian Bridge. The Colosseum can be seen in the background.

sole emperor. With relations between the two men relatively friendly, they met in Milan in 313, where Licinius married Constantine's sister and they both signed the Edict of Milan. Under the rule of Diocletian, the persecution of Christians had been particularly severe, so the edict represented a huge reversal of fortune. The terms of the edict gave people of all religions the freedom to worship, but also singled out Christianity for special treatment, both legalizing it and making provision for the return of property seized under Diocletian's persecutions.

NEW ROME

In the east, Licinius continued to worship the pagan gods of Rome and, although Christians were no longer persecuted, they were not granted any special privileges either. Constantine, in contrast, actively began to promote

Christianity in the west, beginning a program of church building in cities under his control, including the construction of the first church on the site of what is now St. Peter's Basilica in the Vatican City in Rome. By 320, Licinius had reintroduced persecutions, which were, in effect, a challenge to the authority of Constantine. A civil war followed, ending in 324 with victory for Constantine at the Battle of Chrysopolis, making him the ruler of the whole of the Roman Empire.

The following year Constantine decided to move the capital of the empire away from Rome to the Greek town of Byzantium (now Istanbul in Turkey). Here he began a huge program of construction that included massive new city walls, public buildings, and churches. By 330, much of the initial building work was complete and the new city was inaugurated in a ceremony that involved changing the city's name from Byzantium to Constantinople to honor the city's founder.

OFFICIAL RELIGION

It is difficult to pinpoint the exact moment when Constantine converted to Christianity in the same way as we can for St. Paul. If, however, we assume that his conversion really was an expression of his convictions, as the evidence suggests, then its significance for Christianity was almost as great. Legalizing Christianity and allowing free worship under the terms of the Edict of Milan would be the first step to it eventually becoming the official religion of the Roman empire under the later Roman emperor Theodosius I (347–395).

MILVIAN BRIDGE
This fresco depicts the battle in 312 between Constantine and his main opponent Maxentius, who drowned in the river.

TRUE BELIEVER?

The manner of Contantine's baptism in 337, which only happened after it had become apparent that he was dying, has been the main cause of skepticism over his Christian convictions. To those who argue that Constantine wasn't a true convert and that he only promoted Christianity because it suited his wider purpose of gaining control over the whole of the Roman Empire, his choice of the Christian religion was primarily due to it being monotheistic (believing in one god). This, the argument goes, fits in with his intention of replacing the rule of the Tetrarchy with the rule of a single person, thereby leaving the empire with only one emperor and one God. A counterargument might suggest that, if Constantine was a Christian in name only, why did he bother to get baptized at all and why did he spend huge amounts of both his time and money on building so many churches?

The Edict of Milan came into force when only about 10 percent of people in the Roman Empire were Christians, most of whom were from the lower classes, so it would appear that Constantine would have had little to gain politically by favoring the religion of a minority of poor people over that of the majority. His construction of churches across the Roman Empire and many other actions certainly look like those of a true believer rather than somebody going through the motions for the sake of appearances. The Western Roman Empire is conventionally said to have come to an end in 476, by which time Christianity was firmly established in Europe, while the Eastern Roman Empire, usually known as the Byzantine Empire today, continued for a further thousand years as a Christian state, right up until the fall of Constantinople to the Islamic Ottomans.

OUT INTO THE OPEN

Constantine's actions certainly point toward a deeply held conviction and his decision to bring in the Edict of Milan would still rank as one of the greatest ever made in the history of the Church. Without this, Christianity, which was under a constant threat of persecution, may have withered. So, if we can say that St. Paul transformed Christianity from a minor Jewish sect into a separate religion in its own right, then Constantine brought the religion out into the open and set it on the path toward becoming the most widely observed faith today, now followed by an estimated 2.2 billion people around the world.

KING JOHN SIGNS THE MAGNA CARTA

1215

Circumstances: The increasingly despotic rule of a monarch

Protagonists: King John, the barons, and the freemen of England

Consequences: The first expression of the constitutional rights and liberty of the individual

Magna Carta literally means the Great Charter in Latin. In its earliest form, it was the text of a carefully negotiated settlement between King John and a group of English barons who had rebelled at what they thought to be his despotic rule and the heavy burden of taxation he had imposed on them. It dates to July 15, 1215, and was sealed by the king at Runnymede, an otherwise unremarkable field on the banks of the River Thames, just outside London.

Over the years, the Magna Carta has been described as the most important document in the world, the greatest constitutional document of all time, and the foundation stone of parliamentary government. The significance later attached to it was by no means apparent in 1215, not least because the terms of

the settlement were broken within three months of it coming into force. It was not even the first charter sealed by an English king to define their responsibilities as monarch. The Charter of Liberties issued by Henry I at his coronation in 1100 was a direct forerunner of the Magna Carta and set a precedent for monarchs to state their duties in written form, even if they habitually went on to ignore them.

What set the Magna Carta apart was that it represented the first successful attempt by subjects of an English monarch to force their king to accept limitations on his power. It compelled him to respect the liberties of so-called "freemen," who could not be punished solely on the orders of the king and, if accused of a crime, could only be prosecuted through the due process of the law of the land. It said nothing at all

"No free man will be taken or imprisoned or disseised [have their estate seized] or outlawed or exiled or in any way ruined, nor shall we go or send against him, save by the lawful judgment of his peers and by the law of the land. To no man shall we sell, to no man shall we deny or delay, right or justice."

—From the Magna Carta of 1215

PLANTAGENET KING
An eighteenth-century illustration of King
John showing him in about 1200, shortly
after he came to the throne.

rights of women and children and, in
restricting itself to freemen, specifically
excluded serfs, those people who were
held in a form of bonded labor that was
little better than slavery and who made
up something like 70 percent of the adult
male population of England at that time.

Despite its shortcomings, the Magna
Carta can be regarded as the beginning
of the process of constitutional reform
in English, and then British, history,
which would eventually lead to the
representative democracy of today.
King John was compelled to accept
the conditions in the document, so the
historical decision we are dealing with
here is the one made collectively by the
barons who were trying to limit the king's
power over them. The decision of the

barons to rebel in this way may have
been primarily motivated by their own
self-interest, but, whatever their
motivation, the relationship between
monarch and subjects changed and,
once the door to reform had been
opened, there would be no going back.

KING JOHN

John was the youngest son of King
Henry II, the first Plantagenet king of
England, and Eleanor of Aquitaine,
who, when they married, combined their
lands to form an empire stretching from
the southwest of France to southern
Scotland, which included all of England
and much of Wales and Ireland. In 1199,
on the death of his older brother, Richard
the Lionheart, John became king. After
his coronation, he began a long and
costly war in France against the
supporters of Arthur of Brittany, his
nephew and only serious rival to the
throne. After Arthur was captured by
John's army in 1203, he disappeared
from history and, while we don't know
exactly what happened to him, it is
reasonable to assume that he was
murdered on John's orders. But the
removal of his rival did not put an end
to the war and, over the next few years,
John lost almost all of the territory he
ruled in France. He would make a
number of attempts to regain it but by
1214 King Philip II of France had won
control over the majority of the country.

Only four original copies of
the Magna Carta have survived
till today. A later version, dating
from 1297, was sold in New York
in 2007 for $21 million.

FREE MEN

Several clauses in the Magna Carta (one of which is quoted at the beginning of this chapter) deal with individual freedom. They precede laws relating to habeus corpus, the requirement that anyone who has been arrested must be charged and evidence brought before them in a court. Two other clauses relating to the freedom of the Church and the freemen of London also still remain on the statute books of English law today.

THE BARONS

The enormous cost of the war in France was one of the main sources of dissatisfaction among the barons of England, not least because John had extracted as much money as he could from them to pay for it. A particular irritant to a group of barons from the north of England, who would become known as "the Northerners," was scutage, a form of taxation the nobility had to pay in order to buy themselves out of military service. It was only one of numerous taxes and when these were combined with the king's other means of raising money, to include outright extortion (obtaining money by force), it led to a high level of opposition to his rule.

The barons were well aware that they had John over a barrel, so the terms contained in the Magna Carta went far further than the original Charter of Liberties.

The Northerners in particular gained little advantage from John's apparently endless war in France, yet it was costing them a fortune. When the king returned from France in defeat, the opposition erupted into outright rebellion.

THE CHARTER

The barons assembled in January 1215 and, as there was no obvious candidate to replace John as king, they decided to force him to accept a list of their demands. As more people joined them, momentum began to gather behind their cause. When in May they approached London with an army, rather than having to fight, they were welcomed into the city by its freemen. It was a disastrous turn of events for John, who now faced the very real possibility of losing his crown. Rather than risk any further defeats, and in order to buy time to gather his forces, he entered into peace negotiations with the barons at Runnymede.

CIVIL WAR

One of the most important clauses in the charter authorized the creation of a committee of twenty-five barons to oversee John's conduct and ensure that he stuck to the commitments he had made. It represented a direct threat to his authority and, almost as soon as he had placed his seal on the document, John appealed to Pope Innocent III to annul the whole charter on the grounds that it undermined his God-given rights as king and that he had only signed it under duress. The Pope granted John's request, sparking a civil war, known as the First Barons' War, which continued into the following year.

On October 18, 1216, John died of dysentery and was succeeded by his nine-year-old son Henry III, with

RUNNYMEDE
A view across the Thames of the meadow where the English barons met King John and where the Magna Carta was sealed.

Sir William Marshall acting as regent. Marshall was a widely respected man and he immediately reinstated the charter, although with the omission of the clause about setting up a committee of barons, bringing the war to an end.

LIBERTY AND THE LAW

The original Magna Carta, then, only came into effect for a matter of weeks before being annulled, but the principle of limiting royal power had been established and would lead to a gradual shift of power from the monarchy to the people in the form of an elected parliament. The influence of the charter eventually extended far beyond England. The Fifth Amendment to the United States Constitution, for instance, states that people cannot be "deprived of life, liberty, or property, without due process of law," a phrase that can be traced directly back to the original clauses in the first document sealed at Runnymede. It could also be argued that the Magna Carta provided inspiration for American rebels to break away from Britain during the American Revolution because they considered its terms protected them from what they saw as the unlawful interventions of the British Crown in their affairs. This explains why the Magna Carta remains a revered document in America today.

The Magna Carta remains an important document, even if that has more to do with what it represents rather than what it actually says. In setting limits on royal power, the barons of England established a principle of liberty that retains its power today. In recent years, when British politicians attempted to extend the legal period of detention without charge from twenty-eight to forty-two days for suspected terrorists, they were faced with counterarguments based on the liberty of the individual going back to the Magna Carta. The fundamental principles of liberty and unlawful imprisonment may have been the unintended consequences of the Magna Carta, but they are consequences nevertheless and are as worth fighting for now as they ever were.

THE MEDICI OPEN A BANK

1397

Circumstances: A commercial and artistic boom in fifteenth-century Florence

Protagonists: The Medici family and the artists of the Florentine Renaissance

Consequences: The conditions in which some of the greatest art in history was created

During the great cultural flowering of the Renaissance, the learning of Classical Greece was rediscovered and the radical new ideas of humanism, which emphasized freedom of thought and expression, began to challenge the rigid and unchanging doctrine of the Christian Church. Most historians of the period agree that this movement began in the Italian city-state of Florence and reached its height there in the middle of the fifteenth century with the works of such great artists as Leonardo da Vinci and Michelangelo. But there is far less consensus over the question of exactly when the Renaissance began and why it first occurred in Florence rather than in any of the other Italian city-states, such as Milan or Venice. One theory suggests that the presence of so many talented people gathered together in one place was purely coincidental. Others see it as a gradual cultural development beginning in the early fourteenth century with, among others, the writer Dante Alighieri and the artist Giotto.

An alternative school of thought dates the beginning of the Renaissance to a specific moment in 1401 when a competition was held in Florence by the Cloth Importers Guild to find a designer of new bronze doors for the baptistry of Florence Cathedral. After a hard-fought contest, the artist Lorenzo Ghiberti beat the architect Filippo Brunelleschi to the prize and in the process, so the theory goes, introduced a culture of competition among the artists of Florence, who from then on attempted to outdo one another in order to find rich patrons for their work. The problem with these three theories, however, is that they all concentrate on the creativity of individual artists and almost completely ignore the wider social context in which they worked.

By the fifteenth century, Florence had developed into a major commercial center, home to some of the wealthiest bankers in Italy.

FLORENCE

By the fifteenth century, Florence had developed into a major European commercial and financial center, home to some of the wealthiest merchants and bankers in Italy as well as to a large aristocratic class of landowners. One way of expressing this wealth, both for the aristocracy and for social-climbing businessmen, was through the patronage of the arts. The leading family in Florence during much of this period was the Medici, who had made enormous amounts of money through their banking business and other trading activities. While it would be an exaggeration to claim that their money kick-started the Renaissance, it is nevertheless fair to say that their patronage of the arts helped

COSIMO

Portrait of Cosimo de' Medici, Florentine banker and patron, who had a deep appreciation of the arts.

CITIES AND PATRONS

"The causes of the Renaissance were as deep as they were broad. They can be related to the growth of cities and of late medieval trade, to the rise of rich and powerful capitalist patrons, to technical progress which affected both economic and artistic life."

— **Norman Davies**, *Europe: A History*, 1988

to create the conditions in which it could flourish. And it all began in 1397 when Giovanni di Bicci de' Medici (ca. 1360–1429), the head of a well-off but by no means rich Florentine family, decided to use the money he had saved while working for a bank in Rome to start up in business for himself in his home city.

THE MEDICI BANK

Giovanni di Bicci was one of the judges of the competition between Ghiberti and Brunelleschi, indicating that, just four years after opening his own bank in Florence, he had become one of its more notable citizens. This may also have been the moment when the Medici family first became aware of the potential advantages in the patronage of art, which could advertize the wealth of the bank, leading to more people wanting to use its services. Giovanni certainly gives the impression of being an astute businessman, capable of spotting such an opportunity and exploiting it. But he was by no means a gambler, unlike many of today's merchant bankers, relying instead on good business practices and the development of an extensive network of business contacts throughout Italy and in the major trading cities around Europe.

The success of the bank prompted Giovanni to expand, opening branches in a number of other cities, including one in Rome. By far the richest institution of that period was the Catholic Church, and, more specifically, the papacy in Rome, which commanded huge revenues from its churches throughout Europe and beyond, and through such practices as selling "indulgences," a controversial practice that allowed sinners to buy the Pope's pardon. The papacy was undergoing a period of turmoil at this time, in which at least four different people were claiming to be the legitimate Pope. In a daring move in 1402, Giovanni lent a huge sum of money to one of the claimants, a colorful character with little apparent religious conviction called Baldassare Cossa, who had made a fortune through piracy and used it to buy a cardinalship. The loan effectively bankrolled Baldassare's bid and, in 1410, Giovanni's speculation paid off when Baldassare was elected Pope, taking the name of John XXIII and appointing the Medici Bank as the papal bankers.

COSIMO DE' MEDICI

The appointment catapulted the Medici Bank into the forefront of European banking and, as the bank was paid a commission on all the business it did for the Pope, it made Giovanni a very wealthy man. He gave his eldest son, Cosimo, the job of looking after the papal account and, even though only in his early twenties at the time, he proved to be as astute as his father. The prestige

accompanying the position of bankers to the Pope brought a flood of new custom, including royal households around Europe. The huge increase in business, together with the family's many other commercial interests and investments, combined to make the Medici the wealthiest family in Europe. Even after John XXIII was forced to resign his position as Pope in 1415 at the Council of Constance, the Medicis' reputation as loyal and trustworthy bankers ensured that they continued to hold the papal account.

Despite his vast wealth, Giovanni remained a prudent man throughout his life, not given to ostentatious displays or lavish spending. Cosimo followed in his father's footsteps until Giovanni died in 1429, at which point he began to pursue his own personal interests as well as the wider ones of the bank. Giovanni had treated the patronage of the arts as if it were a business transaction, while Cosimo appears to have held a much deeper appreciation of art for its own sake. As well as putting together his own private collection of art and becoming the patron of a number of struggling young artists, notably Donatello and Fra Angelico, Cosimo began to spend large amounts of money collecting manuscripts from around Europe and beyond, bringing together Classical and humanist learning in the great library he established in Florence. He also became fascinated by architecture, constructing

---

The Medici family did not start or inspire the Florentine Renaissance, but its money largely paid for it.

numerous buildings, including the Palazzo Medici as a home for himself, and was involved in the commissioning of Brunelleschi to build the dome of Florence Cathedral, widely regarded today as being the greatest example of Renaissance architecture.

On his deathbed, Giovanni is said to have warned Cosimo not to become involved in the unruly world of Florentine politics, but Cosimo ignored his father's advice, beginning a political dynasty that would rule over Florence and the Grand Duchy of Tuscany for most of the next three hundred years.

LORENZO THE MAGNIFICENT

Patronage of the arts would continue to be a Medici family obsession long after Cosimo's death in 1464, most famously through his grandson Lorenzo the Magnificent (1449–92), who became patron both to Leonardo da Vinci and Botticelli. He also provided the teenage Michelangelo with lodgings in his own house while the artist was an apprentice in the workshop of a Florentine sculptor.

The Medici Bank had been in decline for some years by the time of Lorenzo's death in 1492 and ceased trading completely when the family was expelled from Florence two years later. According to Niccolò Machiavelli, who served in the Florentine government during the Medicis' exile and is now best known for his writings on political science, the bank failed because the Medici had begun to behave more like princes than merchants, neglecting their business so that it collapsed as soon as it faced a crisis.

The extraordinary wealth of the Medici family meant that they were largely unaffected by the failure of the

DONATELLO'S DAVID
This sculpture of David was commissioned by Cosimo de' Medici and now stands in the Bargello Museum in Florence.

banking business. Over the course of the sixteenth century, the family would go on to provide four popes and two queens of France. But they are best remembered for their patronage of the arts during the Florentine Renaissance. During that period artists almost always worked to commissions and most of those came from one member of the Medici family or another. So the decision made by Giovanni di Bicci in 1397 to start out in business for himself must surely be regarded as a great one, because of the enormous consequences it would have for the history of art.

GUTENBERG PRINTS A BIBLE

ca. 1450

Circumstances: A struggling entrepreneur comes up with another scheme to make some money

Protagonists: Johannes Gutenberg, his colleagues, and creditors in Mainz and Strasbourg

Consequences: The beginning of printed books

The invention of the movable-type printing press is widely held to be one of the key technological advances in history—a development that has proved so significant that it has been called the "Gutenberg Revolution" after the man who first developed it, Johannes Gutenberg (ca. 1400–1468). It is hard to overstate the contribution his invention has made to what has been called the "democratization of knowledge," a process in which access to learning and information has changed from being the exclusive privilege of a select few to being available to all. Before printed books began to appear in Europe, books and manuscripts were produced by the slow and laborious process of hand-copying by scribes, making them very expensive and restricting ownership to the wealthy few and the Church.

After Gutenberg developed the printing press, the technology spread rapidly throughout Europe and, as it allowed books to be mass-produced made them much more affordable and more widely available. The radical new ideas of Renaissance humanism and the corresponding rediscovery of Classical learning spread quickly through Europe as a consequence, leading to great advances in knowledge and learning in such spheres as philosophy and science.

Unfortunately for us today, details of Gutenberg's life are, at best, sketchy. What little information we do know about him comes almost exclusively from a few official documents and the

"We should note the force, effect, and consequences of inventions which are nowhere more conspicuous than in those three which were unknown to the ancients, namely printing, gunpowder, and the compass. For these three have changed the appearance and state of the whole world."

—Francis Bacon, *Novum Organum*, 1620

records of a number of court cases he was involved in, so any reconstruction of his working methods has to rely on an interpretation of these sources. One thing we can say is that Gutenberg's invention of movable type and the printing press must have involved numerous decisions, many of which would qualify as being among the greatest ever made because of the impact printing would go on to have. It is not possible to pinpoint exactly when and where these decisions were made because of the scarcity of information about Gutenberg. So what follows is a more general description of how we think he developed his printing method, rather than a detailed dissection of the stages he went through. We also examine his best-known deed: the decision to produce what would become his most famous printed work, the Gutenberg Bible.

JOHANNES GUTENBERG

Gutenberg was born in about 1400, give or take a year or two, in Mainz, a city on the River Rhine in what was then the Holy Roman Empire and is now southwestern Germany. It was a period of fierce rivalry in the city between those of the aristocratic patrician class, including the Gutenberg family, and the merchants and craftsmen of the trade guilds. This conflict would force the family to leave the city on several occasions, when they would go to Eltville am Rhein, where Gutenberg's mother owned an estate. As a young man, Gutenberg is thought to have learned goldsmithing and the minting business, and may also have studied at the University of Erfut. Enrollment records from 1418 include a student named Johannes de

THE PRINTER
Born in about 1400, Johannes Gutenberg developed the early prototype of the printing press, a revolutionary innovation.

Altavilla, which could be him because Altavilla is the Latin name for Eltville. However, Johannes was a common name at the time so it is impossible to say for sure.

Nothing is known about what he did for the next fifteen years, but in 1434, by then in his mid-thirties, he turned up again in Strasbourg, in what is now eastern France. He was the subject of a court case in which a woman claimed that they were engaged to be married and that he had broken his promise to her, but we don't know the outcome of the proceedings, or whether he ever actually got married. Another court case a few years later sheds some light on what he was doing in Strasbourg. It would seem he was involved in developing a method of mass-producing magic mirrors—small sheets of polished metal with religious icons stamped on them, which were thought at the time to be able to capture the holy light given off by religious relics. Apparently he was intending to sell these magic mirrors at a huge profit to pilgrims attending a religious festival in the German city of Aachen, but the scheme foundered when the festival was canceled. The court case involved a group of investors in the scheme who wanted their money back from Gutenberg. He appears to have been in charge of the manufacturing process, which may have involved some

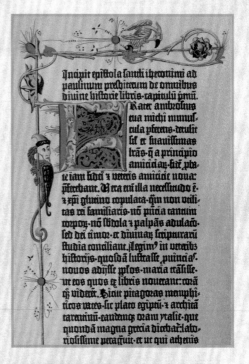

GUTENBERG BIBLE
A detail of a page from an original Gutenberg Bible with illustrations added by hand after it had been printed.

---

sort of press to stamp out the mirrors, enabling him to make thousands of them in a short space of time.

During proceedings, Gutenberg promised to share a secret with the investors to make up for the money they had lost and, while we don't know what that secret was, it is possible that he could have been referring to an early prototype of the printing press. At this vital moment in 1444, just when he may have made the decision to work on the development of the printing press using movable type, we lose touch with him completely and, for the next four years, we have no idea where he was or what he was doing.

Gutenberg's great innovation was to put together several already existing technologies to make his press and then develop those parts of the printing process.

THE PRINTING PRESS

By 1448, Gutenberg was back in Mainz and had borrowed money from Johann Fust, a wealthy citizen of the city, in order to set up a print shop. His great innovation was to put together several already existing technologies to make his press and then develop those parts of the printing process that were necessary for the whole thing to work. The press itself was much the same as those used in wine-making, in which juice was squeezed out of grapes by screwing a board down on top of them. Gutenberg must also have developed the required consistencies of paper and ink, presumably by trial and error, and the method of applying the ink to the typeface with soft leather dabbers.

The typeface itself was composed of small individual blocks, known in the printing trade as "sorts," made in a similar way to how coins were minted— using specially made punches, each carved in the shape of the required letters by highly skilled craftsmen called punch-cutters. The punches were used to stamp out molds, which were then filled with a metal alloy to make the sorts. These sorts had the raised profile of individual letters on their upper faces and could be arranged in a frame to make up the words and sentences of the page to be printed. This was the famous movable type, which, after it had been used once, could be broken up into individual sorts and used again to compose another page. It was the use of this movable type— together with the innovations Gutenberg introduced to make the press and the sorts—which would prove to be his major breakthrough and that would go on to revolutionize the dissemination of knowledge. The techniques of printing were refined and developed over the centuries after Gutenberg first used them, but the essential elements of the process remained much the same right up until the middle of the nineteenth century, when the introduction of the steam-powered rotary press industrialized printing.

At first, Gutenberg used the press to produce individual sheets of text before moving onto books. None of his work was dated, making it difficult to ascertain the exact chronology, but it would appear that the first book he printed was a Latin grammar of the type he had most probably used himself at school and university. It does not appear that the business was very lucrative, because Fust

---

BOOK PRODUCTION

Gutenberg's printing press. The press itself ensured that a uniform pressure was applied over the whole page, to avoid smudges.

brought a court action against Gutenberg in 1451 for not paying the interest on his loan. Rather than collecting the money he was owed, Fust increased the size of the loan, perhaps having been convinced by Gutenberg that his next project would turn the business around.

BEAUTIFUL BIBLE

Wherever the original idea of printing a Bible came from, one thing is certain: it would be a massive undertaking. The Latin grammar book was twenty-six pages long, while Gutenberg's finished Bible ran to 1,275 pages in two volumes. Gutenberg used the money he had borrowed from Fust to set up a second print shop and take on more staff, possibly as many as thirty. Over the course of the next three years, he printed about 180 copies of his Bible, of which 150 were on paper and thirty on vellum (treated calfskin).

It was a staggering achievement, demonstrating the enormous potential of the printing press and producing a truly beautiful book. All 180 copies were sold, but even so, Gutenberg still could not repay his debts and he was sued again in 1455 by Fust, who won the case and took control of the entire business. Fust would go on to run the print shop in partnership with Peter Schöffer, his son-in-law and one of Gutenberg's former employees. It is hard not to come to the conclusion that Fust had waited until Gutenberg had done all the hard work in getting the business up and running and then, realizing its future value, seized it for himself. But,

WORD OF GOD

We don't know the circumstances of his hugely ambitious decision to print a Bible, but, in his book *The Gutenberg Revolution*, John Man speculates that Gutenberg may have been inspired by Nicholas of Cusa (1401–1464), a cardinal in the Holy Roman Empire, who was at the time engaged in a campaign to unify the text of the Bible across all Christian churches. Cusa also wanted to make the word of God much more widely available than it had previously been, and a printed Bible would have gone some way to achieving both of these aims. However, we don't know if Cusa ever met Gutenberg, or if he was even aware of the printing press, so it is impossible to say if he did indeed provide the inspiration for the project.

at the same time, while Gutenberg may have been a great innovator, he doesn't give the impression of being much of a businessman, forever borrowing more money than he could repay.

PROJECT GUTENBERG

Fust and Schöffer went on to produce the second major printed book in 1457, an edition of the Psalms known as the *Mainz Psalter*, which included a publication date

Gutenberg died in 1468 without receiving any recognition for the enormous contribution he had made to the development of the printed word.

WORTHY MONUMENT
This memorial in Mainz, Germany, shows Johannes Gutenberg holding one of his printed bibles. Today, Gutenberg is remembered throughout the world for his remarkable achievement.

and the names of the two printers. Gutenberg was not mentioned. Although he was involved in other printing ventures afterward, he never put his name to them and died in 1468 without receiving any recognition for the enormous contribution he had made to the development of the printed word.

Today the situation is very different; even though we have no idea what he looked like, a statue of him has been erected in Mainz, also the location of the Johannes Gutenberg University. Among numerous other tributes, an asteroid and the first digital library, Project Gutenberg, have been named after him. All of the known forty-eight surviving copies of his Bible are held in major libraries around the world and,

even though there is no chance of any of them being sold, they are considered to be the most valuable books ever printed.

If we were to judge Gutenberg on his business career alone, then his decisions to develop a printing press and to produce a Bible can only be described as being disastrous ones, but if we judge him on the impact these same decisions would go on to have throughout the world, then they must surely rank as being some of the greatest ever made.

FERDINAND AND ISABELLA COMMISSION COLUMBUS

1492

Circumstances: The dream of getting rich by opening a new trading route to the East Indies

Protagonists: A Genoese sailor and the Catholic monarchs of Spain

Consequences: The European discovery of the New World

On October 12, 1492, Christopher Columbus (1451–1506) made landfall on an island that he named San Salvador after five weeks of sailing west from the Canary Islands. He was convinced that he had found an outlying island of the East Indies and, in doing so, had achieved his long-held ambition of opening up a commercial route from Europe to China and Japan. Had he been right, it would have made both him and the people who had invested in his expedition very wealthy indeed. We now know, of course, that his navigational calculations were wildly inaccurate and he had actually landed on one of the many small islands that make up the Bahamas, even if we don't know for certain which one. Columbus had spent the previous seven years lobbying royal courts in order to secure the backing he needed for the expedition — turning first to King João II of Portugal and then to the joint Catholic monarchs of Spain, King Ferdinand II of Aragon and Queen Isabella I of Castile. After so much effort, he was reluctant to admit he had been wrong all along.

Despite mounting evidence to the contrary, Columbus would maintain the

> *"Your Highnesses, as Catholic Christians, and princes who love and promote the holy Christian faith, determined to send me, Christopher Columbus, to the above-mentioned countries of India, to see the said princes, people, and territories, and to learn their disposition and the proper method of converting them to our holy faith; and furthermore directed that I should not proceed by land to the East, as is customary, but by a Westerly route, in which direction we have hitherto no certain evidence that any one has gone."*
>
> **—From Columbus's journal entry for August 3, 1492**

THREE SHIPS
The three ships that took part in Columbus's historic expedition in 1492: the *Santa Maria* (left) the *Pinta* (center), and the *Niña* (right).

conviction for the rest of his life that he had sailed from Europe to Asia rather than stumbling across the New World, as the landmass of the Americas was soon to be called. So, as disastrous as the subsequent colonization of the New World would prove for its indigenous inhabitants, both the initial decision by Columbus to pursue his ambitions and that of Ferdinand and Isabella to back him, even though they must have been aware how unlikely he was to succeed, must be regarded now as being among the greatest in history.

CHRISTOPHER COLUMBUS

In his writings, one of the few things Columbus tells us about his early life is that he first went to sea at the age of ten. He was the son of a weaver, born in 1451 in the Italian city-state of Genoa, which was known for its large navy and extensive maritime trading networks

throughout the Mediterranean and beyond, and he traveled extensively throughout this region as a young man. In some accounts of his life, he is said to have sailed as far as Iceland, where it has been suggested that he could have heard the sagas told about Leif Erikson, the Viking who sailed west five hundred years before Columbus's day and established a colony called Vinland, now thought to be on the coast of Newfoundland in Canada. By 1476, Columbus was living in Lisbon, Portugal, where he had established a successful trading business with two of his younger brothers, and married Filipa Moniz Perestrello, the daughter of the nobleman

CHRISTOPHER COLUMBUS
A portrait of Columbus by Sebastiano del Piombo from 1519, thirteen years after the explorer's death. No portraits from life are known to exist.

different source, but in 1485 he approached João II with a proposal to mount an expedition to search for a trading route to the East Indies by heading west across the Atlantic Ocean. At that time in the late fifteenth century the overland trade routes from China, collectively known now as the Silk Road, had become difficult and dangerous, limiting the enormous commercial potential of importing spices, fabrics, including silk, and other commodities from the Far East. An alternative route by sea would have allowed whoever controlled it to monopolize the highly valuable trade in these goods, making the ambitious proposal put forward by Columbus tempting enough to be taken seriously by the Portuguese king, who appointed a committee of his advisers to assess its potential. Accounts suggesting

and explorer Bartolomeu Perestrello, who was also of Genoese descent and had connections to the court of King João II.

We don't know if Columbus was really inspired by the Icelandic sagas he may have heard or if the idea of sailing west had come to him from an entirely

that João turned Columbus down because the prevailing opinion at the time was that the Earth was flat are inaccurate. The real reason he decided not to back Columbus was, in fact, almost the complete opposite. Portugal was one of the leading maritime nations, with advanced knowledge of geography and navigation, which led João's advisers to conclude, correctly as it would turn out, that the calculations made by Columbus were a huge underestimate of the actual distance from Portugal to China if measured in a westerly direction. In their opinion, it was far too great a distance for ships to sail between provisioning stops to be at all feasible, so, on their advice, João turned the scheme down. At the time, the Portuguese were more interested in establishing a route to the Far East around the African continent and appear to have decided to concentrate on this more practical and achievable solution rather than back a scheme that appeared to be based on fantasy.

THE CATHOLIC MONARCHS

Columbus does not give the impression of having been a man lacking in self-belief and, rather than accept the sensible decision made by João, instead took his proposal to the two Catholic monarchs of Spain. Ferdinand and Isabella had married in 1469, a union that began the process of bringing the modern country of Spain into existence. They were engaged in a long-running program of converting their realm into an entirely

THE AMERICAS

Columbus's calculation of the distance between Portugal and China was indeed vastly inaccurate. The continents he eventually discovered were not part of Asia's eastern outskirts, although he maintained he had landed there. Without even realizing it, he had discovered what came to be known as the New World, or the Americas. The name is most probably derived from that of Amerigo Vespucci, a Florentine explorer who, in the early sixteenth century, established that the New World really was a separate landmass and continent in its own right and not part of Asia.

Christian country, and established the Spanish Inquisition, a tribunal charged with maintaining the orthodox beliefs of the Catholic Church. When Columbus approached them in 1485, they were engaged in a war in Granada against the remnants of the Islamic state of the Moors in the southern Spanish region of Andalusia. Initially, they took the same approach to the proposal as the Portuguese had done, appointing a committee to assess its merits and turning it down once that committee had established it was highly unlikely to succeed. But they did not dismiss Columbus entirely, giving him a grant

Columbus lobbied the royal courts for seven years in order to secure the financial backing he needed to embark on his expedition.

and permission to stay anywhere he chose within Aragon and Castile at no cost, perhaps as a means of preventing him from taking his plan, as unpromising as it was, to any of Spain's rivals.

Columbus had not helped his cause by making outrageous demands in his proposal. He wanted to be appointed governor of any lands he discovered and be made Admiral of the Ocean Seas—titles that would make him one of the highest-ranking members of the Spanish royal court. Over the course of the following few years he began to adopt a more subtle approach, building up support among Ferdinand and Isabella's advisers by persuading them of the merits of his proposal. He stressed how cheaply it could be put into action, and emphasized the opportunity it would present for spreading the Christian message overseas, a tactic almost guaranteed to appeal to the king and queen's missionary zeal. Even so, it would take another seven years before the proposals were accepted, and even then, according to contemporary sources, only because Columbus required just three ships and a hundred men, and perhaps also because the likelihood of him surviving and returning to claim his titles was considered extremely low.

In early 1492, Ferdinand and Isabella had also finally succeeded in defeating the last Moorish outpost in Granada, so they were perhaps in a more agreeable mood than when Columbus had first approached them, and more receptive toward plans for expanding their kingdom, now that Spain was united and internally secure. According to some accounts, Isabella was still reluctant to agree and had dismissed Columbus from her court, only for Ferdinand to send a detachment of his royal guards after him to bring him back. However it came about, the Catholic monarchs had finally

Columbus's decision to try to sail to Asia in fact led to the future colonization of North and South America.

decided to support Columbus and he entered into a series of negotiations with Ferdinand and Isabella's advisers over the exact terms of the contract. In April 1492, an agreement was finally reached, resulting in the Capitulations of Santa Fe, a document setting out the highly favorable terms awarded to Columbus by the Spanish Crown.

THE NEW WORLD

After his first successful expedition, Columbus made three further voyages to the Indies, as he referred to the New World. He served as governor of the Spanish territories in the region until being dismissed in 1500, having been accused of running a regime considered too brutal even by the standards of the monarchs who had set up the Spanish Inquisition. After he died, a long series of lawsuits were brought against the Spanish Crown by his heirs, who were claiming 10 percent of the profits made by Spain from the New World colonies awarded to Columbus under the terms of the Capitulations of Sante Fe. However, the Crown successfully argued that Columbus had lost his right to his share of the profits after being sacked as governor, leading to a settlement in 1536 in which his heirs were awarded a title and land in the New World.

The decision made by Columbus was, then, one of great courage and some foolhardiness, because he set sail into the unknown on the basis of calculations already proved incorrect. The Catholic monarchs, meanwhile, had made their decision because it had not cost them much and, in the unlikely case of it paying off, would bring enormous returns. Neither party could have had any idea of the consequences of these decisions, which would actually be the first steps in the future European colonization of North and South America rather than the discovery of a new trading route to the Far East.

COLUMBUS RETURNS TRIUMPHANT
Columbus presents the treasures of the New World in this painting by Raimundo de Madrazo y Garreta (1841–1920).

THE COUNT OF SALM STANDS STRONG AT VIENNA

1529

Circumstances: A huge Ottoman army arrives at the gates of Vienna

Protagonists: Suleiman the Magnificent, Archduke Ferdinand I of Austria, Count Nicholas of Salm, the Ottoman army, and the defenders of Vienna

Consequences: The gates of Vienna marked the farthest extent of the Ottoman expansion into Europe

The great Ottoman sultan Suleiman the Magnificent arrived at the gates of Vienna in late September 1529 at the head of an army estimated to have been at least a hundred thousand strong (some have put the figure at an unlikely three hundred thousand). Vienna was in effect the capital of the Habsburg territory ruled by Archduke Ferdinand I of Austria, the brother of the Holy Roman Emperor Charles V, and it occupied a vital strategic position on the River Danube. If the city fell to the Islamic forces of the Ottoman Empire, the way would be open for Suleiman to advance into the heart of Christian Europe. Realising his personal safety was at stake, Ferdinand fled the scene, escaping north to Prague and leaving the defense of Vienna to its citizens and a small force of Spanish and German mercenaries (hired soldiers) under the command of the seventy-year-old Count Nicholas of Salm. Altogether, the Viennese forces totaled about twenty thousand and, in the circumstances, the most sensible course of action would have been to surrender to Suleiman. But the Viennese were not about to give up their city so easily and, instead, decided to fight.

CLASH OF EMPIRES

The Ottoman Empire arose out of the westward movement of Turkic tribes from Central Asia into Anatolia. It challenged the supremacy of the Orthodox Christian Byzantine Empire, the remnants of the Eastern Roman Empire, which, by the early fourteenth

> "Suleiman's boast was that he would not lay down his arms before he had erected a monument to his victory on the banks of the Rhine."
>
> —Lord Kinross, *The Ottoman Centuries*, 1977

SULTAN SULEIMAN
A portrait of Suleiman the Magnificent attributed to the Italian master Titian. Suleiman's Ottoman army failed to capture Vienna in 1529.

century, had weakened to the point of total collapse. The Ottomans had already expanded into the European part of the Byzantine Empire before Constantinople, its capital, finally fell in 1453 to the Ottoman emperor Mehmet the Conqueror. From then on the Ottomans consolidated and expanded their empire into one of the largest and most powerful of the day. They controlled much of the Middle East and North Africa as well as the eastern Mediterranean, and had captured the important Balkan cities of Belgrade and Buda (the city that would later unite with Pest on the opposite bank of the Danube to form Budapest, the modern capital of Hungary). This relentless

advance took them right up to the borders of the Habsburg Empire. As Suleiman was well aware, his forces had penetrated straight through the territory of the old Byzantine Empire of Orthodox Christianity, and into the domain of western European Catholicism itself. The resulting tension between the Ottomans and the Habsburgs was set to last into the nineteenth century and only really came to an end with the dissolution of both empires after the end of World War I in 1918.

The Habsburgs themselves were an aristocratic family originally from what is now Switzerland. The family provided kings across Europe, including, from 1273, the Holy Roman Empire, which at its height extended across much of central Europe, from the Low Countries and northern France, through Germany, northern Italy, and up to Poland and Austria. As well as holding the title of Holy Roman Emperor, Charles V was the king of Spain, giving him an extensive empire in the New World and the Far East as well as in Europe. In 1519, when Charles was elected Holy Roman Emperor, he gave control of the Habsburgs' ancestral lands in Austria to his brother Ferdinand, which, together with the independent Kingdom of Hungary, became a buffer zone between his realm and the Ottoman Empire of Suleiman.

OTTOMAN CAMPAIGN

The Ottomans were not the only challenge facing the Habsburgs during this period. Charles was continually fighting with King Francis II of France, a conflict that was as much personal as it was territorial. At that time, France was surrounded by enemies: the Habsburgs in Spain, Italy, and the Low Countries; and the English to the northwest. These threats led Francis to form an alliance with Suleiman that, in 1526, saw them both attacking Habsburg territory at the same time. Francis initiated a war in northern Italy and Suleiman began a campaign to push Ferdinand out of Hungary. The decisive victory for the Ottoman forces at the Battle of Mohács in August 1526 allowed Suleiman to create a vassal state in the south of Hungary. This opened up the way for him to capture Buda, the Hungarian capital, three years later.

THE SIEGE

From Hungary, Suleiman turned his attention to the bigger prize of capturing Vienna, a feat that would remove any further potential threat from Ferdinand and directly challenge Charles and the whole of the Holy Roman Empire.

DEFENDING FORCE

The military force defending Vienna, which was under the command of seventy-year-old Count Nicholas of Salm and made up of Spanish and German mercenaries, was much smaller than the besieging Ottoman army. They were, however, professional soldiers who were not intimidated by the Ottomans, no matter how many there were. The defending force also included a detachment of German *Landsknechte*, mercenary pikemen with a ferocious reputation who could be counted upon, even in the direst situation.

> **Nicholas of Salm's decision to stand and fight at Vienna would have a huge impact on European history.**

The Ottoman campaign of 1529 was dogged by problems from the moment Suleiman led his army out of Constantinople in May of that year. The most serious difficulties were caused by the weather. Heavy rainfall made progress across Bulgaria and Hungary painfully slow so that, even though the resistance the Ottoman army met was light and Buda had fallen quickly, they did not start out toward Vienna until the middle of September. By then, the state of the roads meant that it had become impossible for them to transport their heavy siege guns, which, had they been available, would easily have breached the relatively weak defensive walls of the city.

Even so, Vienna appeared to be there for the taking; Charles was preoccupied with fighting the French and, despite Ferdinand's appeals for help, had left his brother to fend for himself. But if Suleiman had expected the Viennese garrison to submit as quickly as the one in Buda, he was to be disappointed. Ferdinand himself may have departed the scene, but Nicholas of Salm was made of sterner stuff. Although getting on in years, he was a highly experienced military commander who had taken seriously Suleiman's boast of his intention to erect a monument to his victories on the banks of the Rhine, right in the heart of the Holy Roman Empire.

In the short time available before the siege began, Salm did what he could to strengthen the defenses of the city, reinforcing the walls and burning the buildings that lay outside them to create clear lines of fire. In the absence of heavy artillery, Suleiman had to rely on mining under the walls in an attempt to breach them, but the defenders detected where the digging was taking place from the vibrations it caused and easily fought off every attempt to get into the city. Salm also managed to convince the Ottomans that his garrison was much larger than it actually was and that he was expecting the arrival of a relieving army led by Ferdinand. In reality, no such force existed, but this, together with the lack of success and the constant driving rain, weakened Ottoman resolve and, after only two weeks of the siege, Suleiman decided to try one final all-out assault, which, if unsuccessful, would mark the end of the attack. During that final encounter the Viennese inflicted heavy casualties on the demoralized Ottomans before Suleiman finally called off his forces and began a long retreat back to Constantinople.

SIEGE OF VIENNA
An Ottoman depiction of the Siege of Vienna dating to the sixteenth century, with the Sultan's tent in the foreground.

SURVIVAL OF HABSBURGS

The Ottomans would make several further unsuccessful attempts to capture Vienna, most notably in 1683 in what is sometimes referred to as the Battle of Vienna (to distinguish it from the siege of 1529). But none of these later attempts was any more successful in capturing the city and its gates would ultimately mark the maximum extent of the Ottoman Empire in Europe. Ferdinand was the most immediate beneficiary of the decision to stand and fight at Vienna, even though he took no part in the defense himself. The man who actually made that decision to fight and deserved to gain the most credit from it, Nicholas of Salm, was wounded during the siege and died from his injuries the following year. It cost him his life, but Salm's decision would have a huge impact on European history. It allowed the Habsburg monarchy to survive in Austria for more than four hundred years, and prevented Suleiman from establishing a base in the heart of Europe from where he may well have achieved his ambition to reach the Rhine. Had the Ottoman Empire defeated the Holy Roman Empire, it could have resulted in the conversion of much of the population of central Europe to the Islamic faith.

COPERNICUS PUBLISHES ON THE REVOLUTIONS

1543

Circumstances: A lone astronomer makes a great advance in the field but is reluctant to publish it

Protagonists: Nicholas Copernicus and Georg Joachim Rheticus

Consequences: A revolutionary change in our understanding of the universe

In about 1510, when Nicholas Copernicus (1473–1543) was in his late thirties, he wrote a short paper setting out the model he had worked out for the solar system. It placed the sun at the center with the planets, including the Earth, orbiting around it. This heliocentric (sun-centered) model, as it came to be known, challenged the prevailing view of the Earth being at the center of the universe, which dated back over thirteen hundred years to the work of the Greek astronomer Ptolemy (ca. 90–168 CE). Copernicus sent his paper to a very limited number of people, claiming that he was working on a longer version that would include a mathematical proof of his heliocentric model.

Over the course of the next twenty years, he worked on this longer version, although, despite the encouragement of those people who had heard of his work, he refused to publish it. In 1539, a twenty-five-year-old mathematician named Georg Joachim Rheticus came to visit him and apparently talked him into changing his mind. The resulting book, *On the Revolutions of Celestial Spheres*, was published shortly before Copernicus died in 1543 and went on to become a landmark in the history of science. It signaled the start of the Scientific Revolution, a period in the sixteenth and seventeenth centuries when the basic principles of modern science were first established and when great advances were made by such people as Kepler, Galileo, and Newton. Copernicus's decision to publish his book, then, not only revolutionized our understanding of astronomy, but would also lead to the transformation of science as a whole.

THE REVOLUTIONARY

Copernicus does not, at first sight, give the impression of being a revolutionary in any sphere, let alone in science. For forty years, he held the position of canon in the Catholic Church and lived for most of that time in Frombork, a town in northeast Poland that in the sixteenth century was a cathedral city in Warmia, a region governed by its bishop. He was born in 1473 in the Polish city of Torun into a German-speaking family of wealthy merchants. After the death of his

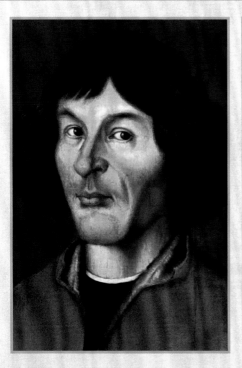

NICHOLAS COPERNICUS
A portrait of Copernicus by an unknown artist. At Frombork, he wrote his first short paper on heliocentricism.

and a range of other subjects without gaining a degree in any. He gives the impression of being what we would now call a perennial student, flitting from one thing to another while avoiding getting a job in the real world. But while he was moving from university to university, he was meeting some of the most eminent mathematicians and astronomers of the day and appears to have engaged in extensive private study of both subjects.

Finally, at the age of thirty, Copernicus was granted a doctorate in canon law and returned to Poland, where he became secretary and doctor to his uncle in Warmia. Watzenrode appears to have expected his nephew to follow him as Bishop of Warmia, but Copernicus showed little inclination to do so. As far as we can tell, he was never ordained as a priest, the first step he would have had to take before he could hope to progress in the Church hierarchy.

After his uncle died in 1512, he moved back to the relatively remote and quiet city of Frombork, where, in his capacity as canon, he was provided with a house and servants. He also bought a tower in the grounds of the cathedral, which he converted into an observatory, although, as he was working in a period before the invention of the telescope, the astronomical equipment he had was very basic. It was at about this time that he wrote his first short paper on heliocentricism, suggesting that he may have decided on the move to Frombork in order to concentrate more fully on his astronomical work and devote more time to his studies.

father when Copernicus was about ten years old, he was supported by his maternal uncle, Lucas Watzenrode, who went on to become the Bishop of Warmia and gave Copernicus the position of canon, which would provide him with a very good income throughout his adult life. Watzenrode also paid for his nephew's education, which continued at a number of universities around Europe, including at Kraców, Bologna, and Padua, where he studied law, medicine,

[*"All the spheres revolve around the sun at their midpoint, and therefore the sun is at the center of the universe."*
—**Nicholas Copernicus,** *Commentariolus,* **1514**]

ON THE REVOLUTIONS

Over the next twenty years he would perform his duties as a canon, make astronomical observations and write the manuscript that would eventually be published as *On the Revolutions of Celestial Spheres*. He seemingly led a quiet and comfortable life, only occasionally disturbed by a brush with Church authorities over some of the affairs he had with women in Frombork, including with one of his housekeepers, which apparently continued after she got married. He maintained regular contact with a number of the astronomers and mathematicians he had met in the universities he had attended and, by this means, the nature of his work became known in academic circles. This is presumably how the young Rheticus, who studied at Wittenberg University, came to hear about Copernicus and, being sufficiently intrigued by what he had learned, made the journey to Frombork to meet the amateur astronomer who was proposing such a revolutionary idea.

Traveling from Wittenberg to Frombork was no small undertaking for Rheticus at that time because he was a Lutheran and was associated with the university where the principal figure behind the Protestant Reformation, Martin Luther, himself worked. As a result, Rheticus was banned from entering the Catholic Kingdom of Poland. Nevertheless he arrived in the town in 1539 and must have made a

> **When Copernicus published his work, astrologers welcomed the mathematical proof they had waited twenty years to see.**

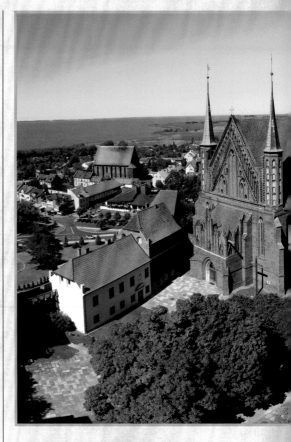

FROMBORK CATHEDRAL
Copernicus used one of the towers in the grounds of the cathedral as an observatory after he moved to Frombork in 1512.

favorable impression with Copernicus because he was taken on as a pupil—the first and only pupil Copernicus would ever have. Rheticus wrote a short summary of the heliocentric model and had it published in 1540. It was favorably received in academic circles, and this may have encouraged Copernicus to consider publishing his own work for the first time. He claimed that his reticence was a consequence of anxiety over how his work would be viewed by other

being given the first printed copy of his book. In truth, first reactions were muted among all except the Church, which predictably criticized it for going against the Bible, and those few astronomers who now welcomed the mathematical proof they had waited twenty years to see. But it would be more than fifty years before his work really began to receive the attention it deserved, when the research carried out by Johannes Kepler (1571–1630) on planetary motion and the astronomical discoveries made by Galileo Galilei (1564–1642) brought the Copernican system, as the heliocentric model is sometimes called, to the attention of a much wider audience.

ON THE REVOLUTIONS
Title page of the third edition of *On the Revolutions of Celestial Spheres*, published in Amsterdam in 1617.

astronomers, but he may also have been worried about his position as a canon in the Catholic Church, an institution that did not always react well to radical new scientific theories. But, whatever the cause of the delay and however Rheticus went about convincing Copernicus that the time was right for his book, he finally made the decision to publish it and they sent the manuscript to a printer.

SCIENTIFIC REVOLUTION

Copernicus did not live long enough to see for himself the reception his book was to have after publication. He suffered from some form of seizure in late 1552 and, according to one account, died after

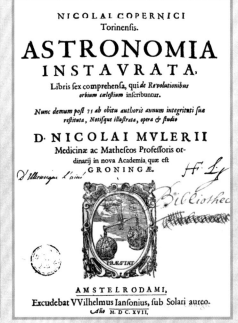

NICOLAI COPERNICI
Torinenfis.

ASTRONOMIA
INSTAVRATA,

Libris fex comprehenfa, qui *de Revolutionibus orbium cælestium* infcribuntur.

Nunc demum poft 75 ab obitu authoris annum integritati fuæ reftituta, Notifque illuftrata, opera & ftudio

D. NICOLAI MVLERII
Medicinæ ac Mathefeos Profefforis or-
dinarij in nova Academia quæ eft
GRONINGÆ.

PRÆSTAT.

AMSTELRODAMI,
Excudebat VVilhelmus Ianfonius, fub Solari aureo.
Año M. D C. XVII.

DESCARTES FINDS HIS REASON

1619

Circumstances: Descartes spends a day and a night in a stove-heated room

Protagonists: Descartes on his own

Consequences: The beginning of a new way of thinking about the world

René Descartes (1596–1650), who has been called the father of modern philosophy, produced a body of work that is still widely studied and debated after almost four hundred years. In it he attempted to begin the study of philosophy anew, starting from its foundations, separating it from the restrictions imposed on thought by religious teachings, and moving it away from a strict adherence to the works of Aristotle and other classical Greek philosophers. In doing so, he established a fundamental method of inquiry based solely on the application of reason and observation, one that did not rely on a supernatural or spiritual explanation for any part of the human experience. He took as his starting point that most quoted of philosophical phrases, *cogito ergo sum* (I think, therefore I am) — the proposition that, if a person is capable of thinking about whether they exist or not, then that act of thinking in itself provides proof that they do exist. This principle provided Descartes with an absolute certainty on which he began to build a method of thinking based on what can actually be known and, in doing so, provided a philosophical underpinning of the sciences that were beginning to develop at that time.

Before beginning his philosophical inquiries, Descartes had already made

> *"I decided to review the various opportunities that are open to people in this life and to try to choose the best one. I thought I could do no better than to persevere in the very same occupation that I already had, that is, to use my whole life to develop my reason and to make as much progress as I could in discovering the truth in accordance with the method I had prescribed for myself."*
>
> —René Descartes, *Discourse on Method*, 1637

RENÉ DESCARTES
A portrait of the great French philosopher by the Dutch artist Franz Hals, now in the Louvre in Paris.

important contributions to the sciences and mathematics. These included establishing the law of refraction in optics (how light changes direction or bends as it moves from one material to another). He also laid the foundations for analytic geometry using a system of coordinates to plot three-dimensional shapes on a two-dimensional axis, familiar to all students of mathematics as the x and y axes of graphs. This would prove crucial for the later inventions of mathematicians and physicists Isaac Newton and Gottfried Leibniz.

Even if Descartes had stopped there, before he began his philosophical inquiries, he would now be considered an important figure in the Scientific Revolution of the seventeenth century,

which goes some way to indicating the overall scale of his achievement. But, rather than considering the work itself, here we are concerned with what led him to take on such a vast project in the first place and, in particular, his decision to devote his life to the pursuit of knowledge. If what he wrote about his life is to be believed, the decision arose as a consequence of the sort of visionary experience his entire philosophy rejected.

EARLY YEARS

Descartes was born into a wealthy land-owning family in the small French town of La Haye, which was renamed Descartes in his honor in 1967. He was educated at a Jesuit college and then studied law at the University of Poitiers, intending to follow his father into the legal profession. In 1618, a year after he left university, he traveled to the city of Breda in the Dutch Republic to join the army of Maurice of Nassau, the prince of Orange. The reason why a Jesuit-educated Catholic Frenchman chose to enlist in the army of a Protestant prince of the Dutch Republic remains a mystery, leading some to suggest that Descartes was working as some kind of spy. No evidence has ever been found to back up such claims and it may well have been that Descartes chose the highly regarded Dutch army because he wanted to study military engineering in the best possible place. But, whatever his motive, it remains a strange decision, not least because at that time Europe was on the verge of the Thirty Years War, a bitter and destructive religious conflict fought in the main between the Catholic Holy Roman Empire and an alliance of Protestant states.

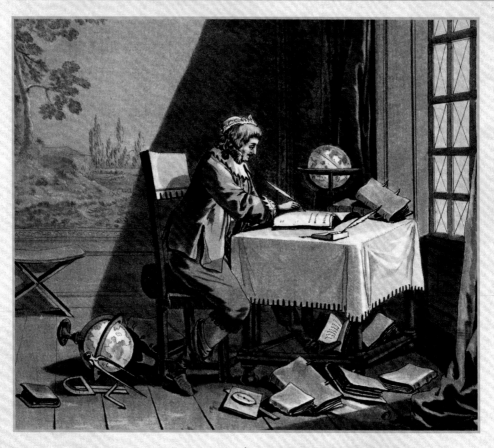

DESCARTES'S VISIONS

While in Breda, Descartes met the mathematician and teacher Isaac Beeckman (1588–1637), who would have a lasting influence on his thinking and who encouraged him to study mathematics, leading to his first serious written work on the subject the following year. By 1619, Descartes had left the Dutch army and joined up with the forces of Duke Maximilian of Bavaria in the Holy Roman Empire, the leading Catholic power of the day. Again there has been speculation about why Descartes did this. On the night of November 10, 1619, Descartes experienced a series of vivid dreams,

WORKING PHILOSOPHER
A 1790 picture of René Descartes working at his desk by the French artist Jean Baptiste Morret.

which, he later wrote, profoundly affected the direction of his life and would lead to a major breakthrough in his philosophical inquiries. In *Discourse on Method*, published seventeen years after the event, he tells us that he was traveling from Frankfurt to Vienna, having attended the coronation of the Holy Roman Emperor Ferdinand II in Frankfurt Cathedral, when he was delayed by a period of bad weather in Bavaria. On the day in question, he says, he was "shut up alone in a stove-heated room, where I was completely free to converse with myself about my own thoughts." These "meditations," as he called them, concerned how he planned to go about working on his philosophical inquiries. They appear to have spilled over into the extraordinary dreams he was to have that night in which he saw how he could find the solutions to the problems he had posed himself.

His interpretation of these dreams, taken together with the meditations of that day, left him feeling as if he had experienced some form of awakening in which he could suddenly see the way to achieving his aims in philosophy. Without specifying the exact time and place, Descartes goes on to tell us that, after that extraordinary day, he decided to commit himself to philosophical inquiry for the rest of his life and, in particular, to answering the question, "What can be known for certain?" by the use of the application of reason and logic.

COGITO ERGO SUM

The *cogito ergo sum* argument apparently came to Descartes not long after his decision to commit himself to philosophy, but it would take many years for him to find a way of communicating it fully in writing. In 1620, he left the army and spent the following nine years traveling in Europe, before finally settling in the Dutch Republic, where he would live for

---

Descartes spent the rest of his life committed to philosophy, asking, in particular, the question: "What can be known for certain?"

VIVID DREAMS

After experiencing what he described as "meditations" during the day, Descartes is said to have had extraordinarily vivid dreams that night, in which he could instantly see a way forward in his study of philosophy. He woke on two occasions during the night and wrote down the details of what he had been dreaming in a notebook, and again in the morning after one last dream. He is said to have kept the notebook with him for the rest of his life, but unfortunately it has not survived. Its contents are known to us only from the writing of other people who had either seen it themselves or had heard what was in it from others.

almost all of the remaining twenty years of his life. The reason he chose this area is not known, but the Dutch Republic had a reputation for tolerance at that time, so perhaps Descartes felt that he would encounter less opposition to his radical new ideas.

Whatever the reason, it was during this period that *Discourse on Method* and *Meditations on First Philosophy* were first published—the major works on which Descartes's fame now rests. He died in February 1650, at the age of fifty-four, after contracting pneumonia while he was in Stockholm. His work had been controversial during his lifetime, particularly in Catholic countries, but was nevertheless widely recognized as being of fundamental importance in the history of philosophy, as it remains today.

NEWTON GOES BACK TO SCHOOL

1659

Circumstances: Isaac Newton's mother considers what the future holds for her son

Protagonists: A scientific genius in the making, his mother, his uncle, and his former schoolmaster

Consequences: A farmer's son from Lincolnshire, England, revolutionizes the natural sciences

The list of the achievements of Isaac Newton (1645–1727) is a long and impressive one. He is most famous for his work on gravity and for the three laws of motion, all published at the same time in the monumental *Philosophiæ Naturalis Principia Mathematica* (Mathematical Principle of Natural Philosophy). However, he also made many other important contributions to mathematics, optics (the study of light), physics, astronomy, and a range of other subjects. He is still widely regarded as one of the greatest of all scientists. During his lifetime he held the positions of Lucasian Professor of Mathematics at Cambridge University, President of the Royal Society, Member of Parliament, and Master of the Royal Mint, and was knighted by Queen Anne.

YOUNG ISAAC

As accomplished as he was in the natural sciences and mathematics, there were fields in which he did not excel, namely the management of his family's farm in Woolsthorpe, a small village in the English county of Lincolnshire. Unlike many of the great scientists and thinkers of that period, Newton came from a fairly humble background. At the age of sixteen, having finished his schooling in the nearby market town of Grantham, he returned home to work on the farm. Young Isaac proved himself such a

> "The alteration of motion is ever proportional to the motive force impressed; and is made in the direction of the straight line in which that force is impressed."
>
> —Newton's Second Law of Motion, first published in *Philosophiæ Naturalis Principia Mathematica*, 1687

hopeless farmer that his mother soon realized that there was no future in it for him. She talked the matter over with his uncle, William Ayscough, and John Stokes, his former schoolmaster in Grantham, and between them they decided that he should return to school for a course of special tuition aimed at gaining entry to the University of Cambridge. Rather than struggle with a life on the land, they pointed him in the direction of a life of the mind, even if they could not have predicted the extraordinary outcome of their decision.

FAMILY LIFE

The stone farmhouse where Newton was born is now protected by the National Trust, and is restored to its seventeenth-century appearance. It is a beautiful old house but, despite its grand name, Woolsthorpe Manor, it is clearly the sort of property lived in by a successful farmer rather than a member of the landed aristocracy. Newton's father, also called Isaac, died three months before his son was born, and his mother, Hannah, married again when he was three. Her new husband, Barnabas Smith, was, at sixty-three, almost forty years older than her and, as well as being the rector of a neighboring parish, had a substantial private income. Hannah moved to the rectory, leaving young Isaac in the care of his grandparents in Woolsthorpe.

Some have argued that being abandoned by his mother must have had a psychological impact on Newton, particularly as he never married and is not known to have had a physical relationship in his life. Amateur psychologists have also made a great deal of a list Newton wrote at the age of nineteen in which he set out what he

considered to be the sins he had committed in his life, which included threatening to burn down his stepfather's house. This has been taken to indicate that Newton had a difficult relationship with his stepfather, but, as Smith died when Newton was ten, this is perhaps an exaggeration.

Hannah had three children with Smith and, after she was widowed for a second time, she brought them back to Woolsthorpe with her. She had inherited much of Smith's wealth and, together with a good income from the farm, was now a relatively wealthy woman. Newton was sent to the grammar school in Grantham at the age of twelve, where he did well in his studies despite preferring to work on his own projects rather than those officially set out in the

ISAAC NEWTON

A portrait of Newton painted in 1689 when he was aged forty-six and had been appointed Lucasian Professor of Mathematics at Cambridge University.

curriculum—a preference for individual work he would display throughout his life. He certainly did enough to suggest to his schoolmaster John Stokes that he had the potential to study at university at Cambridge, and Stokes was the one who recommended he apply.

Before returning to school, Newton spent almost a year on the farm, where he appeared intent on demonstrating that farming was not for him. He would leave all the work to the farm's laborers while he read a book and, on one occasion, managed to return from the market in Grantham carrying the bridle of the horse he had ridden to town, having absent-mindedly left the horse itself behind. If his plan had been to convince his mother that he would be better off back at school than wasting his time in a half-hearted attempt at farming, it certainly worked.

OPTICS

Isaac Newton examines the nature of light with the aid of a glass prism.

UNIVERSITY LIFE

Newton was successful in his attempt to gain entry to Cambridge University and, in 1661, at the age of nineteen, he was admitted to Trinity College as a sizar, which meant that he had to work to pay for his board and lodgings. In a college dominated by the wealthy upper classes, Newton initially appears to have struggled to fit in, keeping to himself and embarking on his own program of study rather than following the college syllabus. He was by no means an outstanding student, although the often-repeated story that he failed his degree is probably not true. It appears that he was beginning to conduct his own experiments as an undergraduate and he spent more time doing this than studying for exams.

NEWTON'S APPLE

Shortly after Newton finished his degree in 1665, the university closed down for a period as a precautionary measure due to the outbreak of the Great Plague in London. He returned to Woolsthorpe, where he stayed for much of the next two years, continuing to conduct his own experiments. He was particularly interested in examining Kepler's work on the motion of the planets. Finding that the type of calculations he needed to work on were not possible using the available mathematical techniques, he invented his own method, which he called "fluxions" and which would later form the basis for the development of "infinitesimal calculus."

The famous incident of Newton finding the inspiration for his theory of gravity after seeing an apple falling from a tree in the orchard at Woolsthorpe also occurred at this time and, as it was a story that Newton told himself, probably had

WOOLSTHORPE MANOR
The farmhouse in Lincolnshire where Newton was born and where he formulated his theory of gravity.

some basis in truth, even if its importance may have been exaggerated in the telling. Newton was certainly thinking about the question of why the Moon continued in its orbit around the Earth during this period and arrived at the solution of it being the result of the pull of the same force, gravity, which caused an apple to fall from the tree to the ground. It would be twenty years before he was finally persuaded to publish his law of universal gravitation in the *Principia*. This provided the foundation stone of classical mechanics

for more than three hundred years, until it was finally replaced in 1916 by Einstein's general theory of relativity. This was quite an achievement for a man who, if it hadn't been for his mother's decision to send him back to school, might otherwise have spent his life as a Lincolnshire farmer.

If Isaac Newton's mother hadn't sent him back to school, where he gained entry to the University of Cambridge, Newton might have lived his life as a farmer in Lincolnshire.

PETER THE GREAT REFORMS RUSSIA

1698

Circumstances: A country that had been left behind by the political, social, and technological advances made in Western Europe

Protagonists: Peter the Great, his Russian and European advisers, and the Russian people

Consequences: Russia becomes a major player in European affairs for the first time

Toward the end of the seventeenth century, the Romanov tsar Peter the Great (1672–1725) introduced a series of reforms that began the process of transforming Russia. By the end of his reign, Russia was no longer a medieval kingdom but a modern state capable of competing in both military and economic terms with the all of the more advanced Western European countries and the Ottoman Empire.

The first major obstacle to Peter's ambitions was geographical; at that time Russia had no western sea ports to give it access to the Baltic Sea or Black Sea.

This prevented the country from fully exploiting its vast natural resources through commercial links with Europe, where more developed countries had built their prosperity on maritime trade. The eastern Baltic was largely controlled by Sweden, while the Black Sea was entirely within the control of the Ottoman Empire, either directly or through vassal states (states dominated by another). As a consequence, the first step in Peter's plan to modernize Russia had to involve the expansion of the territory he controlled to include a sea port in one or both of these locations.

"The Great Embassy was one of the two or three overwhelming events in Peter's life. The project amazed his fellow countrymen. Never before had a Russian tsar traveled peacefully abroad; a few had ventured across the border in wartime to besiege a city or pursue an enemy army, but not in time of peace."

—Robert K. Massie, *Peter the Great: His Life and World*, 1980

PETER THE GREAT
A portrait of the Emperor of All the Russias, the title adopted by Peter in 1721, painted in 1838 by Paul Delaroche.

THE GREAT EMBASSY

In 1695, Peter attempted to take the fort of Azov on the northern coast of the Black Sea, which was under Ottoman rule and controlled access to the Sea of Azov, an inlet of the Black Sea. An initial attack by land was unsuccessful, causing Peter to rethink his tactics and begin to build ships to form the first Russian navy. Further attacks from the land and bombardment from the Black Sea led to the capture of Azov, but, with the Ottomans controlling the rest of the Black Sea, Russia still needed a suitable trading port.

Peter realized that in order to stand any chance of gaining the necessary territory, the army would have to be modernized and a navy developed almost from scratch. The expertise required to achieve these goals did not exist in Russia at that time, so Peter began to look to other countries that had already made advances in military technology and naval engineering. He decided to send out a huge diplomatic mission, known as the Great Embassy, to travel extensively through Europe. His objective was to develop relations with the Christian countries of Europe that opposed the Ottoman Empire, but also to learn as much as he could about European military and naval methods. The embassy was led by some of his closest advisers, but Peter also traveled with the mission, concealing his identity so that he didn't have to spend all his time performing ceremonial duties in the countries he visited. It was an unprecedented move by a Russian tsar, not least because Peter was leaving his country, which had a turbulent political history, for eighteen months.

The diplomatic mission failed to achieve its aims of forming alliances against the Ottomans because the major European powers were involved in various disputes, which would lead to the War of the Spanish Succession in 1701. While they were preparing to fight one another, they had no wish to provoke the Ottoman Empire by siding against it with the relatively insignificant Russians.

While this largely unsuccessful diplomacy was going on, Peter spent his time visiting shipyards, armament

> Peter sent out a huge diplomatic mission known as the Great Embassy, which traveled throughout Europe. Peter also traveled with the mission himself.

factories, and military bases, all the while learning as much as he could about how different European countries organized their affairs in general. In the Dutch Republic, for instance, Peter was given access to the shipyard of the Dutch East India Company, the largest and most advanced of its time, where he worked for four months on the construction of a ship.

MODERNIZING RUSSIA

By the summer of 1698, Peter was forced to return to Russia after an uprising in one part of the army. The uprising was put down quickly and brutally before Peter had even arrived back in the country, leaving him free to implement the many reforms he had been planning while he had been away. An extensive

BEARD TAX

As part of a set of sweeping reforms designed to modernize Russian society, Peter also brought in a tax on beards. Impressed by the clean-shaven Westerners he had seen on his travels around Europe, he was determined that Russians should follow suit. Those who paid the beard tax were required to carry at all times a copper or bronze token as proof of payment. The coin depicted a Russian eagle on one side and the lower half of a face complete with beard on the other side, inscribed with the two phrases: "the tax has been taken" and "the beard is a superfluous burden."

shipbuilding program was undertaken and the new Russian navy was modeled on those of Britain and the Dutch Republic. The army was reorganized along the lines of the Prussian and Swedish military, then widely recognized as being the best armed forces of the day. Peter had employed many experts in various different fields during his travels, who arrived in Moscow to begin work on modernizing the country as a whole. As well as military advisers, there were engineers, scientists, architects, and a whole range of other experts. As part of the overall plan, people living in Moscow were encouraged to adopt Western dress, a practice that would famously result in Peter bringing in a tax on beards.

SIEGE OF NÖTEBORG
A painting by Alexander von Kotzebue showing Peter directing his army during the Great Northern War.

ST. PETERSBURG

In what would prove to be the only diplomatic success of the Great Embassy, Peter formed an alliance with Poland and other countries with interests in the Baltic against the dominance of Sweden in the region. This led to the outbreak of the Great Northern War in 1700, and for the first time Russia gained territory on the Gulf of Finland, an eastern extension of the Baltic Sea. To ensure that Russia could maintain this territory and make the most of its access to the Baltic, Peter ordered the founding of a new city on a stretch of unpromising marshland, about 3 miles (5 km) inland from the gulf. He used the foreign engineers, architects, and city planners he had employed to make the bogland habitable, and then constructed the first buildings of what would become St. Petersburg.

In 1712, Peter moved his capital city from Moscow to St. Petersburg, which became known informally as the "Window on the West," both because of its geographical position and the Western-leaning attitude of its people. The city would also become famous for its beautiful buildings, many designed by the Italian architect Domenico Trezzini.

Peter's decision to reform Russia and engage with Western Europe had far-reaching consequences for Russian society and would lead to the country becoming a major power in the region. He also initiated a huge expansion in the territory under his control, forming what would from 1721 be known as the Russian Empire. In this respect, he is now remembered as one of Russia's greatest leaders, even if he was capable of great brutality against his own people if they opposed his rule.

But there was one institution that Peter did not attempt to reform or modernize in any way—the Russian tsardom would remain an absolute monarchy with unrestricted powers for the next two hundred years, until it was finally overthrown in 1917 by the Bolsheviks of the Russian Revolution.

> **Peter's decision to reform Russia and to engage with Western Europe had far-reaching consequences for Russian society.**

THE COLONISTS SIGN UP FOR INDEPENDENCE

1776

Circumstances: Colonists who were not represented in the British Parliament objecting to being taxed without consultation

Protagonists: Thomas Jefferson, John Adams, Benjamin Franklin, and all the other delegates attending the Second Continental Congress

Consequences: The United States of America

On July 2, 1776, the Second Continental Congress, an assembly of representatives from all thirteen American colonies, decided by a vote of twelve in favor and one abstention to declare independence from the British Empire. At the time of the vote, the delegates from New York did not have the constitutional authority from their state legislature to vote for independence, so they were forced to abstain (not vote). A week later, they obtained the required authority and voted, making the decision in favor of independence for what would soon become known as the United States of America a unanimous one.

Two days after the vote, and after some alterations to the document as it was first written by Thomas Jefferson, the formal statement, the Declaration of Independence, was adopted by the Congress and sent to the printer for publication. It is this date, July 4, that is celebrated in America as Independence Day.

THE REBELLION

The revolt by the thirteen American colonies against British rule, which led to the American Revolutionary War, started at the Battles of Lexington and Concord on April 19, 1775. The roots of the rebellion, however, can be traced back to the French and Indian War, also known as the Seven Years War.

The French and Indian War (1756–1763), fought primarily between Britain and France over disputed colonial interests, had been vastly expensive for both countries. In France, the military defeat to Britain and the financial strain it placed on the economy partly led to the French Revolution in 1789. In Britain, despite accomplishing most of its war aims, the national debt doubled.

Much of the debate surrounding independence was held in the back rooms of taverns and coffee houses around Philadelphia.

The cost of defending the British Empire remained a huge burden on public spending, leading the government to attempt to raise more revenue in the colonies by introducing new systems of taxation.

In the thirteen colonies of the British Empire on the eastern seaboard of North America, the first direct tax, the Stamp Act of 1765, caused widespread protests, including a boycott of British goods. As they had no representation in the British Parliament, the colonists argued that their consent was required before direct taxes could be raised, leading to the slogan "No taxation without representation." The Stamp Act was repealed, but, in 1767, the duty imposed on a number of commodities, such as paper and tea, was increased, leading to further organized protests and outbreaks of mob violence. The British responded by increasing the number of troops garrisoned in the colonies, inevitably leading to a number of ugly incidents and the deaths of some protesters.

BOSTON TEA PARTY

The British Parliament again repealed the tax increases on everything except tea and when, in 1773, the East India Company was granted the monopoly to supply tea to the colonies, it provoked a furious response. This was known as the Boston Tea Party of December 16, 1773, in which all the tea in the holds of three East India Company ships was thrown into Boston Harbor by a protest group calling themselves the Sons of Liberty. Rather than recognize the legitimate grievances of the protesters, the British

encouraged the colonists to escalate their protests into outright rebellion.

THE TWO CONTINENTAL CONGRESSES

Called in direct response to the Coercive Acts, the First Continental Congress met in Philadelphia on September 5, 1774. It was made up of fifty-six delegates sent from twelve of the thirteen colonies (the exception was Georgia, which did not want to antagonize the British because it wanted their help in a frontier war). Over the course of the next few months, the delegates decided to implement a ban on the import of British goods if the conditions imposed by the Coercive Acts were not removed and to petition King George III in an effort to find a solution to the grievances held in the colonies. Whatever the personal opinions of the delegates, there was no suggestion at this stage of a move toward independence from Britain. Their intention was to reach an agreement so that the colonies could

government instead decided to impose its authority on the colonies by closing Boston Harbor until compensation had been paid for the destroyed tea. This was followed by a number of further punishing measures taken against Massachusetts, collectively known as the Coercive or Intolerable Acts, which were intended to quash colonial resistance to the authority of the British Parliament. Instead, the measures had the opposite effect, causing widespread outrage among many people throughout the thirteen colonies at what was seen as an arbitrary violation of their rights. Rather than intimidating people into accepting British rule, the British response actually become more self-governing but remain within the British Empire.

One further decision reached by the First Continental Conference was to set a date for a second meeting, May 10, 1775, at which the delegates intended to consider the results of their actions, in particular the petition sent to the king. By the time the Congress met again, events on the ground had moved beyond petitioning George III because fighting in a revolutionary war had already broken out. The American forces were made up of numerous separate militias and, in an effort to coordinate them into an effective fighting force, one of the first decisions made by the Congress was to form the Continental Army and appoint George Washington as its commander-in-chief. The prospect of a return to negotiations was ended after the British issued a Proclamation of Rebellion in August 1775, decreeing that the American rebels, including the delegates at the Second Continental Conference, were traitors. As a result, rather than finding a resolution to the conflict, the Second Continental Congress ended up managing the war effort, making it, in effect, the government of the thirteen colonies.

TOWARD INDEPENDENCE

The Congress included a section of delegates with loyalist sympathies — those who wanted the colonies to remain a part of the British Empire — so the path toward the Declaration of Independence was by no means a straightforward one. Much of the debate surrounding independence was not held in the formal setting of the Congress but went on instead in the back rooms of taverns and coffee houses around Philadelphia, making it difficult to reconstruct the exact sequence of events that led to the Declaration. But before anything could be debated, the delegates had to get authorization from their own legislatures, which, in effect, meant that each of the thirteen colonies had to come out in favor of independence before their delegates could vote for it at the Continental Congress. The Boston lawyer John Adams, who had long been in favor of independence, played a key role in the political maneuvering that

"We, therefore, the Representatives of the United States of America, in General Congress, Assembled, appealing to the Supreme Judge of the world for the rectitude of our intentions, do, in the Name, and by Authority of the good People of these Colonies, solemnly publish and declare, That these united Colonies are, and of Right ought to be Free and Independent States; that they are Absolved from all Allegiance to the British Crown, and that all political connection between them and the State of Great Britain, is and ought to be totally dissolved."

—From the conclusion to the US Declaration of Independence

paved the way for this to happen. On June 7, 1776, a resolution was brought before Congress by Richard Henry Lee of the Virginian delegation, which proposed:

> *... that these United Colonies are, and of right ought to be, free and independent States, that they are absolved from all allegiance to the British Crown, and that all political connection between them and the State of Great Britain is, and ought to be, totally dissolved.*

LIFE AND LIBERTY

The preamble to the Declaration of Independence initially received little attention. The first sentence read:

"We hold these truths to be self-evident, that all men are created equal, that they are endowed by their Creator with certain unalienable Rights, that among these are Life, Liberty, and the pursuit of Happiness."

These words would become some of the most quoted in the English language and, in a single sentence, managed to sum up the entire ethos of the country that would become the United States of America. The fact that the sentence provoked almost no response at the time, however, suggests that people were far more concerned with the main aim of the document—to declare independence from Britain—than with the stating of lofty ideals.

The Declaration of Independence formally changed what had started out as a rebellion to an all-out revolution.

Loyalists, led by John Dickinson of the Pennsylvanian delegation, argued vigorously against the resolution, but were defeated in the ensuing vote. A committee, including John Adams and Benjamin Franklin of Pennsylvania, was established to draft a formal declaration, although the job of writing the document was given to another of the committee members, Thomas Jefferson of Virginia.

Over the next few weeks, Jefferson wrote a first draft and, in consultation with Adams, made numerous changes before the committee was happy with it. It was ready by June 28, at which point Congress decided to let it "lie on the table" for a few days to give everybody a chance to consider their responses. In the vote on July 2, a number of key opponents of independence, including Dickinson, abstained, allowing the resolution for independence to be adopted. The main body of the finished document published on July 4 consisted of a list of grievances against George III, some of which were what had led to the rebellion in the first place, such as, "For imposing Taxes on us without our Consent," and "For depriving us in many cases of the benefit of Trial by Jury." One or two others were a little more fanciful, seemingly thrown in to increase the volume of charges leveled against the king.

EQUALITY FOR ALL?

Critics of the declaration soon picked up on the lack of attention it paid to the rights of both women and American

FINAL DRAFT
The Declaration of Independence, published July 4, 1776. Made up of a list of grievances, it also conveyed the ideals of the United States of America.

A FREE NATION

If these criticisms can be left aside, however, the significance of the event is abundantly clear. In the Declaration of Independence, the American colonies set out their plain intention to separate from Britain and gave their reasons for doing so. This formally changed what had started out as a rebellion against the way authority had been imposed on the colonies to an all-out revolution aimed at getting rid of the British from America for good. It would take another eight years for this aim to be realized, until the decisive victory at Yorktown and the subsequent peace treaty in which Britain officially recognized the United States of America as a free and independent nation.

The success of the revolution and the creation of a new independent state must surely mean that the vote in favor of independence was the single most important decision made in American political history.

Indians, a major oversight in a document of this nature. Any mention of slavery was also removed from the final draft before it was published, leaving the Founding Fathers, as the men who signed it came to be called, open to accusations of hypocrisy because their declaration promoted equality and the liberty of the individual, yet a sizable number of its signatories, including Thomas Jefferson, were slave owners. It could be argued that the failure to deal with the issue of slavery at this early stage laid the foundations for the civil war that erupted eighty-five years later and all but ripped the country apart.

THE STORMING OF THE BASTILLE

1789

Circumstances: The volatile atmosphere of Paris in the summer of 1789

Protagonists: A Parisian mob, the defenders of the Bastille, King Louis XVI of France

Consequences: The start of the French Revolution

The French public holiday of Bastille Day on July 14 marks the moment when the French Revolution began in 1789 with the storming of a Parisian prison known as the Bastille. It led to the fall of the despised *ancien régime* (the Old Order), the removal of the monarchy, and the eventual establishment of a republic.

Today, nothing much is left of the Bastille, once a huge fortress and prison that had originally been built in the fourteenth century to guard the eastern approach to Paris. After the building was stormed, it was demolished and the stone was either used again in new construction work or made into souvenirs of the revolution.

In overcoming the garrison of troops stationed within the building, the Paris mob that took part in the attack actually achieved very little in practical terms. The Bastille had long since ceased to have any military role and, at the time the revolution erupted, held only seven prisoners in its cells. The significance of its capture had much more to do with what it represented than what it really was. It had become a symbol of the power of the king and in storming what was supposed to be an impregnable fortress, the mob not only demonstrated that it was possible to take the building, but also that it was possible to take on the monarchy and win.

News of the fall of the Bastille quickly spread throughout France, prompting similar outbreaks of revolt and, even though the king quickly backed down from any further confrontation with the people of Paris, the scene was now set for a full-scale revolution.

The Bastille had become a symbol of the power of the king, and in storming what was supposed to be an impregnable fortress, the mob showed it could take on the monarchy and win.

LOUIS XVI
The King of France as a prisoner, painted by Jean-François Garneray (1755–1837). Grotesque inequalities and dissatisfaction with Louis's rule led to revolution.

PARIS MOB

It is not possible to single out one individual who was responsible for making the decision to attack the Bastille. Instead, we must look at the actions of a mob of people who, whipped up by the heat of the moment, made spontaneous decisions to undertake an extremely dangerous and, had it been considered rationally, seemingly impossible venture.

Ultimately, however, regardless of how the decision was reached, the consequences, both for France and more widely around the world, would prove to be enormous and, as the Bastille Day celebrations in France show, ones that remain with us today.

THE PATH TO REVOLUTION

The political commentator Alexis de Tocqueville, writing with the benefit of hindsight in the 1850s, said of the French Revolution that, "Never was any such event so inevitable yet so completely unforeseen." He was making the point that France was heading in the direction of some form of major social upheaval in the late eighteenth century and that, if the revolution had not been ignited by the storming of the Bastille, then it would probably have begun in some other way.

The Enlightenment ideas of republicanism and the liberty of the individual as expressed by such French writers as Voltaire and Rousseau were widely known and much discussed. They had also been influential in the political philosophy of the American Revolution, which had successfully expelled the British only six years previously. Taken together with the disastrous state of the French economy at the time and a widespread dissatisfaction with the rule of King Louis XVI, this created a great desire for change across much of French society. Despite numerous promises of reform by the king and his government, this dissatisfaction had found little outlet for its expression.

The Seven Years War (1756–1763) fought against Britain, and then France's support for the American Revolution, had effectively bankrupted what had previously been one of Europe's wealthiest countries. In an effort to raise money, taxes were increased and, as so often happens, the burden fell disproportionately on those less able to pay. The French aristocracy used their influence with the king's government to ensure that they remained untouched by

THE ESTATES-GENERAL

The French government's general assembly, known as the Estates-General, was made up of representatives of the three estates of French society: the clergy (the First Estate), the nobility (the Second Estate), and everybody else (the Third Estate) made up of the middle-class bourgeoisie, together with common people and peasants, who in reality played almost no part in proceedings.

the economic problems of the country, while the king himself continued to live a life of extravagance and excess. In an effort to placate the French people, the government called a general assembly, known as the Estates-General, with the aim of finding a solution to the financial disaster.

NATIONAL ASSEMBLY

The Estates-General first met on May 5, 1789, and it immediately became apparent that the nobles intended to dominate the assembly, shattering any illusions that the Third Estate—who represented the middle-class, common people, and peasants—may have had about finding a fair and equitable solution to France's economic problems.

The Third Estate began to meet separately and, in June, declared itself to be the National Assembly. The king attempted to bypass the newly established assembly and, when that did not work, he locked the doors of the room they were using and posted soldiers there to prevent the delegates from gaining access.

They met instead in the nearby royal indoor tennis court, where they swore an oath to continue with the assembly until a new constitution had been implemented that limited the power of the king. The Tennis Court Oath, as it came to be called, was a pivotal moment in the beginning of the revolution, as it was the first occasion in which the power of the king had been directly challenged by a group of citizens.

BASTILLE DAY
The Storming of the Bastille and Arrest of the Governor Marquis de Launay by an unknown artist. De Launay was eventually beaten and killed by the mob in the street.

GROWING UNREST

Meanwhile, the situation in Paris steadily deteriorated due to rapidly increasing food prices. To add to the economic difficulties, the previous two years had seen very poor harvests, pushing the price of bread, the staple food of the poor, in the summer of 1789 to a higher level than at any other time during the whole of the eighteenth century. With unrest growing daily, the king ordered an increased military presence in the city, including regiments made up of soldiers from Switzerland and Germany. The Gardes Françaises, the regiment usually stationed in Paris, was thought to be largely sympathetic to the plight of the people, while foreign mercenaries were considered more reliable and would, if ordered, not hesitate to open fire on the French masses. The presence of these troops, widely distrusted by Parisians for exactly the same reason, only inflamed the situation even further. Added to this, the king decided on July 11 to sack his finance minister Jacques Necker, the only member of the government who had shown any support for the Third Estate and the new National Assembly.

THE ATTACK

The situation in Paris in the middle of July had become highly volatile. A widespread desire for reform, together with the inflammatory actions of an much despised and out-of-touch king, combined to create an atmosphere that was ready to explode. Rumors were circulating that the king intended to use his foreign mercenaries to restore order by force and, on the morning of July 14, a large crowd gathered outside Les Invalides, a hospital and retirement home for wounded soldiers. As an arsenal of weapons was known to be stored here, the crowd intended to arm themselves against the threat posed by the king's troops. The unit of Gardes Françaises stationed there did not make any effort to stop the crowds from forcing their way into the cellars, where they found about thirty thousand muskets and several cannons, but very little gunpowder or shot. It was at this point that people in the crowd began to turn their attention to the Bastille, perhaps following a prearranged plan to gather as many weapons as possible, but more likely through a mob reaction to a shout from a single individual or from an accumulation of rumors that had spread through the crowd that caused a spontaneous movement in the direction of the fortress.

The Governor of the Bastille, the Marquis de Launay, admitted two representatives into the fortress for talks, which dragged on into the afternoon. The crowd outside was rapidly growing impatient at the apparent lack of progress. By now they had been reinforced by soldiers from the Gardes Françaises.

HEAVILY GUARDED

The Bastille held a huge stockpile of gunpowder and was guarded by about eighty old soldiers, who were reinforced in the days leading up to July 14 with a detachment of thirty-two Swiss grenadiers. A regiment of five thousand regular French Army troops was also stationed a short walk away, who, if they had chosen to, could easily have dispersed the crowd, which is thought to have numbered no more than a thousand. Instead, they opted not to intervene at any stage during the day.

After the attack, the king returned to Paris wearing a tricolor cockade, the red, white, and blue ribbon that had become the symbol of the people.

Early in the afternoon, people surged forward into the outer courtyard of the building, where an exchange of musket fire broke out between the attackers and defenders. It is not clear which side began the shooting, but it continued intermittently through the afternoon until, at five o'clock, the governor ordered a ceasefire and, in a note pushed out through a crack in the inner gate, offered terms for his surrender. The terms were refused, but the governor surrendered anyway, perhaps fearing that if the situation deteriorated any further, it would lead to a bloodbath. He ordered the inner gates to be opened and the mob surged into the fortress.

AFTERMATH

As a consequence of the attack, ninety-eight of the attackers had been killed, compared with only one of the defenders. In the aftermath, eight of the garrison were killed by the mob, including de Launay, who was dragged out of the Bastille into the street, where he was beaten, stabbed, and then beheaded.

The officer in charge of the Swiss troops survived and later wrote a report highly critical of de Launay, blaming his indecision and prevarication for the loss of the supposedly impregnable fortress. In the days following the fall of the Bastille, the king, finally realizing how dangerous the situation had become, backed down. He sent out an order for the troops in and around Paris to go back to their barracks, reinstated Necker, and

GUILLOTINED

An engraving of the execution of Louis XVI on January 21, 1793, three and a half years after the storming of the Bastille.

then returned to Paris himself, where he wore a tricolor cockade, the red, white, and blue ribbon that had become the symbol of the people.

The National Assembly then began the process of writing a new constitution, in which the king was to have almost all of his powers removed and become the figurehead of a constitutional monarchy. A period of relative calm returned to Paris, but it would only be a matter of time before more radical revolutionaries, who were advocating a republic without a monarchy, returned to the streets to continue the struggle. So, even if the intention of the mob who stormed the Bastille had primarily been to capture its arsenal and gunpowder, the outcome was to spark one of the great turning points in European history. Once the absolute power of the monarch had been successfully challenged in this way, the scene was set for a full-scale revolution.

THE LOUISIANA PURCHASE

1803

Circumstances: The American government makes France an offer to buy the port of New Orleans

Protagonists: Thomas Jefferson, Robert Livingston, James Monroe, and Napoleon Bonaparte

Consequences: A doubling in the size of the United States of America for a knockdown price

The purchase of the Louisiana Territory by the United States of America was formalized on April 30, 1803, by the signing of an agreement between US envoys Robert Livingston and James Monroe and the French Treasury Minister François Barbé-Marbois. The price was $15 million, made up of $11.75 million in cash and the cancellation of $3.25 million of France's debt to America. The exact expanse of the territory was not known at the time because most of the region had not been mapped, but it would encompass approximately 825,000 square miles (2.1 million square km), an area almost four times the size of France and one that would double the size of America.

Livingston and Monroe had been authorized by President Jefferson to offer up to $10 million solely for the port of New Orleans. They had no instructions for what they should do when France unexpectedly put the whole of the territory on the table. They decided to agree to the price asked by the French, concluding that it was too good an offer to turn down. In doing so, on their own initiative, they struck what must rank as the greatest real-estate deal of all time.

WEST OF THE MISSISSIPPI

After victory in the Revolutionary War over Britain, achieved in 1783, America began to expand westward from its original thirteen states. It advanced through the Appalachian Mountains and into the valleys of the Ohio and Mississippi rivers, which provided vital transport links for the import and export of goods by river transport through the port of New Orleans. Up until 1800, the land west of the Mississippi had been owned by Spain.

In a secret treaty, Spain had handed over the entire region between the Mississippi and the Rocky Mountains—the Louisiana Territory—to Napoleon Bonaparte's France, even though some of the land on the western bank of the Mississippi had already been settled by Americans. When Thomas Jefferson became president in 1801, he immediately became concerned that Napoleon intended to incorporate the territory into the French Empire, which would prevent the further westward expansion of America and bring access to the Mississippi through New Orleans under French control. The Spanish, who were formally still in control of the city, had closed it to American shipping on a number of occasions in the past and Jefferson was looking for a permanent solution to the problem. One option was to take New Orleans by force, risking a war with both Spain and France, or, alternatively, America could enter into an alliance with Britain to make it difficult for Napoleon to take up his possession.

Jefferson did not like either of these options, so, despite being concerned

The Louisiana Purchase doubled the size of America at a cost of less than four cents an acre.

about the constitutional legality of purchasing territory, he decided to make Napoleon a cash offer for New Orleans and, if that failed, approach the British about an alliance. To that end, in March 1803, Jefferson dispatched James Monroe, a future president, to assist the American ambassador to France, Robert Livingston, in the ensuing negotiations.

NAPOLEON BONAPARTE

Before Napoleon could make any use of his new American territory, he had to make peace with the British, who had the naval power to prevent him from establishing a French Empire on the American continent. The Treaty of Amiens accomplished that aim in March 1802, even if it was to prove a short-lived peace settlement.

By that time Napoleon was already attempting to establish a base on the Caribbean island of Saint-Domingue, now Haiti, having dispatched an army there to put down a slave revolt so that he could then use the island as a stopping place en route to America. The French forces met much stiffer resistance from the Haitian rebels than had been expected and their numbers were decimated by disease. The resulting defeat for the French appears to have persuaded Napoleon to give up his ambitions in the New World. Without a base in the Caribbean, and with Florida remaining a Spanish possession, Napoleon knew that a colony in Louisiana would have proved

ROBERT LIVINGSTON
The American ambassador to France, who, together with James Monroe, was responsible for negotiating the Louisiana Purchase.

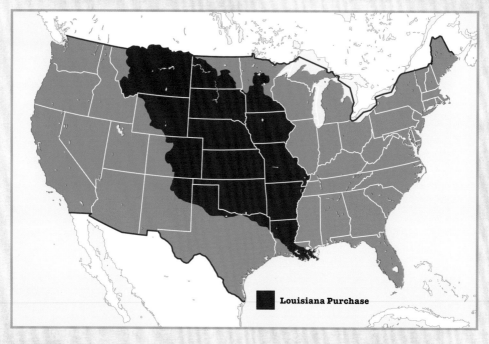

Louisiana Purchase

LOUISIANA PURCHASE

The extent of the area sold to America by Napoleon was unknown at the time, but it would double the size of the country.

impossible to defend against either the Americans or the British.

By the spring of 1803, hostilities with the British were on the brink of reigniting and Napoleon was making plans for an invasion of Britain, which he would later abandon. In order to pay for the buildup of an invasion force, he needed money quickly and, with his attention now firmly back on Europe, he decided to make the Americans an offer they could not refuse.

NAPOLEON'S OFFER

The offer put to the American negotiators was to sell the whole of the Louisiana Territory for $15 million. Waiting for an answer from Jefferson would have taken

several months, and Napoleon was well known for his tendency to change his mind. Rather than give him the opportunity to do so, Livingston and Monroe made the decision to accept the offer themselves and on April 30, 1803, as quickly as it could be arranged, signed the treaty with Barbé-Marbois to make the agreement official.

On July 4, Jefferson publicly announced the sensational deal, which doubled the size of the country at a cost of less than four cents an acre (about nine cents per hectare) and without a shot being fired. The deal was not universally welcomed in America at the time, particularly after doubts about its legality began to emerge. Napoleon, it turned out, had no more constitutional authority to sell the territory than Jefferson had to buy it. Moreover, at the time the treaty had been signed, Spain had still not formally transferred the title of the land to France. And, of course, nobody at the time stopped to consider that the American Indian tribes living across the region could, had they been consulted and given legal advice, have claimed that the territory belonged to them in the first place through right of possession.

LEWIS AND CLARK

Before the Louisiana Purchase, Jefferson had always insisted on acting in accordance with the US Constitution, but he was a landowner himself and could appreciate how extraordinary a deal it was for America. So, on this occasion he put his misgivings aside and, legal or otherwise, decided to accept the deal as it stood. The Spanish were not so accommodating, challenging the extent of the territory being claimed by the United States and insisting that the deal had only been for New Orleans and the land on the western bank of the Mississippi, not for all the territory right up to the Rocky Mountains.

Jefferson had already been considering sending expeditions into the territory before the purchase and now commissioned the first of several. Their main aim was to assess the economic and commercial potential of the new territory, but also to survey the land in the belief that the country with the best maps would have the better claim to the territory. In May 1804, the expedition, which was led by the US soldiers Meriwether Lewis and William Clark, embarked west along the Missouri River, making, for the most part, friendly contact with the American Indian tribes they encountered. They then headed farther to the west through the disputed Oregon Territory and on to the Pacific Ocean.

The Lewis and Clark Expedition into the Louisiana Territory was followed by several later expeditions, which explored the Red River Basin and the area farther south. The maps drawn up by these expeditions would subsequently play a part in negotiations between America and Spain to establish the western boundary of the territory. In the Adams-Onís Treaty, signed in 1819, the American negotiator John Quincy Adams not only set the border between American and Spanish territories, but also secured the purchase of Florida from Spain, making it one of America's greatest diplomatic successes.

AFTER LOUISIANA

The United States was to grow larger still after the Louisiana Purchase. In the 1840s, territory west of the Rockies came into American possession through a process of annexation and negotiation with Mexico, and by a treaty with Britain over the Oregon Country, establishing the border between America and Canada on the 49th parallel. The Alaska Purchase of 1867, in which America paid Russia $7.2 million for a huge area of what was then considered a barren Arctic wilderness, added almost as much territory to the United States as the Louisiana Purchase had done. The addition of Hawaii in 1959, after Hawaiians voted in favor of accepting statehood rather than remaining as a US territory, completed the fifty states of America as they are today.

SETTLING THE PEACE AT THE CONGRESS OF VIENNA

1814–15

Circumstances: The end of the Napoleonic Wars

Protagonists: Diplomatic representatives from the Great Powers

Consequences: The reorganization of European states and the establishment of the Concert of Europe to maintain peace through the balance of power

After more than twenty years of almost constant war, the Great Powers of Europe came together at the Congress of Vienna, beginning in November 1814. Their objectives were to negotiate a peace settlement and establish a system of diplomacy that would avoid further wars in the future.

The French Revolutionary Wars, beginning in 1792, had been followed by the Napoleonic Wars, which had led to the dissolution of the Holy Roman Empire and left much of the continent in disarray. Napoleon was defeated at the Battle of Leipzig in October 1813 and subsequently exiled to the island of Elba, off the coast of Italy. France then formally surrendered to a coalition of forces primarily made up of the other four Great Powers: Britain, Russia, Austria, and Prussia. In the immediate aftermath of the French surrender, the members of the alliance decided to state formally in a treaty that they would remain as allies for at least the next twenty years and to hold the Congress of Vienna to sort out all the outstanding issues arising from years of war.

BALANCE OF POWER

The outcome of the negotiations led to the reorganization of much of Europe, affecting almost every continental European state. It established a system of maintaining the balance of power by diplomatic means—known as the Concert of Europe—in which the Great Powers could settle disputes by negotiation rather than war. The Congress has attracted a great deal of criticism over the years, largely because of the Great Powers' preference for reinstating monarchies over the more liberal and enlightened systems of government that had begun to develop as a result of the French Revolution.

Nevertheless, the negotiated settlements achieved through the Concert of Europe helped to prevent

> **The main area of contention during much of the remainder of the nineteenth century concerned the decline of the Ottoman Empire.**

another major European war for almost fifty years, and it wasn't until a hundred years later, at the outbreak of World War I, that all the Great Powers were involved in a war. Overall, the decisions made at the Congress of Vienna, despite being motivated by self-interest, were nevertheless effective in their aims of maintaining peace in Europe and they established a precedent for the conduct of future diplomatic meetings between the Great Powers.

CONCERT OF EUROPE

The Congress met in Vienna under the chairmanship of the Austrian Foreign Minister Prince Klemens von Metternich, an accomplished diplomat and statesman who would remain highly influential in both Austrian politics and European diplomacy for several decades afterward. The subsequent meetings held between the Great Powers in order to maintain the balance of power are now widely known as the Concert of Europe, but at the time were often referred to as being part of the Metternich System because Metternich was acknowledged as the man behind the development of this approach. He was also known for his conservative attitude, favoring rule by monarchies and aristocratic families, a stance that fitted well with the main negotiators from the other three Great Powers.

The Russian delegation was directed by Tsar Alexander I, who remained in Vienna for the entire period, while the Prussians were led by their chancellor, Prince Karl von Hardenberg. The British delegation was initially led by Lord Castlereagh, but he was replaced by the Duke of Wellington, who himself had to leave the Congress to lead the campaign

NAPOLEON BONAPARTE
The Congress of Vienna was convened after the defeat of Napoleon Bonaparte at the Battle of Leipzig and the subsequent surrender of the French forces.

against Napoleon, who had escaped from exile and returned to France, beginning a period known as the Hundred Days. The British delegation was then led by the diplomat Richard Trench, the Earl of Clancarty, who would remain in Vienna until the settlement's conclusion.

At first, the French were excluded from the Congress because they were held responsible for the wars that had made it necessary in the first place. They were admitted later, however, after skilled diplomatic maneuvering by their foreign minister, Charles Talleyrand. One of the early decisions made by the Congress was to restore the Bourbon dynasty, in the shape of King Louis XVIII, to the throne of France in succession to Napoleon.

THE SETTLEMENT

Although delegations from every other European state, of which there were almost two hundred at the time, were involved in the formal discussions, they had little influence on the decisions made because most of the real negotiations occurred in informal meetings held in private between the representatives of the Great Powers. An almost constant round of balls and dinner parties was held to entertain the huge numbers of aristocratic delegates who had arrived in Vienna for the Congress, many of whom are said to have done more dancing than talking.

The final settlement was signed by all participants on June 9, 1815, nine days before the Battle of Waterloo. One of the principal intentions of the reorganization of European states was to create a buffer zone of independent states around France, which was forced to revert to the borders it had before the start of the French Revolutionary Wars. Prussia was given territory in the Rhineland, on its northwest border with France, while Switzerland's neutrality (unaligned with any country) was guaranteed. The Kingdom of Piedmont-Sardinia was restored as a constitutional monarchy and given territory on the eastern border of France. To the north, the Kingdom of the Netherlands was created out of the Dutch Republic and those adjacent parts of the French Empire that would later split away to form Belgium.

The other major decisions included giving Finland and part of Poland to Russia, with the rest of Poland going to Prussia, together with several of the smaller German states of the former Holy Roman Empire. All the remaining German states, principalities, and grand duchies, of which there were more than a hundred, were absorbed into about thirty states and united as the German Confederation, while Italy was also reorganized into seven states, and Norway, which had previously been governed by Denmark, was given to Sweden without the Norwegian people being consulted.

A NEW EUROPE

By the end of this process, the map of Europe had been almost completely redrawn, with most of the new states both large and small being placed under the rule of either an absolute (all-powerful) monarch or a constitutional monarchy

KLEMENS VON METTERNICH
The Austrian foreign minister, Metternich chaired the Congress of Vienna, which established the Concert of Europe, also known as the Metternich System.

(where the powers of the monarchy are restricted by principles set out in a constitution). The only one of the Great Powers to remain the same after the settlement was Britain, which was more interested in its overseas empire than in any particular territories in Europe.

The complete lack of concern showed by the Great Powers for the wishes of the people in countries being reorganized would lead to problems in the future, as would the failure to acknowledge the desire for reform felt in many parts of Europe. A revolution would erupt in Belgium in 1830, and in 1848 a series of revolutions and uprisings that began in France would spread across much of the continent. But these revolutionary struggles did not develop into wider wars and for the most part the conflicting interests of the five Great Powers continued to be managed through the Concert of Europe. The main area of contention during much of the remainder of the nineteenth century concerned the decline of the Ottoman Empire, in which some of the Great Powers, particularly Britain and Russia, competed with one another to gain the greatest benefit as Ottoman influence eroded.

BEGINNING OF THE END

This "Eastern Question," as the Ottoman situation was known, was behind the Crimean War, fought between 1853 and 1856 by the Russian Empire and a coalition of European states led by Britain and France. The failure of the Great Powers to find a negotiated solution to this conflict can be seen as the beginning of the end for the Concert system established by the Congress of Vienna. It was further undermined by the unification of Germany in 1871,

AIMS ACHIEVED

The peace settlement reached after the end of World War I provides an illustration of how successfully the Congress of Vienna had dealt with the issues arising out of the Napoleonic Wars. The punishing measures taken against Germany in 1919 as part of the Treaty of Versailles were one of the direct causes of World War II, so much so that some historians have described the twenty-year gap between the wars as being nothing more than a break in hostilities.

which had the industrial and military capacity to dominate Europe, disrupting the balance of power created by the Congress. The Great Powers sought to form individual alliances between one another rather than to maintain strong diplomatic relations across the continent. While these alliances were by no means the only cause of World War I, they certainly played a major part in the crisis that developed in July 1914.

The decisions made at Vienna did not take into account the more liberal atmosphere that had developed in Europe by that time, nor did they foresee the later rise of nationalism in many European countries. But even the left-wing historian Eric Hobsbawm, no friend of dynastic monarchies, described the settlement as "reasonable and sensible." It is hardly a ringing endorsement, but, considering the circumstances, being "reasonable and sensible" was not a terrible way of settling differences either.

KARL DRAIS INVENTS THE LAUFMASCHINE

1817

Circumstances: The rising price of oats in Baden

Protagonists: Karl Drais, an inventor trying to find a way of replacing the horse

Consequences: The first two-wheeled self-propelled mode of transport, the forerunner of the modern bicycle

The largest volcanic eruption in the last two thousand years began on April 10, 1815, on the island of Sumbawa in the Dutch East Indies, now Indonesia. A huge buildup of magma underneath Mount Tambora caused an immense explosion, throwing an enormous amount of debris out into the atmosphere. The German historian Hans-Erhard Lessing has proposed a surprising connection between this devastating event and the subsequent invention of the laufmaschine, the earliest form of the bicycle.

Other than the fact that the invention took place only two years after the eruption, this connection might seem a little stretched, but Lessing's theory makes sense. The ash and dust thrown high into the Earth's atmosphere by the eruption caused a rapid cooling in the climate across the northern hemisphere, leading to what became known in Europe as the Year Without a Summer. The poor harvest experienced that year resulted in famine in some European countries and caused a spike in food prices across much of the rest of the continent, including in the city of Mannheim in what was then the Grand Duchy of Baden, where the forestry official and inventor Karl Drais lived. A dramatic increase in the price of oats made feeding horses an expensive business and, at least according to Lessing, this led to Drais's decision to revisit an unsuccessful project he had worked on a few years previously. His plan was to develop a horseless carriage, only this time, rather than the four-wheel contraption he had originally envisaged, he concentrated on a version with two wheels. He called this the laufmaschine, literally the "running machine."

A dramatic increase in the price of oats made feeding horses an expensive business and this may have motivated Drais to develop his laufmaschine.

EDUCATION

Karl Drais was born on April 29, 1785, in the city of Karlsruhe, the capital of Baden. His father, who held the title of baron, was a senior civil servant in the government of the Grand Duke of Baden, working as the chief administrator of the forestry department, an important role because the Black Forest covered a large area of the Grand Duchy. The grand duke became Drais's godfather and through family connections and the duke's patronage,

Drais joined the forestry service himself in 1803, but found himself without a role for several years while he waited for a suitable position to become available. In the meantime, he studied sciences at the University of Heidelberg and, if he had not already developed a fascination for mechanical devices beforehand, he certainly appears to have done so while at the university.

After finishing his studies, and while still waiting for a position in the forestry service, Drais taught for a few years at the local school run by his uncle, which specialized in forest administration. After two more years of waiting, a position finally opened up, but by this time Drais appears to have become much more interested in mechanical engineering than in forestry.

In 1812, Drais was granted indefinite leave from the forestry service on a full salary, allowing him to concentrate all his time on designing and building mechanical devices.

KARL DRAIS
A portrait of the inventor from about 1820, a few years after he had constructed the first laufmaschine.

RUNNING MACHINE
Riders on Karl Drais's laufmaschine had to propel it with their feet as if they were walking or running.

MECHANICAL HORSE

The complete lack of interest in his horseless carriage most likely caused Drais to rethink, and was perhaps also behind his decision to concentrate on developing a mechanical horse to be ridden by a single rider. By the summer of 1817, Drais had built his first laufmaschine, consisting of two small wooden coach wheels with metal rims, connected by a beam with a seat on it and with a pivot and handlebars above the front wheel so that it could be steered.

On June 12, Drais took the laufmaschine out for a demonstration ride, propelling it with his feet as if he were walking or running. In a little over an hour he had covered 9 miles (15 km). In the following month, and having made a few adjustments, he traveled from Gernsbach to Baden-Baden, a distance of 32 miles (50 km), in four hours, more than twice as quickly as anybody could reasonably walk the distance.

HORSELESS CARRIAGE

A string of inventions followed, including in 1814 his first attempt at a horseless carriage, which was driven by a crank handle turned by its passengers. Drais demonstrated the carriage to some of the nobles who had gathered for the Congress of Vienna later in that year, but it provoked little interest in them or, in truth, in anybody else. He shelved the idea, concentrating on other projects, such as the stenotype machine he had invented for recording musical notation by punching holes in paper.

Drais did not explain the reasons behind his decision to return to the idea of a self-propelled mechanical vehicle, but the scarcity of animal feed during the winter of 1816 certainly provides a reasonably convincing one. German newspapers from that time carried reports of the rising price of oats and of horses having to be put down because they could not be fed, so it is entirely possible that this was a motivating factor behind his decision.

INSTANT DEMAND

The two demonstrations received extensive coverage in German newspapers, leading to an instant demand for the laufmaschine. Drais was awarded a grand ducal privilege to enable him to exploit his invention, but although this

In Britain, the laufmaschine was nicknamed the dandy horse because it was mostly ridden by dandies (well-dressed men) showing off.

protected his invention in Baden, he did not have a wider patent so there was nothing to stop anybody else from outside the region copying his idea. Many other people began to make their own versions of the laufmaschine, and a craze began throughout Germany and in other parts of Europe. The original name, however, did not catch on and different versions of Drais's invention were known as the velocipede and the draisine. But, like all crazes, once the initial excitement for something new had died down, the laufmaschine gradually became less and less popular, until it remained in use only by a few die-hard enthusiasts.

TWO PEDALS

In truth, riders on their velocipedes and draisines did look faintly ridiculous and its popularity was not helped by the scorn it attracted from newspapers or by the poor state of most roads at the time. They were often deeply rutted and uneven from the passage of carriages and carts. The bad publicity may account, at least in part, for why it took fifty years for somebody to think of adding pedals to their velocipede so that it could be propelled without the rider having to run along the ground, an innovation that might now appear obvious.

The first person usually credited with making a bicycle in this way is Pierre Michaux, a blacksmith and carriage maker from Paris, who attached pedals directly to the front wheel of his velocipede in 1868, allowing him to move forward by turning the wheels with the pedals even if it made steering difficult. The problem was solved by the addition of a chain drive to propel the back wheel rather than the front, allowing the rider to steer much more easily and improving the weight distribution and balance of the bicycle.

The first of these to be produced commercially, the Rover Safety Bicycle, was made in Coventry, UK, in 1885 by the English inventor and industrialist John Kemp Starley. It was the first recognizably modern bike and began a second craze for individual mechanical horses that, with a few adjustments and modifications over the years, continues to this day.

> "These machines move at the rate of from 6 to 10 or 12 miles an hour, according to the peculiarities of the road traveled and the dexterity of the rider. The agreeable and moderate exercise they afford help to promote digestion, invigorate the corporeal system, insure health to those who are indisposed: and thus save the doctor's, druggist's, and housekeeper's bills."
>
> —From an advertisement offering velocipedes to rent in the *Connecticut Herald* on June 15, 1819

MONROE STATES HIS NON-INTERVENTION DOCTRINE

1823

Circumstances: The possibility of a resurgence of European colonization in the New World

Protagonists: President James Monroe and Secretary of State John Quincy Adams

Consequences: Establishment of a key principle of US policy

The tradition of the US president giving an annual message to a joint session of Congress, which is now known as the State of the Union Address, was initiated by George Washington in 1790 during his first term of office and only two years after independence. President James Monroe (1758–1831) used the occasion on December 2, 1823, to set out the American position on a particular point of foreign policy, a stance that would become known as the Monroe Doctrine. This was the principle that European powers should no longer consider any of the states of either North or South America as being potential colonies. He went further, saying that the United States would respect European colonies already in existence and would not intervene in the internal affairs of any European country. However, it would regard European interference anywhere in the Americas as an act of aggression against the United States.

This robust statement was the result of a decision reached over the course of several cabinet meetings held that November in which the Secretary of State John Quincy Adams (1767–1848), the son of the second US president John Adams, who would succeed Monroe to the presidency two years later, argued forcibly against a proposal to issue much the same declaration jointly with the British.

In deciding to go it alone, the US government was both asserting its independence on the world stage and establishing a principle of foreign policy that remains today. The way in which the Monroe Doctrine has been interpreted over the years has sometimes been controversial, being used, for instance, as a justification for US intervention in Central and South American states. The original decision, however, to formulate

> In going it alone, the US government was both asserting its independence on the world stage and establishing a principle of foreign policy that remains today.

JAMES MONROE
A portrait of the fifth president of the United States of America by Samuel Morse, the man who invented Morse code.

The Peninsular War, the theater of the Napoleonic Wars fought across Iberia, had left Spain in political turmoil, all but bankrupt, and incapable of maintaining its colonies in the New World when challenged by independence movements. Earlier in the year, a French army had intervened in Spain to restore the Bourbon king Ferdinand VII as the absolute monarch of the country and, after that successful campaign, rumors in diplomatic circles suggested that an alliance of Spain, France, and Russia was now planning to use force to restore the Spanish Crown's former colonies in the Americas as well.

At the same time, the Russian Tsar Nicholas II had been making statements about extending Russian territory in North America. The Americans and British had yet to agree a border between their own territories in the northern regions and the last thing either country wanted was a third party like Russia becoming involved and complicating matters even further.

the doctrine must surely rank as a great one in US diplomatic history because it has formed the basis of its foreign policy for almost two hundred years.

SUMMER OF 1823

One of the reasons why the Monroe Doctrine has lasted for so long is because it was stated in language that did not make it specific to an individual set of circumstances, even if it arose as a consequence of a particular moment in history. By the summer of 1823, America had formally recognized those Latin American countries that had won their independence from Spain after the end of the Napoleonic Wars in Europe.

EYE ON THE PRIZE

In formulating his view that the United States of America would look stronger if it issued the statement on its own rather than with the British, John Quincy Adams may have had an eye on his own interests as well as those of his country. By this time, he may well have already decided to stand in the presidential election of 1825, so being seen by the American people refusing a British request and enhancing America's reputation on the world stage would certainly have helped to boost his profile in America.

The British held a dominant position over much maritime trade, and ships following commercial routes came under the protection of the Royal Navy, which, at that time, really did rule the waves. It was not in Britain's interests for other European powers to become any more established in the New World than they already were, so, as well as opposing Russian expansion in the north, Britain was firmly against the restoration of Spanish rule in the south, particularly if that rule was imposed with the help of France, which would then surely use the opportunity to regain a foothold in the region.

Relations between Britain and America had been improving in the previous few years, even if the war of 1812 was still fresh in the memory. In August 1823, the British Foreign Secretary George Canning proposed that the two countries issue a joint statement disapproving of any outside intervention in the former colonies of Spanish America. The statement was to be worded in the usual diplomatic language, which did not actually mention the names of the countries it concerned, although it was obvious to everybody that its purpose was to warn off both France and Russia.

GO IT ALONE

Before discussing the British proposal with his cabinet, Monroe consulted with two of his predecessors, Thomas Jefferson and James Madison, both of whom expressed the opinion that it would be wise to go along with Canning. The first cabinet debate on November 7 appeared to be heading for a decision in line with the advice given by Jefferson and Madison, until Quincy Adams spoke. He put forward his view that

"The American continents, by free and independent condition which they have assumed and maintain, are henceforward not to be considered as subjects for future colonization by any European powers."

—From the address given to Congress by President James Monroe on December 2, 1823, setting out the principle that would later be known as the Monroe Doctrine

QUINCY ADAMS
The Monroe Doctrine was named after the president, but was principally the work of the secretary of state, John Quincy Adams.

region whether or not they issued a joint statement.

STATEMENT
In the weeks that followed, Quincy Adams's views were accepted by Monroe, who asked him to write a statement that could be incorporated in the presidential address to Congress. So, even though the resulting declaration was named after Monroe, it was largely the work of Quincy Adams.

America would look stronger as a nation if it issued a statement on its own rather than doing so with the British and then relying on the Royal Navy to police the ensuing policy. He was also certain that the threat from France and Russia had been exaggerated and in his opinion neither had any intention of intervening in the New World on behalf of Spain. This being the case, the United States had the opportunity to make its position clear without risk to itself and without having to enter into an alliance with the British, who, nevertheless, would still want to protect their interests in the

Critics of the doctrine immediately picked up on the point that, in reality, there was little America alone could have done if any European country had chosen to ignore it. Despite this, the Monroe Doctrine came to be seen as a defining statement of the separation of the Old World and the New, which demonstrated their different values, from Europe's continuing attachment to monarchies to the republicanism of America. It also pointed to a newfound confidence in what was then still a relatively young country: America was beginning to assert itself on the world stage.

DARWIN JOINS THE VOYAGE OF HMS *BEAGLE*

1831

Circumstances: A young naturalist is presented with a great opportunity, although not everyone sees it that way at first

Protagonist: Charles Darwin, John Henslow, Robert FitzRoy, Robert Darwin, and Josiah Wedgwood II

Consequences: A revolutionary change in our understanding of the natural world and our place within it

On August 30, 1831, the twenty-two-year-old Charles Darwin returned from a geological tour of North Wales to his family home in Shrewsbury, England, to find a letter waiting for him from John Henslow, one of his tutors at the University of Cambridge. In the letter Henslow explained that an opportunity had arisen for a naturalist to join the Royal Navy ship HMS *Beagle* on its next voyage, beginning in a month. The voyage was planned to last for two years and was primarily concerned with surveying the coast of South America.

Darwin was not being offered the position of the voyage's official Royal Navy naturalist, duties that would normally be undertaken by the ship's surgeon, but the role of "gentleman companion" to the captain, Robert FitzRoy. This meant that whoever took up the position would not be financed by the navy and would have to pay his own way. Nevertheless, it offered the chance to undertake a study of the natural history of the places visited by the *Beagle*, which, in the course of its voyage, would sail around the globe. At that moment, Darwin was about to return to Cambridge to begin the study of divinity with a view to becoming an Anglican clergyman, but, as soon as he read Henslow's letter, he decided that he wanted the position. The only problem he now faced was to convince the man who would have to foot the bill, his father, Robert Darwin, that delaying his studies for two years while he sailed around the world was a sensible thing to do.

UNIVERSITY LIFE

As it would turn out, the voyage of the *Beagle* would last for five years rather than the two initially planned. It would set Darwin not only on course to become the most famous naturalist of his day, but also the most celebrated figure in the history of the biological sciences.

But, as a young man, it was by no means apparent that Darwin would go on to become so successful in his chosen field. After leaving school, he first went to the University of Edinburgh at the age of sixteen to study medicine, following in

HMS BEAGLE
An engraving of the Royal Navy brig on which Darwin set sail in December 1831 for a five-year voyage around the world.

financial investments. Once at Edinburgh, Darwin found the lectures dull and the practical demonstrations nauseating, leading him to the conclusion that the medical profession was not the right one for him. Rather than studying medicine, he spent most of his time going out with friends and indulging his enthusiasm for shooting and fishing, while at the same time keeping up his childhood interest in natural history.

After two years studying medicine, Darwin left Edinburgh and, again on the advice of his father, moved to the University of Cambridge to take a Bachelor of Arts degree, the necessary first step to becoming an Anglican clergyman. It is hard to imagine now, given the reaction of the church to his later work, that anybody could think this would be a suitable career choice for Darwin, but he agreed to the plan even though he had never expressed any great interest in religion. He appears to have been quite taken with the idea of becoming the vicar of a country parish, where he could continue his interest in natural history and perhaps follow in the footsteps of

the footsteps of his older brother, Erasmus, and his father, who ran a successful medical practice in Shrewsbury and had become very wealthy through a series of shrewd

The voyage gave Darwin the chance to study the natural history of the places visited by the *Beagle*, as it sailed around the globe.

CHARLES DARWIN
A photograph taken in 1854 when Darwin was forty-five, more than twenty years after he had embarked on the voyage of the *Beagle*.

Gilbert White, the author of one of his favorite books, *The Natural History of Selborne*, who famously studied the bird life in and around a Hampshire village during the late eighteenth century.

THE NATURALIST EMERGES

At first, Darwin carried on at Cambridge much as he had done at Edinburgh, enjoying the social side of being a student more than academic study. But over the course of the next three years he gradually became more serious and studious, an attitude that brought him to the attention of a number of his tutors, including the geologist Adam Sedgewick and John Henslow. Country sports were replaced by beetle collecting and walking tours to study geology, and he not only began to attend lectures but also to read around the subjects that he was studying. One of the books that left a lasting impression on him was *Personal Narrative of a Journey to the Equinoctial Regions of the New Continent* by the German scientist and explorer Alexander von Humboldt, who traveled through the New World between 1799 and 1804. The book would influence Darwin's account of his own journey, known today as *The Voyage of the Beagle*. It began by describing an extended stay Humboldt had made on Tenerife in the Canary Islands in which he made observations of its unusual geology and natural history. At the end of his three-year degree course, Darwin planned to mount his own expedition to Tenerife, but before setting out for the island he accompanied Adam Sedgewick on his annual summer geological tour of North Wales to learn more about the practical and technical aspects of geological investigation.

LETTER FROM HENSLOW

On returning home after this trip to find Henslow's letter offering him a position on the *Beagle*, Darwin was suddenly presented with a much greater opportunity to study natural history overseas than his planned trip to Tenerife. Henslow knew about Darwin's desire to travel and considered that he had the potential to make a fine naturalist. Joining the *Beagle* would be the perfect way to extend his knowledge and it would also bring him to the attention of the wider scientific community.

Robert Darwin, on the other hand, was far from convinced and initially refused to provide his son with the necessary funds, no doubt thinking that Darwin was in the process of throwing away a respectable career in the clergy just as he had done with medicine. But he did not completely rule out the idea either, telling his son that he would reconsider if Charles could find a man of common sense who would support the scheme. To Charles, it was clear who his

father was referring to, as Robert Darwin had often said that his brother-in-law, Josiah Wedgwood II, was the most sensible man he had ever met. If Charles could persuade Uncle Jos, as he was known, of the merits of the scheme then his father would agree to it as well.

Darwin made a list of his father's objections, of throwing away his career before it had even started and of it being a "wild scheme," and went to see Uncle Jos at his country estate 30 miles (50 km) away in Staffordshire. Wedgwood immediately supported his nephew and wrote a letter to Robert Darwin addressing all of his objections, but then, after posting it, changed his mind about the best way of dealing with the matter and immediately drove over to Shrewsbury in his carriage to see his brother-in-law in person.

By the time Wedgwood arrived in Shrewsbury, Robert Darwin had already changed his mind, probably knowing all along what his brother-in-law's opinion would be. With his father now supporting him, and prepared to pay for everything, Darwin's decision was finalized and, after gaining the approval of the Admiralty and of Captain FitzRoy himself, he spent a frantic few weeks gathering all the equipment he would need for the voyage.

THE *BEAGLE* SAILS

As it would transpire, the *Beagle* did not actually leave Britain until the end of December, setting sail on the first leg of its voyage to cross the Atlantic to South America. Darwin turned out to be a terrible sailor, becoming seasick almost as soon as the ship left port, and he spent as much time as he could on land whenever the opportunity presented

SPECIMENS

Various specimens of mollusks that were collected by Charles Darwin during the *Beagle* voyage.

itself. But the voyage would prove to be the major formative experience of his life, giving him the opportunity to study the geology and natural history of a wide variety of habitats, from the Amazon rainforest of Brazil to tiny coral atolls in the Pacific Ocean.

GALÁPAGOS ISLANDS

On the Galápagos Islands, 600 miles (1,000 km) off the coast of Ecuador, Darwin could not fail to be struck by the remarkable geological formations and diversity of animals and plants he encountered, which, he noted in his journal, were very different from what he had seen on the South American mainland. It was only when he returned to Britain that he would begin to formulate his theory of evolution through natural selection, which would explain these differences.

In the introduction to *On the Origin of Species*, published in 1859, Darwin would reflect on this period of his life, saying:

When on board HMS Beagle, *as naturalist, I was struck with certain facts in the distribution of the inhabitants of South America, and in geological relations of the present to the past inhabitants of the continent. Those facts seemed to me to throw light on the origin of species — that mystery of mysteries, as it has been called by one of our greatest philosophers. On my return home, it occurred to me, in 1837, that something might perhaps be made out of this question by patiently accumulating and reflecting on all sorts of facts which would have any bearing on it.*

"Considering how fiercely I have been attacked by the orthodox it seems ludicrous that I once intended to be a clergyman. Nor was this intention and my father's wish ever formally given up, but died a natural death when on leaving Cambridge I joined the Beagle *as Naturalist."*

—From an autobiographical sketch written by Darwin in 1876

NATURAL SELECTION

Darwin embarked on an intense period of study once he got back to Britain, and sorted out the various collections he had made during the voyage. He kept a series of notebooks on his study of the "transmutation of life," or evolution as we call it now.

These would in October 1838 crystallize into the theory of natural selection after he read *An Essay on the Principle of Population* by Thomas Malthus. In the book, Malthus set out his thoughts on the likelihood of human population growth outstripping the availability of resources and the ensuing struggle for existence that this would cause.

By combining Malthus's theory with his own work and observations, Darwin arrived at the theory of natural selection, in which species of animals and plants change over time as a consequence of the competition for resources between individuals of the same species. Those individuals that were best adapted to their environment would be the ones

Darwin arrived at the theory of natural selection, in which species of animals and plants change over time as a consequence of the competition for resources.

most likely to survive and reproduce, thereby passing on their characteristics to their offspring.

ON THE ORIGIN OF SPECIES

However, it would be another twenty years before Darwin was prepared to publish his theory, and only then because another naturalist, Alfred Russell Wallace, had come to a similar conclusion from his own studies. In *On the Origin of Species*, Darwin presented the evidence he had accumulated over the years, some of which went back to the work he had undertaken during the voyage of the *Beagle*.

The book proved to be a turning point in the biological sciences and was highly controversial among those who considered that it challenged the biblical account of creation. Despite overwhelming evidence supporting the theory, it remains controversial in some circles today. But the decision made by Darwin, with the help of his father and Uncle Jos, to join the voyage of the *Beagle* would lead to him dedicating his life to his work, which he described as being "one long argument" in favor of evolution. In doing so, he did more than anybody else before or since to further our understanding of the natural world, changing the way we think about ourselves and the world in which we live.

LINCOLN FREES THE SLAVES IN THE SOUTH

1862

Circumstances: The US president considers what can be done about a series of reverses in the Civil War

Protagonists: President Abraham Lincoln and his cabinet of ministers

Consequences: The end of slavery in the United States of America

President Abraham Lincoln made the decision to issue a proclamation to free the slaves of the thirteen states of the Confederacy on July 12, 1862. He first mentioned it the following day to two of the members of his cabinet, Secretary of State William H. Seward and Secretary of the Navy Gideon Welles, who noted in his diary that Lincoln had said the issue had "occupied his mind and thoughts day and night" for several weeks.

By that time the Civil War had been raging for more than a year and it had not been going well for the Union (the northern states of the US that opposed the southern states of the Confederacy that had broken away from the Union in 1860–61). Lincoln intended issuing the proclamation as a war measure, which he was entitled to do under the US Constitution as commander-in-chief of the armed forces, citing the use of slaves by the Confederacy in their war effort. At a cabinet meeting on July 22, Lincoln discussed his intention with his colleagues and accepted the advice of Seward not to issue the proclamation until the Union had achieved a significant victory on the battlefield, otherwise it would look like a desperate measure adopted by the side losing the war. It took two months for a suitable occasion to arise and, in the aftermath of the Battle of Antietam, the president made public his intention of issuing the Emancipation Proclamation, stating that it would come into force in all those

> "While Washington sweltered through the long, hot summer [of 1862], Lincoln made the momentous decision on emancipation that would define both his presidency and the Civil War."
>
> —Doris Kearns Goodwin, *Team of Rivals*

Confederate states that had not rejoined the Union by January 1 of the following year. In doing so, Lincoln officially broadened the war aims of the federal government, from opposing the rebellion in the southern states and preserving the Union to include the liberation of the slaves of the Confederacy.

By any standards, the Emancipation Proclamation was a momentous decision and a defining moment in both the Civil War and in the history of America as a whole—even if its immediate effect was limited and it did not actually apply to those slaves held in the border states that had not joined the Confederacy, but in which slavery was still legal.

NORTH AND SOUTH

There can be no doubt that slavery was a major issue during the Civil War, but the extent to which it actually caused the war in the first place has become one of those difficult historical debates because the answer is a matter of opinion. But the division of the states fighting on either side of the war essentially came down to those in the North, where slavery had either been abolished or had never been legal in the first place, and the southern slave states, which formed the Confederacy after Lincoln, the candidate of the antislavery Republican Party, won the 1860 presidential election. Unlike in the rapidly industrializing North, the economy of the southern states largely remained an agricultural one, primarily based on the lucrative cotton trade. It relied on the plantation system and slavery, and, even though the majority of white people in the South had never owned a slave, most of their political representatives came

ABRAHAM LINCOLN

A portrait taken on November 8, 1863, by which time the Emancipation Proclamation had been in force for ten months.

from the slave-owning class. They were not prepared to risk their positions and wealth by allowing what they considered to be interference in a state issue by a federal government dominated by those who favored the abolition of slavery, known as abolitionists.

SLAVERY AND CIVIL WAR

The crux of the matter was in whether the newly emerging states created as a result of the westward expansion of America should be slave states or free states. The opinion at the time was that, if these new states were free, then the institution of slavery would gradually wither away throughout America. This was because the slave states would become an increasingly small minority in Congress and would eventually have to agree to abolition even if they did not agree with the moral arguments against slavery.

This split had already led to violent confrontations in the 1850s during what is known as the Bleeding Kansas era, in which immigrants from both sides, slave-owning southerners and northern free-staters, fought over the status of the territory in the Midwest. This would become the free state of Kansas in January 1861, three months before the Confederate attack on Fort Sumter in South Carolina that started the Civil War. So it could be argued that the Confederacy went to war to maintain the

> Even though the majority of white people in the south had never owned a slave, most of their political representatives came from the slave-owning class.

LINCOLN'S CABINET

The First Reading of the Emancipation Proclamation of President Lincoln by Francis Bicknell Carpenter, now in the US Capitol building in Washington.

right of individual states to determine their own laws and that the North went to war to preserve the Union, as Lincoln said himself on numerous occasions. However, the poisonous issue underpinning everything was slavery.

ABRAHAM LINCOLN

The extent to which Lincoln was genuinely committed to the abolitionist cause rather than using it as a political

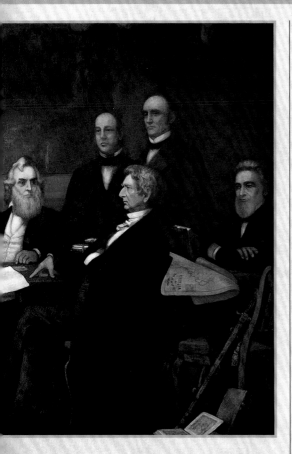

the time, the president did not possess the power required to abolish slavery on his own. To make any proposed constitutional change legal it had to be approved by both houses of Congress and by the legislatures of each state of the Union. The Republican Party may have been in a majority in Congress, but Lincoln was well aware that at least some of the states, particularly those border states where slavery was still legal, were not going to support any abolitionist legislation, making it impossible for him to push a constitutional change through by this method.

One strategy Lincoln adopted in an attempt to overcome this deadlock was to persuade the Congressional representatives of the border states to accept a deal he called "compensated emancipation." It proposed that states would introduce laws to put an end to slavery in return for slave owners receiving compensation (repayment) for the loss of their property, the loss being the slaves they owned. He held several meetings in the White House to discuss this proposal, but could not reach an agreement with the representatives of the border states. After one particularly fruitless encounter that took place on July 12, 1862, the day of his momentous decision, Lincoln came to the conclusion that, no matter what he did, the border states would never agree to it.

CHANGE OF MIND

By this time, the Union Army had also suffered major defeats in Virginia prompting Lincoln to pursue the war more vigorously. After concluding that he was never going to get anywhere with the border states, he also changed his approach to abolition, making the

tool to help the Union win the war has been the cause of almost as much speculation as the role slavery played in the start of the war. He has been characterized by some as being no more than a political manipulator, using any means he could to achieve his aims. Others see him as an idealist whose main purpose in seeking election as president and then in fighting the Civil War was to abolish slavery. The truth of the matter probably lies somewhere between these two extremes and, at least according to the current trends in historical research, now tends toward the latter argument.

The major obstacle facing Lincoln was that, under the US Constitution at

ROBERT E. LEE
Commander of the Confederate
Army of Northern Virginia (1865).

decision to free the slaves held in Confederate states first because he had the power to do so without the approval of Congress or the state legislatures. It was, Lincoln said, "a military necessity absolutely essential for the salvation of the Union." In response to Confederate claims that it was unconstitutional, he stated, "The rebels could not simultaneously throw off the Constitution and evoke its aid."

LEE FIGHTS BACK

A few weeks before July 1862, the Union had suffered a major setback in the war. The Union Army of the Potomac had attempted to capture Richmond, the Confederate capital in Virginia, but were defeated in a series of encounters with a Confederate Army under the command of Robert E. Lee. These became known as the Seven Days Battles, and the Union Army had been forced to retreat. Lee's successes on the battlefield prompted rumors that both Britain and France were considering recognizing the Confederacy as the legitimate government of the southern states. This would have forced Lincoln into a settlement, putting an end to his hopes of preserving the Union.

BATTLE OF ANTIETAM

Over the course of the following two months, the war continued to go badly for the Union. Lee advanced through Virginia until his army was only 20 miles (30 km) from Washington, but then turned north and crossed the Potomac River into the Union state of Maryland, before finally being stopped on September 17 at the Battle of Antietam.

The battle was the single most costly day of the war, with a combined total of twenty-three thousand casualties, of which thirty-five hundred were killed. In reality it was fought to a stalemate, even if it was treated like a victory by the Union forces because it prevented Lee advancing farther into Maryland. Lincoln also claimed victory and used the occasion to publicly issue his provisional proclamation.

EMANCIPATION

None of the Confederate states complied with the terms of this proclamation by returning to the Union before January 1, 1863, leading to the Emancipation

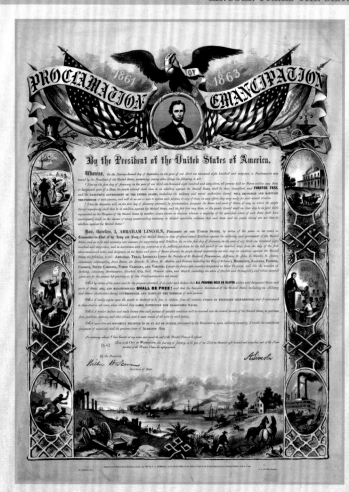

THE PROCLAMATION
A reproduction of the Emancipation Proclamation issued by Lincoln on January 1, 1863, which freed the slaves in the Confederate states.

THIRTEENTH AMENDMENT

As the war was drawing to a close, Lincoln, knowing that the Emancipation Proclamation could be thought of as being only a temporary war measure, proposed an amendment to the US Constitution to make slavery illegal throughout America. It read, "Neither slavery nor involuntary servitude, except as a punishment for crime whereof the party shall have been duly convicted, shall exist within the United States, or any place subject to their jurisdiction."

Proclamation entering into law on that date. Approximately four million slaves in the Confederacy became technically free that day, even if almost half a million more in the border states remained enslaved. Over the course of two and a half years, the advancing Union Army gradually freed those slaves in the Confederate territory that they captured.

By December 6, 1865, it had been approved by Congress and all the states of the Union, thereby coming into law as the Thirteenth Amendment nine months after Lincoln had been assassinated by the Confederate sympathizer John Wilkes Booth.

The amendment to the US Constitution that made slavery illegal throughout America came into law as the Thirteenth Amendment on December 6, 1865.

THE WRIGHT BROTHERS BUILD AN AIRPLANE

1903

Circumstances: Two brothers indulge their childhood fascination with flying

Protagonists: Wilbur and Orville Wright

Consequences: The beginning of the age of the airplane

On December 17, 1903, Orville Wright flew the *Wright Flyer 1* for a distance of 120 feet (37 m), which took him about twelve seconds. It was the first in a series of four successful flights that day, with Orville and his brother Wilbur alternating as pilot. It was Wilbur who was at the controls for the longest flight of the day, which lasted for almost a minute and on which he traveled 852 feet (260 m). It might not have been very far, but according to the Smithsonian Institute, the *Flyer* was "the first powered, heavier-than-air machine to achieve controlled, sustained flight with a pilot aboard," or, to the rest of us, the first proper airplane.

FASCINATION WITH FLIGHT

Before becoming aviation pioneers, the Wright Brothers had opened a bicycle shop together in their home town of Dayton, Ohio. Here they constructed and repaired their own version of the safety bike, and both had been fascinated by the idea of flight since childhood. The inspiration behind their decision to attempt to build their own airplane came from reading a newspaper report of the death of the German flyer Otto Lilienthal on August 10, 1896. He had made more than two thousand gliding flights before losing control of his hang glider, as we would now call it, and broke his neck in the subsequent crash. Many people would have been put off the idea of flying by such a report, but Wilbur and Orville were inspired by it. They differed from all the other early pioneers of flight by adopting a much more rigorous and methodological approach to the design and testing of their machines. Flying was clearly a dangerous business and, while it was not possible to eliminate all the risks, the Wright Brothers intended to leave as little to chance as possible.

CONTROL

The fundamental problem preventing all the pioneers of flying from making a sustained flight was not so much staying in the air, since the aerodynamics of lift—the movement of air around a solid body in flight—had already been worked out. The key problem was how to keep control of the airplane when it was in flight. Lilienthal's system of control had simply involved moving his body both to maintain the balance of his glider and to change direction. While this worked up to a point, as Lilienthal and various other pilots of the day had found out to their cost, it made their gliders difficult to handle in the changing wind conditions encountered in the air. This problem would only be worse for powered flight, in which airplanes with engines and propellers would be much heavier. Anybody attempting to achieve powered flight, and survive the attempt, would first have to find a solution that allowed them to control the three potential ways for the airplane to move. In aviation this is known as the pitch, roll, and yaw, the ability of an airplane to move in three dimensions around its point of balance.

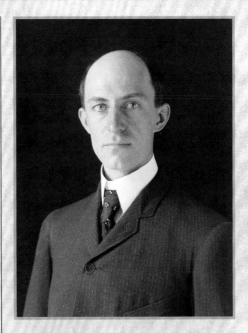

WILBUR WRIGHT

Four years older than Orville, Wilbur is acknowledged as the innovator of the control system used in the *Wright Flyer*.

ORVILLE WRIGHT

The younger of the Wright brothers piloted the first powered flight on December 17, 1903, near Kitty Hawk, North Carolina.

SOLVING THE PROBLEM

The earliest evidence we have that the Wright Brothers were working on finding a solution to the control problem comes from 1899, three years after they first began to investigate powered flight. Wilbur, who was the innovator of the two brothers, wrote to the Smithsonian Institute to request any material the institute might have on the subject of mechanical flight. This suggests two things: either that the brothers were only just beginning the serious study of aerodynamics three years after Lilienthal's death or that Wilbur had already arrived at the solution to the problem and wanted to be sure nobody else had beaten him to it. He would later say that his first inspiration for the mechanical control system that he had devised came from his observations of birds in flight. He had noticed how a pigeon leaned into a turn in a similar way to how a person shifted their weight to take a corner on a bicycle. The pigeon achieved this by moving the long feathers on both its wing tips. This altered the angle of air flow over its wings, allowing the pigeon to turn without losing control of its flight.

But, even if this was the way a bird maneuvered in the air, it was far from obvious how that could be transferred to an airplane, which would need to have wings flexible enough to move and light enough to allow the plane to fly, but still strong enough to cope with the pressure being placed on them. Wilbur figured out how to design wings combining all of these features after he picked up a long

WATCH THE BIRDS

"There are only two ways of learning to ride a fractious horse; one is to get on him and learn by actual practice... the other is to sit on a fence and watch the beast awhile... To ride a flying machine; if you are looking for perfect safety, you will do as well to sit on the fence and watch the birds; but if you really wish to learn, you must mount a machine and become acquainted with its tricks by actual trial."

From a speech given by Wilbur Wright to the Western Society of Engineers in Chicago on September 18, 1901.

thin box that had previously contained the inner tube of a bicycle tire and then twisted it at either end. When he released the pressure he had applied to the box, it naturally sprang back into its original shape. This led him to envisage a biplane (an early plane with two pairs of wings) in which the lower and upper pair of wings was separated by struts to form the shape of a box. The pilot from the cockpit could twist them to alter the air flow over the wings by means of wires attached near their tips.

THE *WRIGHT FLYERS*

Before risking their lives with a full-scale version of the biplane, the Wright brothers tested their idea with a series of kites and unmanned gliders that made use of the so-called wing-warping technology Wilbur had developed. In the autumn of 1900 they began to travel to Kitty Hawk on the coast of North Carolina, where wind conditions were suitable for conducting tests and where they could work in privacy.

During the next few years they conducted experiments with larger manned gliders in which they both developed their skills as pilots, learning to keep the glider balanced in a similar way to how people learn to ride a bike. Over the course of these experiments, they increased the size of the wings to gain more lift and, as well as the wing-warping to control roll, added a forward elevator (a hinged flap) and rear rudder to control pitch and yaw.

When the brothers were satisfied that everything worked, they decided the time had come to add an engine. With nothing suitable available to buy, they had to design and build both it and the propeller themselves. They were helped by Charlie

WRIGHT FLYER
The *Wright Model A*, a two-seater version of the *Wright Flyer III* and the first airplane to be commercially produced.

Taylor, a mechanic in their bicycle shop, who built a lightweight engine from their plans in just six weeks.

From start to finish, the *Wright Flyer I* took seven years to design and build—a truly remarkable achievement considering that the brothers had no outside investment and had done all of the required design and construction themselves, either in the back of their bicycle shop or from a camp on the sand dunes near Kitty Hawk.

MAJOR ACHIEVEMENT

At first their achievements received little attention in the press, in part because they worked in secret to prevent anybody stealing their ideas, but also because few people believed that two brothers who ran a bicycle shop could really have built a working airplane. Over the next few years they worked on improving the design of their plane to make it more stable. In 1905, they built the first truly practical airplane, the *Wright Flyer III*, which Wilbur flew for forty minutes, covering 24 miles (39 km) and demonstrating beyond doubt that he and his brother had overcome all the problems involved in powered flight.

The Wright brothers' major breakthrough was undoubtedly their system of control, the basic ideas of which remain in use in fixed-wing airplanes today.

D. W. GRIFFITH MAKES A MOVIE IN HOLLYWOOD

1910

Circumstances: A director looks for an outdoor location for his next movie

Protagonists: The director D. W. Griffith and the early pioneers of American film

Consequences: The establishment of Hollywood as the center of the movie industry

The first movie to be shot in Hollywood, now the world center of films, was made in 1910 by D. W. Griffith, one of the great innovators of early cinema. He was working for the Biograph Company at the time and decided to use a location in the Hollywood Hills for the outdoor scenes of one of his productions. Like most movie companies in those early days, Biograph was actually based in New York, initially using a studio built on the roof of what is now the Roosevelt Building on Broadway, before moving to an indoor studio in 1906 on East 14th Street. Griffith joined the company in 1908, first as an actor and then, within a matter of months, as its main director.

In January 1910, Biograph sent Griffith and his company of actors out to Los Angeles to take advantage of the sunny weather of southern California.

GRIFFITH THE DIRECTOR

Griffith had come to New York from Kentucky hoping to make his name as a playwright. After achieving little success in that field, he switched to acting and then, after the previous principal director at Biograph had been forced to retire through illness, to making movies rather than being in them. The role of director appeared to suit Griffith, who was something of a workaholic, regularly churning out movies at the rate of three a week. All of them were shot on single reels of film, the industry standard at the time, making them shorter than twenty minutes in length, but even so this was an incredible achievement, not least because of the high quality of the movies he made.

Griffith innovated by employing the latest techniques in movie-making, which he either devised himself or adapted from the work of others, moving film away from being made solely with a fixed camera pointed at a stage and establishing it for the first time as an art form in its own right.

"Griffith did everything. He preceded Hollywood in everything that has been done since. It is an abiding mystery and a scandal to me that an ungrateful industry has not raised a statue to him ninety feet tall at the intersection of Hollywood Boulevard and Vine Street."

—Lionel Barrymore, *We Barrymores*, 1951

HOLLYWOOD

In January 1910, Biograph sent Griffith and his company of actors, which included Mary Pickford and Lilian Gish, out to Los Angeles to take advantage of the bright, sunny weather of southern California. They wanted to shoot outdoor locations rather than be limited to the

D. W. GRIFFITH

The pioneer of early film directed more than five hundred movies and was the first to shoot a movie in Hollywood.

indoor studio in New York. Independent movie-makers had been working in Los Angeles for a number of years by that time, having moved out of New York to get as far away as possible from the Motion Picture Patents Company (MPPC), an organization started by Thomas Edison in order to protect the licenses he and several other film companies held over almost all of the equipment and film stock used in movie-making. The methods employed by the MPPC to prevent illegal filming could be brutal, on occasion resorting to hiring groups of thugs to break up film sets by force. It is therefore no coincidence that the independents picked southern California not only because it was far from New York, but also because the California authorities had a relaxed attitude to patent laws. It was also conveniently close to Mexico in case they had to flee the country in a hurry.

Biograph had no such concerns. They were members of the MPPC and had come to Los Angeles because of the weather and to assess the potential for a permanent move to California. Griffith maintained his extraordinary work rate, shooting in an outdoor studio erected on a vacant lot in Los Angeles and, on the odd occasion when he wasn't actually shooting a movie, scouting locations for a future project. For the film *In Old California*, set in early nineteenth-century

Spanish America, he needed rural locations and, having chosen the Hollywood Hills, decided to establish a base at a hotel in the small town of Hollywood itself, which was conveniently near to the locations and only a few miles outside the city of Los Angeles.

The resulting movie, in truth, has little to distinguish it other than being the first to be shot in Hollywood. It was thought to have been lost completely until 2004, when it was rediscovered and shown for the first time in more than ninety years. It proved to be a seventeen-minute melodrama concerning a Spanish woman who has to choose between two suitors for her hand in marriage, picking the one who turns out to be a worthless drunk rather than the one who goes on to become the governor of California. It is only really notable for Griffith's camera work in photographing the scenery of the Hollywood Hills.

FIRST STUDIOS

In the following year, the first studio, the Nestor Motion Picture Company, opened in Hollywood, which by this time had become incorporated as a suburb of Los Angeles. In 1914, Cecil B. DeMille shot the feature-length movie *The Squaw Man* there, which really put it on the map. Over the next few years Paramount, Warner Brothers, and RKO all opened studios in Hollywood, while Universal moved to a huge new studio nearby. By this time D. W. Griffith had left Biograph, wanting to make features

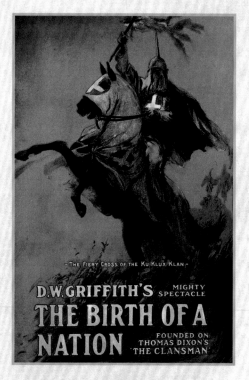

GRIFFITH'S MASTERPIECE
The movie was technically brilliant but highly controversial because of the racist nature of the material.

longer than an hour, rather than continue to be restricted to the single-reel films still favored by the company.

THE BIRTH OF A NATION

In 1915 he released what is considered to be his masterpiece, *The Birth of a Nation*, an epic story set in the Civil War and the following period of reconstruction. It was controversial at the time, as it remains today, for its overtly racist content.

Griffith shot the first movie in Hollywood and over the next few years Paramount, Warner Brothers, and RKO all opened their studios there.

It set a new standard as far
as technical filmmaking goes
but, while it can still be
appreciated from this
perspective, the appalling
characterization of black
people and the depiction of
the Ku Klux Klan as heroes
are now so offensive as to
be almost laughable, giving
the impression that it was
actually intended to be a
parody rather than a work
of serious drama.

INTOLERANCE

Screenings of *The Birth of a
Nation* provoked riots in
several American cities and the
controversy it provoked no doubt boosted
its audience, people going to see it to find
out for themselves what all the fuss was
about. Griffith's next movie, *Intolerance*,
was an even grander and more expensive
affair, intercutting four separate stories
and lasting well over three hours. It was a
commercial failure and, although Griffith
continued to make movies into the 1930s,
he would not have another success.

EARLY PIONEER

Griffith may have been the first to make
a movie in Hollywood, but he died in
1946, at the age of seventy-three, without
receiving any of the recognition that his
achievements in the history of American
film deserved. This was partly, no doubt,
as a consequence of the controversial
nature of *The Birth of a Nation*, but also
because Hollywood had simply moved
on, leaving many of its early pioneers
behind. It would be stretching the
truth to suggest that Griffith founded
Hollywood; his decision to shoot one of
his movies in the Hollywood Hills may
have opened up the way for others to
follow his lead, but it was the big movie
studios buying up real estate on the
outskirts of Los Angeles, where land
was available and relatively cheap, that
really resulted in the town becoming
the movie-making center of the world.

Nevertheless, D. W. Griffith showed
the way, as he did for so much of the
industry, and deserves to be recognized
not only for that but for all the other
contributions he made to early film.
Charlie Chaplin summed it up after
Griffith died, saying, "He was the
teacher of us all."

GANDHI PRACTICES CIVIL DISOBEDIENCE

1917

Circumstances: The struggle against British imperial rule in India

Protagonists: Mahatma Gandhi and the people of India

Consequences: The independence of India

By the time the forty-six-year-old Mohandas K. Gandhi returned to India in January 1915, he had already been internationally recognized for his work campaigning for the civil rights of the Indian community in South Africa, where he had worked as a lawyer for the previous twenty-one years. He was widely known as Mahatma, an honorific title in India meaning "great soul," and as Bapu (father) to his followers in the communities, or ashrams, he founded in South Africa and in his home province of Gujarat. It was a natural progression for him to become involved in the civil rights movement in India and the struggle for its independence from Britain, leading to him joining the Indian National Congress, the leading political party campaigning for an end to British rule.

While still living in South Africa, he had been advised by the leader of the Congress Party, Gopal Krishna Gokhale,

---

Gandhi was widely known in India by the name Mahatma, meaning "great soul."

---

to take at least a year to get to know the complicated political situation in India before taking on any active role himself. Gandhi took this advice, later describing the moderate and sensible Gokhale as his mentor and guide.

INDIGO FARMERS

At a Congress meeting in December 1916 Gandhi was approached by Rajkumar Shukla, a farmer from Champaran in the Himalayan foothills of Bihar state, who asked him to come to the region to help with a dispute between the indigo farmers and their British landlords. Gandhi was initially reluctant to get involved, having never heard of Champaran and with no knowledge of indigo farming (indigo was used in the industrial process of making dye). But Shukla persisted, turning up at every meeting Gandhi attended until he finally agreed to come.

On arriving in Champaran, Gandhi found the farmers to be in a desperate situation, which, if nothing was done, could result in famine. As part of their rental agreements, the farmers were forced to plant a proportion of their land with indigo, rather than food crops.

They were also forced to sell the indigo at a fixed price to their landlords, who, despite refusing to pay more for the crop, were in the process of raising rents beyond what the farmers could afford to pay. When they attempted to take their grievances to the local authorities, the farmers were dismissed out of hand because the Bihar government was in the pockets of the landlords.

It was a straightforward case of rich and powerful colonialists using their position and influence to exploit the poor and powerless. In the light of what he had observed in Champaran, Gandhi decided that the time had come to test the methods of civil disobedience he had developed in South Africa against British colonial rule in his homeland.

CIVIL DISOBEDIENCE

Gandhi trained as a lawyer in London and then worked for a shipping company run by wealthy Indian Muslims in Durban, South Africa. He would later say that he had experienced a personal "awakening" in May 1893 after being thrown off a train in Pietermaritzburg because of the color of his skin, writing, "I discovered that as a man and as an Indian I had no rights."

From then on Gandhi began to campaign for social reform, developing the concept of satyagraha, which literally means "truth-force," as a means of nonviolent resistance to oppression. This philosophical stance put forward the belief that people who are oppressed but have the force of being morally right on their side can ultimately defeat a stronger oppressor by accepting the need for personal suffering and sacrifice in order to achieve their aims.

Gandhi had developed his method of protest into active civil disobedience rather than passive resistance by the time he became involved in the dispute between the indigo farmers and their landlords. He was joined in Champaran by a number of his followers, who helped him to hold meetings in which evidence showing the mistreatment of the farmers was collected and protests and strikes organized. The British authorities in Bihar arrested Gandhi and ordered him to leave the region, creating in the process a news story that had already been reported nationally but was now attracting international interest because it involved such a well-known figure.

MAHATMA GANDHI IN 1910
Before returning to India in 1915 Gandhi worked as a lawyer in South Africa campaigning for civil rights.

Gandhi refused to comply and was put on trial. The national government intervened, no doubt aware that the actions of the British landlords and the corrupt nature of their relationship with the officials in the local government would not stand up to close scrutiny. The charges against him were dropped and an official inquiry, with Gandhi on the committee, examined the causes of the dispute. This would eventually lead to a change in the law to prevent British landlords from forcing Indian farmers to grow indigo and to place limits on any rent increases.

It was a victory for Gandhi and his method of satyagraha, which he would

AN AWAKENING

Gandhi experienced a personal awakening when traveling on a train in South Africa. A white man who had boarded at Pietermaritzburg objected to his presence in the first-class compartment. The conductor on the train told him to move to third-class seating but, as he had the correct ticket, Gandhi refused. A police officer was called and he was forcibly removed from the train. Over the next few hours, as he waited for another train, he came to the decision not to ignore this relatively minor incident and, from then on, resolved not only to stand up for his own rights, but also to do so for the rights of the wider Indian community in South Africa, many of whom were routinely treated much more severely than he had been.

go on to use on numerous occasions in other disputes across India. The British had no idea how to deal with him, at times negotiating and at other times throwing him into jail, but never gaining the moral high ground and almost always giving in to his demands in the end.

THE SALT MARCH

One of Gandhi's most famous protests happened in March 1930 when he began a satyagraha against the tax the British had imposed on salt, which effectively gave them a monopoly (exclusive control) on its collection and sale. A few months earlier the Congress Party had issued a Declaration of Independence, ignored by the British, and many of Gandhi's political associates were left baffled by his insistence on concentrating on what they saw to be a relatively minor injustice compared to the much bigger issue of independence.

Gandhi began the protest by walking with a group of his followers from his ashram to Dandi on the coast of Gujarat, a small village where salt was produced. It was a distance of 241 miles (390 km) and the walk, which became known as the Salt March, took twenty-four days and was extensively covered by newspapers and newsreels from around the world. Once at the coast and in front of thousands of people, Gandhi picked up a handful of salty mud and said, "With this, I am shaking the foundations of the British Empire," before going on to break the law by boiling the mud in seawater to make salt without paying the tax.

Millions of Indians followed Gandhi's example and at least sixty thousand were arrested by the British authorities, including Gandhi himself, who was held in prison for almost a year before being

released in early 1931 to enable him to negotiate a settlement to the dispute with the Viceroy of India.

SALT MARCH
Gandhi and his followers shown in 1930 walking to Dandi on the coast of Gujarat to protest about the British tax on salt.

INDEPENDENCE

The negotiations resulted in Gandhi agreeing to end the campaign of civil disobedience if the British would agree to discuss constitutional reform in India. The salt protest was to reinvigorate the independence movement among ordinary Indians and return it to prominence both in India and around the world. It would take another sixteen years before the British eventually agreed to leave India, a period in which Gandhi initiated further campaigns of civil disobedience. On August 15, 1947, India became a Dominion within the British Empire, giving it the status of a separate country. But it was a bittersweet victory for Gandhi, who had promoted Hindu and Muslim unity throughout his life. British India was partitioned along religious lines into India and Pakistan, a division that resulted in terrible violence and the deaths of up to a million people.

Gandhi did not live to see India become a republic on January 26, 1950. He died on January 30, 1948, after being shot by a Hindu extremist. But he left a legacy of tolerance and nonviolence that remains in India today, and his methods have been adopted by others in their struggle against oppression, including Martin Luther King Jr. in his campaign for civil rights in America and Nelson Mandela in the anti-apartheid movement in South Africa. Gandhi is remembered today as the Father of India, a man who was prepared to stick to his principles throughout his life no matter what the consequences and succeeded because he was fighting for a just cause and the rights of the Indian people to justice.

ROBERT JOHNSON MAKES A DEAL AT THE CROSSROADS

1930s

Circumstances: A blues singer records some of his songs

Protagonists: Robert Johnson and other bluesmen of the Mississippi Delta

Consequences: A small but highly influential body of work

These days, when a record company promotes one of their artists as "authentic," it usually means that either nobody has ever heard of them or they write their own songs but don't have a very good singing voice. The blues revival of the late 1950s and early 1960s had no need of such marketing spin as a new audience, mostly made up of young white college boys, rediscovered the original blues singers of the 1930s and 1940s from the Mississippi Delta.

Many of the singers had not actually disappeared but continued to perform throughout their careers. Many had followed their audience north to Chicago and to other industrial cities and were now playing electric guitars rather than the acoustic ones most of them had started out with. John Lee Hooker, Muddy Waters, Howlin' Wolf, B. B.

King, to name just a few of the best known, all had their roots in the Delta. Then in 1961 Columbia Records released *King of the Delta Blues Singers* by Robert Johnson, a man unknown to almost everybody, including many of the other artists from the Delta. (Just to be confusing, the Delta in this context refers to the flat agricultural plain between Vicksburg, Mississippi and Memphis, Tennessee, immediately to the north of the actual delta of the Mississippi River in Louisiana.)

EARLY INFLUENCE

The release was the idea of the Columbia executive and record producer John Hammond, a blues enthusiast, who in 1938 had traveled to Mississippi in an attempt to sign Johnson up for a blues concert he was organizing at Carnegie

"Robert Johnson has become the ultimate blues legend, and it is easy to forget that he was once just a man who sang beautifully and played expert guitar."

—Elijah Wald, *Escaping the Delta*

DELTA BLUESMAN
Like many of the great blues singers, including Robert Johnson, Muddy Waters was born and raised in rural Mississippi.

Hall in New York, only to find when he got to the Delta that Johnson had recently died. The record released in 1961 contained sixteen of Johnson's songs, recorded in two sessions in 1936 and 1937, and, despite the scratchy nature of the recording, his fine guitar playing and the mournful quality of his voice, together with some truly great songs, would make it a landmark release. Even so, it took a number of years for the record to be appreciated beyond a small circle of blues enthusiasts. Over the following ten years, both Eric Clapton and Keith Richards would acknowledge Johnson as a major influence on their own music and would record a number of his songs, bringing

him to the attention of a much wider audience and fueling an interest in the man himself, about whom almost nothing was known.

CROSSROADS

In the absence of any certain facts, stories began to circulate about Johnson, in particular one that still attaches to his name today. It was said he had gone to a crossroads at midnight where the devil offered to make him a great guitarist in exchange for his soul.

Now, let's be honest, none of us really believes that Robert Johnson actually decided to sell his soul to the devil. No doubt he became a great guitarist the same way as every other great musician has done it, through long hours of practice. But it was the haunting nature of the lyrics to his songs and the unearthly quality of his voice that suggests he was deeply troubled by something. Without any biographical detail to shed some light on what that trouble might have been, it became possible for people who were

CROSSROADS
The crossroads of highways 49 and 61 in Mississippi, claimed by some to be where Johnson made his deal with the devil.

> **The haunting nature of his lyrics and unearthly quality of his voice suggest that Johnson was deeply troubled by something.**

listening to his music for the first time more than thirty years after he died to believe anything they wanted to believe about him. It turned him into the archetypal bluesman, a tortured and misunderstood genius who died at that most rock 'n' roll age of twenty-seven. It was the same age that Jimi Hendrix, Jim Morrison, and Janis Joplin had all been when they died. Brian Jones, the original member of the Rolling Stones who first introduced Keith Richards to Johnson's music, was also twenty-seven when he drowned in his swimming pool. Adding Johnson's name to this list of musical legends who died young was an easy enough jump to make, and the mythology that grew up around him only served to add another layer of intrigue to fascinate people who listened to his music.

A MAN EMERGES

It was inevitable, given the renewed interest in Delta blues and in the mysterious life of one of its greatest singers, that people would begin to investigate the circumstances of Robert Johnson's life. From interviews with other Delta blues musicians and with people living in the Delta who had known him personally, a picture of the man himself has gradually emerged, even if some of the stories told about him have not always proved very reliable.

Johnson was born in Hazelhurst, Mississippi, in May 1911 and grew up in Memphis and various rural villages in the Delta. The noted blues musician Son House remembered him living in Robinsonville sometime in the 1920s, describing him as a "little boy" who could already play the harmonica but was a poor guitarist. By the time he was twenty, he was earning a living as a musician, traveling around Mississippi

ELECTRIC BLUES
Robert Johnson's contemporary John Lee Hooker left the Delta in the 1940s for the northern industrial cities.

playing on street corners, in juke joints, and for Saturday-night parties. Other musicians, like Johnny Shines and David "Honeyboy" Edwards, sometimes accompanied him on his travels, occasionally going to Memphis and cities in Texas as well as Chicago and New York. Johnson apparently had girlfriends in numerous different towns, staying with them when he was passing through or picking up somebody else after one of his gigs. According to some accounts of his life, his promiscuity eventually got him into trouble with the husband of one of his girlfriends, who is said to have poisoned a bottle of whiskey and then offered him a drink. Despite claims by some researchers to have identified his murderer, no credible evidence has ever come to light. All we can say with any certainty is that he died on August 18, 1938, near Greenwood, Mississippi, and could have been buried in an unmarked grave at the Mount Zion Missionary Baptist Church not far away.

JOHNSON'S GRAVE

A small tombstone erected in 1990 in Greenwood, Mississippi, marking the possible grave site of Robert Johnson (although there are other contenders).

"DEVIL'S MUSIC"

These biographical details are, it must be admitted, only the bare bones of a life, but one account of an incident involving Johnson, told by the family of the girl involved, could shed some light on the origins of the stories about him. In February 1928, at the age of seventeen, Johnson married the sixteen-year-old Virginia Travis, who was pregnant at the time and died in childbirth not long afterward. Johnson was not present during this terrible event, having left his heavily pregnant young wife to play a gig somewhere out of the district. By the time he returned, she was already dead and buried, a tragedy that some religious members of her family would later claim

was divine retribution for his decision to leave her to play what they described as the "devil's music."

We can only speculate now what Johnson's reaction to this may have been, but he never settled in any one place for long afterward and the "hellhound on his trail" could have been his own guilt over the death of his wife.

Whatever the truth of the matter, the great decision we are dealing with here is not really what Robert Johnson did or didn't do with his soul, but it is simply his decision to learn to play the guitar and sing the blues in the first place. It may have taken a very long time for his music to be fully appreciated, but the fact that it emerged at all is miracle enough.

ROOSEVELT'S NEW DEAL

1933

Circumstances: The Wall Street Crash leads to the Great Depression

Protagonists: Franklin D. Roosevelt, the Brain Trust, and the American people

Consequences: America emerges from the Great Depression

I n Franklin D. Roosevelt's speech accepting the Democratic Party's nomination as presidential candidate for the November 1932 election, he used the words "new deal" without laying any particular emphasis on the phrase and with no apparent intention to give it any greater significance than anything else he said. But the newspapers picked up on it in the days after the speech and it came to embody the American Government's policies aimed at dealing with the economic and social disasters created by the Great Depression of the early 1930s. In his election campaign, Roosevelt did not specify exactly what he intended to do once elected and even on occasion issued contradictory statements, promising at one moment to cut public spending and, in the next, to fund huge programs to get people back to work.

In truth, Roosevelt could have said almost anything and still won. His predecessor, President Herbert Hoover, had been quick to claim credit for the financial boom America had enjoyed immediately before the Wall Street Crash of October 1929 and the Great Depression. He had then done his best to deflect blame for the depression onto everything and

> *"I pledge you, I pledge myself, to a new deal for the American people. Let us all here assembled constitute ourselves prophets of a new order of competence and of courage. This is more than a political campaign; it is a call to arms. Give me your help, not to win votes alone, but to win in this crusade to restore America to its own people."*
>
> **—From a speech given by Franklin D. Roosevelt on July 2, 1932, accepting the presidential nomination of the Democratic Party**

FDR
Upon becoming the president of the United States, Franklin D. Roosevelt introduced the New Deal, policies designed to drag America out of the Great Depression.

Roosevelt to tackle the Depression. He also brought together a group of advisers, later known as the Brain Trust, to help him devise his own plan, but what he didn't do in this period, just as he hadn't during the election campaign, was spell out what it was going to entail. He didn't offer much more in his inaugural address, in which he blamed the Depression on the irresponsibility and corruption of bankers and financiers and famously said, "The only thing we have to fear is fear itself." Many people were left wondering if Roosevelt really had any idea what he was going to do, but, as he also made clear in his inaugural speech, the time for talking had come to an end. The time had now come to make some big decisions and to put the New Deal, whatever it was, into action.

everybody else other than himself, so he hardly gave the impression of being the right man to lead America back to prosperity.

LANDSLIDE VICTORY

Roosevelt went on to win a landslide victory in the election and, in the period between his election and the inauguration ceremony, from November 1932 to March 1933, he spent his time appointing members of his future government and doing his best to ignore Hoover, who wanted to find a way of working with

WALL STREET CRASH

The complete crash of the stock market, known as the Wall Street Crash, began on October 24, 1929. Panic selling of stocks, which are shares in the ownership of companies, led to a further fall in prices so that by October 29 (known as Black Tuesday) stock prices had collapsed completely, with shares worth only a fraction of their original value. The results were disastrous: banks lost millions, businesses closed, unemployment soared, and the public stopped buying goods. The resulting depression, poverty, and hardship would ripple across the US and many parts of the world.

CAUSE AND EFFECT

There are as many different explanations for the onset of the Great Depression as there are economists attempting to explain it—a similar situation to the recent financial crisis of 2008. Most of them have come to conclusions that have supported their own particular points of view in the first place, giving the impression that they have little better idea about what happened than the rest of us have. At the time, some economists were making the case for massive state intervention in the economy, while others called for the complete opposite: reduce public spending and the role of the government in the economy to allow the market to correct itself. But if there was little agreement over the best way of dealing with the Depression, the effects were obvious for everybody to see.

DESPERATE POVERTY

The winter of 1932–33 had been a desperate one for many people. The unemployed and homeless were visible everywhere and what amounted to shanty towns, known as Hoovervilles, sprang up on the outskirts of many American towns and cities. Children all over America were not only going without shoes, but were not getting enough to eat. The unemployment rate was running at almost 25 percent, and there were thirteen million people without work, while industrial production had dropped by 45 percent since the 1929 crash.

> **Roosevelt's greatest achievement was in restoring confidence among ordinary Americans.**

DUST BOWL
A dust storm in Stratford, Texas, in April 1935, caused by dry weather, strong winds, and unsuitable farming practices.

As if that were not enough, the Dust Bowl in America's agricultural heartlands was just getting underway, in which unusually dry weather conditions combined with unsuitable farming practices caused topsoil to be blown away in giant dust storms from huge areas of what had once been productive farmland.

THE HUNDRED DAYS

The problems facing Roosevelt, then, as he first stepped into the White House, were immense. To his great credit, he did not pursue an ideological agenda in an attempt to find a solution (some have argued that he didn't have an ideology to pursue in the first place). Rather, he developed policies, from whatever source they came, on the basis of whether or not they were likely to work. Members of the Brain Trust, including Raymond Moley and Frances Perkins, the first woman to serve in the US Cabinet as Secretary of State for Labor, contributed ideas on reforming the banking system and the labor markets.

In what became known as the Hundred Days, Roosevelt introduced numerous new bills into Congress and all of them were passed, supported by Democrats and Republicans alike. The process established the tradition that is still followed by the American media who like to assess how a new president has fared after their first hundred days in office.

THE FIRST NEW DEAL

One of the first measures Roosevelt took was to close every bank in the country while he introduced an emergency banking bill. This was designed to deal with one of the most pressing problems, the failure of banks, many of which had crashed as a result of bank runs (people removing all their savings from a bank because they feared it was about to go bust and, in doing so, actually causing the bankruptcy).

Roosevelt explained what he was doing to the American people in the first of what became regular "fireside chats," in which he described the closures as being a "bank holiday." The Banking Act was passed on the same day as it was introduced to Congress, March 9, having only been read through once. It made unlimited loans available to accredited banks through the Federal Reserve, effectively guaranteeing all deposits. When the banks reopened four days later, people were lining up outside, many of them to deposit the money they had previously withdrawn because it would now be much safer in the bank than under the mattress. A blizzard of legislation followed the Banking Act, on farming, industry, housing, labor. Prohibition (outlawing the manufacture or sale of alcohol) was also repealed—a move that proved enormously popular with the American people, and it increased the tax revenue of the government as well. Not all of the new legislation was as successful as the banking reform, but overall the program appeared to be working, gradually dragging the American economy out of the Depression it had endured for the previous three years.

MAN OF ACTION

As it would turn out, March 1933 was the lowest point of the Great Depression in America. Roosevelt's greatest achievement

SECOND NEW DEAL

In what is sometimes called the Second New Deal, Roosevelt attempted to build on the success of his first raft of measures, introducing legislation between 1936 and 1938 to deal with a variety of pressing social issues. As has always been the case in America, federal government involvement in such social matters as health insurance and social security would prove much more controversial than the initial economic measures he had introduced. It reopened splits between liberals who supported the reforms and conservatives who most definitely did not, not unlike the more recent situation over President Obama's healthcare reforms.

in bringing in what became known as the First New Deal, the first two years of his program of legislation, was in restoring confidence, creating conditions in which ordinary Americans felt secure enough to carry on with their lives without worrying about losing their jobs and homes.

Where Hoover had typically given the impression of being defeated by the size of the problems the country faced, Roosevelt looked like a man of action, prepared to do whatever was necessary to get the American economy moving again and to get people back to work. Banks and businesses began to return to their normal modes of working, industry began to pick up and rehire some of the many employees who had been laid off. The Depression was by no means over, but many people could now foresee a brighter future than had previously been apparent.

NOT FAR ENOUGH?

In the years since the New Deal was first introduced criticisms of it have followed a similar pattern, some arguing that Roosevelt went too far in allowing the state to become involved in people's lives, while others have argued that he did not go far enough and should have introduced the full range of social measures that have since been adopted in many European countries.

But, however the outcome of the New Deal is assessed, Roosevelt's initial decision to take direct action to combat the deepest and most damaging depression in both American and world history must surely be regarded as one of the greatest political decisions ever made in America.

The effects of Roosevelt's New Deal continued to be felt for decades after it

FIRESIDE CHAT
Roosevelt discusses the economic situation and addresses the nation during one of his famous "fireside chats" on September 30, 1934.

was first introduced and some of the programs remain in place today. It also caused a fundamental realignment in American politics, known as the Fifth Party System, in which voters of a more liberal persuasion began to support the Democratic Party, while conservatives tended toward the Republicans, a situation that has largely remained the same to this day.

Roosevelt continued as US president until his death in 1945, serving into but not completing an unprecedented fourth term. So, as well as dealing with the Great Depression, he was responsible for taking America into World War II, giving him plenty more big decisions to make.

Roosevelt's initial decision to take direct action to combat the deepest and most damaging depression in both American and world history must surely be regarded as one of the greatest political decisions ever made.

THE BRITISH CABINET RESOLVES TO FIGHT ON

1940

Circumstances: The desperate situation for Britain at the beginning of World War II

Protagonists: Winston Churchill, Neville Chamberlain, Lord Halifax, Clement Attlee, and Arthur Greenwood

Consequences: No negotiation with Hitler

Toward the end of May 1940, the war against Nazi Germany was going very badly for Britain. Norway, Denmark, the Netherlands, and Belgium had either already surrendered or were on the brink of doing so and, after a lightning invasion of France, beginning on May 13, the British Expeditionary Force was stranded on the beaches of Dunkirk, where a desperate attempt was being made to evacuate as many of them as possible before they were either destroyed or captured. The fall of France was a matter of days away, leaving Britain on its own and facing the threat of an imminent German invasion. Winston Churchill had only been appointed to the position of prime minister on May 10, three days before the invasion of France began, and, on May 28, he called a meeting of his war cabinet to discuss the disastrous situation Britain faced.

THE WAR CABINET

On becoming prime minister, Churchill had formed a national government comprising a cabinet of ministers from all three of the main political parties.

"Even though large parts of Europe and many old and famous states have fallen or may fall into the grip of the Gestapo and all the odious apparatus of Nazi rule, we shall not flag or fail. We shall go on to the end, we shall fight in France, we shall fight on the seas and oceans, we shall fight with growing confidence and growing strength in the air, we shall defend our Island, whatever the cost may be, we shall fight on the beaches, we shall fight on the landing grounds, we shall fight in the fields and in the streets, we shall fight in the hills; we shall never surrender..."

—From the speech made in the House of Commons by Winston Churchill on June 4, 1940, and repeated on the radio that evening

V FOR VICTORY
A characteristic gesture from Churchill, who vigorously argued against negotiating with Hitler during a war cabinet meeting in May 1940.

He also appointed a much smaller war cabinet to make the decision-making process relating to the war effort as efficient as possible. The war cabinet had five members: Churchill; two Conservative ministers, former prime minister Neville Chamberlain and Foreign Secretary Lord Halifax; and two Labour Party ministers, Clement Attlee and Arthur Greenwood.

The discussion held during the meeting on May 28, which would remain secret until thirty years after the end of the war, primarily revolved around a proposal received two days previously from Benito Mussolini, the dictator of Italy. He was offering to act as a mediator in negotiations aimed at reaching a peace settlement between Britain and Germany. Halifax was in favor of the offer, arguing that Britain would be able to achieve more favorable terms if a settlement was reached before France fell and it would also avoid the threat of an invasion. Churchill was enraged by such a suggestion and argued forcibly against any negotiations with the German leader, Adolf Hitler.

Churchill had the support of both Attlee and Greenwood, but Chamberlain was wavering. Before coming to a final decision, Churchill spoke to the full cabinet of twenty-five ministers, telling them that he had been considering the proposal to enter into negotiations with "that man," as he called Hitler, and thought any deal achieved would lead to Britain becoming a "slave state" of the Nazi regime. He finished by saying:

> *I am convinced that every man of you would rise up and tear me down from my place if I were for one moment to contemplate parley or surrender. If this long island story of ours is to end at last, let it end only when each one of us lies choking in his own blood upon the ground.*

His short speech was met with cheers and applause, showing that most of the cabinet was behind him and bringing Chamberlain firmly onto his side as well. Only Halifax remained unconvinced, writing in his diary for that day, "I thought Winston talked the most frightful rot." But the decision had been made; there would be no deals with Hitler and Britain would fight on alone.

LORD HALIFAX
After arguing in favor of negotiating with Hitler, Halifax lost the confidence of Churchill and was later removed from the war cabinet.

LORD HALIFAX

When Churchill became prime minister, the only other serious contender for the position had been Halifax. We can only speculate now what could have happened if he had become prime minister rather than Churchill, but the most obvious conclusion, given his stance at the war cabinet meeting, is that he would have entered into negotiations with Hitler. Churchill thought that it would have been interpreted as a sign of weakness by Hitler and could only have encouraged his plans to invade Britain. From that moment on, Churchill's already weak confidence in Halifax evaporated. Halifax remained in the war cabinet for a further nine months, until Churchill replaced him with Anthony Eden.

FINEST HOUR

Later that same night Churchill issued a memo to the cabinet and senior civil servants. The message was clear. The decision to fight on had been made and Churchill was not going to tolerate any public signs of defeatism. With bombs falling on British cities and the situation at Dunkirk looking worse by the minute, the last thing Churchill needed was to be undermined by his own government.

Over the next few days more than three hundred thousand troops were evacuated from Dunkirk and, although it was nothing short of miraculous, the overall extent of the defeat was obvious to all. With such thoughts on his mind, Churchill made one of the greatest speeches of his life in the House of Commons on June 4, quoted at the beginning of this chapter, which he then repeated to the nation by a radio broadcast that evening.

Further stirring words were required two weeks later after the French surrender on June 16, in which Churchill said, "What General Weygand [the Commander-in Chief of the French army] has called the Battle for France is over. I suspect that the Battle of Britain is about to begin," and continued:

> ... if we fail, then the whole world, including the United States, including all that we have known and cared for, will sink into the abyss of a new dark age made more sinister, and perhaps more protracted, by the lights of perverted science. Let us therefore brace ourselves to our duties, and so bear ourselves, that if the British Empire and its Commonwealth last for a thousand years, men will still say, 'This was their finest hour.'

WILL TO FIGHT

If further evidence of Churchill's resolve to fight were needed, his decision, made on July 3 together with the war cabinet, to issue an ultimatum to the commander of the French Navy ships stationed at the port of Mers-el-Kébir in Algeria made the British position crystal clear. The ultimatum demanded that the French ships be handed over to the British to prevent them from falling into the hands of the Germans. When the French commander refused, the Royal Navy opened fire, killing almost thirteen hundred French sailors. By any standards, it was a ruthless and cold-blooded attack on a country that had been an ally only weeks before. If Hitler had doubted the British will to fight, then this terrible event must surely have persuaded him to think again.

BATTLE OF BRITAIN

At the same time as the attack at Mers-el-Kébir, the Battle of Britain was getting underway and the Battle of the Atlantic was intensifying. At sea, German U-boats and warships were attempting to sever Britain's vital supply lines from North America. In the skies over southern England the fighter pilots of the Royal Air Force (RAF) and German Luftwaffe engaged in aerial dogfights while the German bombing campaign of British cities continued. To mount an invasion of Britain, Hitler knew that he had first to achieve air superiority over the English Channel and the coast. In July and August the aerial onslaught did not let up.

After the war, German documents revealed that Hitler had earmarked September 15 as the day for the invasion and on that day some of the most intense aerial battles were fought. Losses on both

THE FEW

On August 16, 1940, Churchill visited the headquarters of 11 Group Fighter Command in Uxbridge and sat in the gallery over the operations room watching as wave after wave of German planes crossing the Channel were marked out on the map table below. At one point during that day, every squadron in the group was in the air at the same time, prompting Churchill to say afterward, "Never in the field of human conflict has so much been owed by so many to so few." The remark echoed the St. Crispin's Day speech from Shakespeare's *Henry V*, in which the king rallied his army on the eve of the Battle of Agincourt. Churchill would include it in a later speech, demonstrating again his uncanny ability to sum up the mood of the nation in words.

sides were heavy but more than twice as many German crew were to lose their lives during the Battle of Britain. The Luftwaffe were at a disadvantage because the fighting occurred over England, where the German planes could only remain for a few minutes before having to return to France to refuel.

After September 15, and as the Luftwaffe switched to nighttime raids, it became clear that the Battle of Britain had been won. The German advance across Western Europe had been halted, justifying the decision made by Churchill to fight on however bleak the prospects had looked at the time.

THE SIGNING OF THE ATLANTIC CHARTER

1941

Circumstances: A diplomatic exchange between America and Britain four months before America entered World War II

Protagonists: President Franklin D. Roosevelt, Prime Minister Winston Churchill, together with military and diplomatic representatives from America and Britain

Consequences: The formation of a close working relationship between Roosevelt and Churchill and a charter that would lay the foundations for the formation of the United Nations

On August 9, 1941, US President Franklin D. Roosevelt and British Prime Minister Winston Churchill met for what would be the first of many occasions during World War II on board the USS *Augusta*, anchored in Placentia Bay off Newfoundland and within sight of the recently constructed American naval base of Argentia. The base had been acquired from Britain six months previously as part of the land-lease agreement between the two countries in which America supplied Britain with war materials in exchange for, among other things, the lease of a number of military facilities in the Caribbean and North Atlantic. The two men had been in regular communication by telephone and telegraph since the outbreak of the war in September 1939, when Churchill had held the position of First Lord of the Admiralty in the British war cabinet. Both set great store in face-to-face meetings in which they could assess the character of the person they were dealing with and establish personal relations, so they had been receptive to the suggestion of US diplomat Harry Hopkins to arrange the meeting. While Churchill crossed the Atlantic aboard HMS *Prince of Wales*, Roosevelt sent a double to take a trip on board the presidential yacht so that no one would know he was attending the secret meeting in Newfoundland.

THE AGENDA

The main purpose of the Atlantic Conference, as the meeting was called, was to discuss the shared aims of Britain and America during the war and to decide on the organization of the postwar world (assuming the Allies were on the winning side). As well as these stated objectives, there could be little doubt that both sides were pursuing their own agendas at the conference. The British were hoping for a deeper commitment to engaging in the war from the Americans, going beyond supplying

ATLANTIC CONFERENCE
Churchill and Roosevelt on board HMS
Prince of Wales. Roosevelt's son Elliott, to
the right, provides his father with support.

materials and support to actually
becoming militarily involved.

Churchill was aware of the political
reasons preventing Roosevelt from
announcing an American entry into the
war. These included a perceived lack
of public support in America and the
long-standing foreign policy of the
American government, going back to
the Monroe Doctrine of 1823, of not
becoming involved in European wars.

With the US presidential election
coming up that November, in which
Roosevelt was hoping to be elected for a
convention-busting third term, he could

not be expected to take any action that
would alienate a large proportion of the
electorate. Nevertheless, Churchill was
hoping for a private commitment from
Roosevelt to enter the war when the
time was right.

The unstated aims of the American
delegation were rather more subtle and
long term. They were looking for a way
to reduce the long-standing British

MESSAGE TO HITLER

The Atlantic Charter was not a binding document in the form of a treaty between Britain and America. Even though the press release stated that it had been signed by both Roosevelt and Churchill, in reality neither had done so. Churchill had been on his way back to Britain before the final draft was finished. Even so, the charter was an important document in a number of respects, not least because it sent a clear message to Hitler that America was firmly on Britain's side and expected Nazi Germany to lose the war.

influence on world affairs and to promote republicanism (government with an elected president as its head, rather than a monarch) preferably based on the American model. This would replace British imperialism (rule over colonies), thereby initiating a new world order in which the wealth and strength of the American economy would allow them to take over Britain's former position as the dominant world power.

THE CONFERENCE

The conference began on August 11 and consisted of three separate sets of meetings. As well as the talks held personally between Roosevelt and Churchill, the chiefs of staff of both countries came together to discuss military strategy, having been instructed by the two leaders to find a way of working together so that they could manage areas where American and

British interests overlapped. The third set of meetings was between American and British diplomatic staff, who had the job of preparing a joint statement that set out the objectives agreed by Roosevelt and Churchill for postwar planning. After two days of talks, the conference broke up; the following day, August 14, the finished document was released to the press under the title *Joint Statement by President Roosevelt and Prime Minister Churchill*, soon renamed the Atlantic Charter in newspaper reports.

THE CHARTER

The purpose of the charter was not to set out the details of postwar planning, but to establish the general principles governing how it would be conducted. The first three of the charter's eight clauses, quoted opposite, concerned the territorial settlements that might be reached after the war was over, stating that any changes to boundaries must be done in consultation with the people who were affected and that they had a right to choose their own government.

Without actually spelling it out, this was obviously aimed at those regions of the British Empire, such as India, where independence movements had sprung up. It was a clear signal of American anti-imperialistic sentiment, indicating that their negotiators had been in a position of strength in the talks because Britain needed American support for its war effort. Some historians have pointed to this moment as being the one in which the balance of power in world affairs decisively tipped away from Britain and toward America.

The next four clauses concerned trade, social security, and the freedom of the seas, and gave the assurance, "that all

1. Their countries seek no aggrandizement, territorial or other.
2. They desire to see no territorial changes that do not accord with the freely expressed wishes of the peoples concerned.
3. They respect the right of all peoples to choose the form of government under which they will live; and they wish to see sovereign rights and self-government restored to those who have been forcibly deprived of them.

—**The first three clauses of the Atlantic Charter**

the men in all the lands may live out their lives in freedom from fear and want."

The final clause read in full:

They believe that all of the nations of the world, for realistic as well as spiritual reasons, must come to the abandonment of the use of force. Since no future peace can be maintained if land, sea, or air armaments continue to be employed by nations which threaten, or may threaten, aggression outside of their frontiers, they believe, pending the establishment of a wider and permanent system of general security, that the disarmament of such nations is essential. They will likewise aid and encourage all other practicable measures which will lighten for peace-loving peoples the crushing burden of armaments.

These were fine words to finish off such a document, even if it could be argued that they were roundly ignored by both countries after the war came to an end. But the clause also raised the possibility of the development of an international organization that would attempt to maintain peace and security in the postwar world. In this sense, the Atlantic Charter can be regarded as the direct precursor of the Charter of the United Nations, the treaty signed in 1945 that set up the UN.

NEW WORLD ORDER

The joint decision by Roosevelt and Churchill to hold a conference to discuss the postwar world and then to issue the Atlantic Charter had far-reaching consequences and also established a close relationship between the two men who, along with Joseph Stalin of the Soviet Union, would lead the Allied war effort. The process of establishing a new world order that had been started by an old guard of politicians was taken up by others, a process that continues with varying degrees of success today.

The Atlantic Charter can be seen as the direct precursor of the Charter of the United Nations, the treaty signed in 1945 that set up the UN.

EISENHOWER PLANS FOR INVASION ON D-DAY

1944

Circumstances: Rough weather forces a postponement of the invasion of Normandy

Protagonists: General Dwight D. Eisenhower and the Allied invasion force on D-Day

Consequences: The beginning of the end for Nazi Germany in Western Europe

Even though he was from America, General Dwight D. Eisenhower could be forgiven if he indulged in the British national obsession with the weather during the first few days of June 1944. He was the commander-in-chief of SHAEF, the Supreme Headquarters Allied Expeditionary Force, and as such was responsible for the planning and execution of Operation Overlord, the code name given to the plan for the invasion of Normandy in France and the land battle that would follow it.

OPERATION OVERLORD

The invasion plan was by far the largest and most complicated amphibious invasion ever attempted, with more than one hundred and fifty thousand American, Canadian, and British troops landing on the Normandy beaches on the first day of the invasion alone, who were to be followed over the next months by almost two million more. That first day, known as D-Day, was the most critical part of the whole operation; its success or failure would determine not just the immediate prospects for Nazi-occupied France, but the outcome of the entire war.

STORMY WEATHER

Eisenhower had provisionally set D-Day for June 5 and throughout much of May the weather had been ideal on those days of the month when the combination of the tides on the Normandy coast and the

"My decision to attack at this time and place was based on the best information available. The troops, the air, and the navy did all that bravery and devotion to duty could do. If any blame or fault attaches to the attempt, it is mine alone."

—A note written by Eisenhower on the eve of D-Day in case it all went wrong

moonlight had been right for an invasion. As D-Day approached, the weather turned and by the evening of June 3, when the order to go or to stand down needed to be given, storms in the Channel and low-lying cloud over much of northern France meant that launching the invasion on the morning of June 5 was all but impossible. The risks of sending an amphibious invasion force out in stormy weather were clear enough and the overcast conditions meant that protection from airplanes could not be provided for the landings. They also meant that the airborne operation involving troops landing inland by parachute and glider to capture strategic locations could not go ahead.

Eisenhower made the decision to hold off for a day and, knowing that if he postponed again it might be weeks before everything could be reorganized, faced an even harder decision at the same time on the following day. He listened to his chief weather forecaster, who thought there might be a short break in the weather in the early morning of June 6. He then asked for the opinions of the military commanders at SHAEF, some of whom thought it was worth the risk, while others advised caution.

EISENHOWER

Ike with paratroopers from the US 101st Airborne Division on June 5, 1944, as they prepared for the first assault on D-Day.

144399

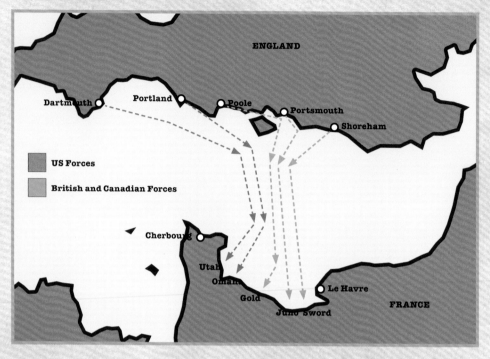

The map shows the departure ports in England (Dartmouth, Portland, Poole, Portsmouth, Shoreham) and the landing beaches in France (Utah, Omaha, Gold, Juno, Sword) with locations including Cherbourg, Le Havre.

US Forces

British and Canadian Forces

The final decision rested with Eisenhower and getting it wrong could cost the lives of thousands of the men under his command. At about 9:45 pm on the evening of June 4 he made up his mind and gave the order to go.

IKE

Ike, as Dwight Eisenhower was almost universally known, may have been in overall command of Operation Torch, the American invasion of North Africa beginning in November 1942, and then of the invasions of both Sicily and the Italian mainland in the following year, but he was by no means the only candidate for the command of SHAEF.

Winston Churchill had promised the job to General Allen Brooke, the British Chief of the Imperial General Staff, while in America General George Marshall, the Chief of Staff of the US

NORMANDY LANDINGS

On D-Day 150,000 Allied troops crossed the English Channel to take part in the assault on the Normandy beaches.

Army, was the hot favorite for the job. But Churchill came to realize that an American had to be given the position because the British Army was already at full stretch, so many of the men and materials for the latter stages of the war would have to come from America. Meanwhile, President Roosevelt wanted Marshall to stay in Washington as his Chief of Staff, leaving the way open for the appointment of Eisenhower.

Some senior military figures were not happy about Eisenhower's appointment, however, despite his success in planning and overseeing three major operations involving amphibious landings. He was regarded by his critics as being a career staff officer who had no first-hand battlefield experience and had risen slowly through the ranks of the US Army in peacetime because he was a good administrator and diplomat rather than through any proven ability as a military commander.

But, as it turned out, it was exactly these qualities of organization and man-management that made him the perfect man for the job. On numerous occasions in the buildup to the Normandy landings he proved himself capable of dealing with the huge egos of many of the senior politicians and military commanders involved. These included Churchill himself as well as the British commander of land forces General Bernard Montgomery and the US General George Patton, who both gave the impression of being almost as keen on fighting with each other as they were on fighting the Germans.

PLANNING FOR INVASION

By the time Eisenhower had been appointed as commander of SHAEF, the beaches of Normandy had already been selected as the site of the landings ahead of Pas-de-Calais, the only other really viable alternative to the north. His first decision on being shown the plan, made together with Montgomery, was to increase the scale of the initial invasion force and widen the area where it would be landing. In doing so, the original

> **Erwin Rommel, the commander of the German defenses in France, was well aware of the massive buildup of American troops and equipment in Britain.**

planned date for the invasion in early May had to be put back to June to ensure that the extra men and equipment necessary for the larger-scale attack would be ready in time.

It was to be the first of numerous decisions made by Eisenhower over the course of planning such a major undertaking, many of them made while disagreements and disputes raged between almost everybody else involved. During the months of planning, the need for secrecy was paramount. Erwin Rommel, the commander of the German defenses in France, was well aware of the massive buildup of American troops and equipment in Britain, which could only mean that an invasion was being planned. As soon as he was given the command, Rommel had ordered the Atlantic Wall, the line of defensive structures along the Channel coast of northern France, to be strengthened and reinforced. If he had found out exactly when and where the attack would come, giving him the opportunity to direct his forces against the landing zones, the operation would have been almost certainly doomed to failure.

FALSE INFORMATION

As well as planning for the invasion itself, a huge effort, known as Operation Fortitude, was directed at deceiving the Germans into thinking that the invasion was going to come at Pas-de-Calais. Dummy divisions were formed on England's east coast and radio traffic of the sort created by a massive buildup of forces was broadcast, while German-speaking secret agents were used to feed false information to the Nazi intelligence service. It was so effective that, even after the D-Day landings had started,

NORMANDY LANDINGS
Robert F. Sargent's famous photograph
Into the Jaws of Death showing the US
Army First Division assaulting Omaha
Beach on D-Day.

some German commanders remained convinced that the real thing in Normandy was actually part of the deception plan, leading to German armed units remaining near Calais weeks after an Allied position had been established on the coast farther south.

It was another reason for Eisenhower to order the invasion to go ahead. A delay would not only increase the likelihood of secrecy being compromised, but would also give the Germans more chance of discovering the nature of the deception plans. It was impossible to disguise the level of activity at ports on the south coast of England, which faced Normandy rather than Calais. In any case, returning the first wave of troops, who had already embarked on ships for

SURPRISE ATTACK

When the invasion was launched, the level of surprise achieved was remarkable, given that the German forces defending the French coast had been expecting an attack. In the end, the bad weather even played into the hands of the Allies. A number of senior German commanders, believing that an attack was not possible while the rough weather persisted, had taken leave. Rommel himself had gone back to Germany for a few days to be with his wife on her birthday.

the invasion, back to the ports where the next wave was being prepared would have been a logistical nightmare and doing so would have damaged the morale of all the army units involved.

THE ORDER TO GO

Everything was in place for the invasion to proceed on time; the only obstacle stopping it was the weather, the one thing nobody could control. On that evening of June 4, as Eisenhower paused for a moment after consulting with his advisers, he must have been feeling the tremendous responsibility of command, even if he remained calm and collected.

After making the decision to go, he turned to his advisers and military commanders and said, "I am quite positive we must give the order. I don't like it, but there it is." After a brief pause, everybody cheered and the mess room they had been using for the meeting immediately emptied as the rush began to get the order out.

D-DAY

At H-Hour of D-Day, 6:30 in the morning of Tuesday, June 6, 1944, the landings on the Normandy beaches began, the airborne assault having commenced a few hours earlier.
The Americans went first, landing on the beaches designated as Omaha and Utah, and they were followed by the British and Canadians on Gold, Juno, and Sword.

The location of the landings caught the Germans by surprise and the initial German response was chaotic and uncoordinated. Despite this, the Germans put up fierce resistance, particularly on Omaha Beach, where the Americans took heavy casualties before managing to overcome the German defenses. Over the next few weeks the Allied forces established a strong position in Normandy where they could build up their forces and then, from early August, liberate France, before crossing the River Rhine into the heartland of Germany.

VICTORY IN EUROPE

Eisenhower remained in command of SHAEF until victory in Europe was achieved in May 1945, after which he served as the military governor of the US zone of occupied Germany. In later life, Eisenhower entered politics. He won the presidential election of 1952 for the Republican Party and held it for a second term before retiring to his farm in Gettysburg, Pennsylvania, where he died in 1969 at the age of 78.

Some have viewed Eisenhower's political career unkindly, but there can be no doubt about his role in the buildup to the invasion of Normandy. He not only made one of the biggest decisions of World War II, but took responsibility for it before the successful outcome of D-Day had been established. For that alone, he must surely be regarded as one of the great leaders of the twentieth century and one of the greatest military decision-makers of all time.

NORMAN BORLAUG CHANGES CAREERS

1944

Circumstances: The offer of a job in Mexico researching stem rust in wheat

Protagonists: Norman Borlaug and numerous other agricultural researchers around the world

Consequences: The Green Revolution

When the Nobel Committee attempted to contact Norman Borlaug in October 1970 to inform him that he had been awarded the Nobel Peace Prize, he was outside at the agricultural research station in Mexico where he had worked since 1944, conducting field trials on new varieties of wheat that he and his team of researchers had bred. His wife, Margaret Borlaug, took the call from the committee and it took her some time to convince him that he really had won the prize because, at first, he thought she was joking.

Even when Borlaug received the award, he made sure he did so on behalf of agricultural research as a whole rather than for himself, saying that, in giving him the award, the Nobel Committee was "selecting an individual to symbolize the vital role of agriculture and food production in a world that is hungry."

He was trying to stress that he did not work in isolation. Nevertheless, the difference he was making in parts of the developing world at a time when rapidly increasing populations and stagnating agricultural production seemed to be leading to widespread famine and mass starvation certainly deserved to be individually recognized.

MOVE TO MEXICO

After completing a Ph.D. in plant pathology and genetics at the University of Minnesota in 1942, Borlaug got a job with the DuPont chemical company. When he was thirty, he was offered a job researching wheat disease at a newly established agricultural research facility in Mexico. Married with a child and with another on the way, Borlaug initially turned the position down as he already had a steady, well-paid job.

Having grown up on a farm in Iowa, however, and studied agriculture at university, where he specialized in the control of stem rust, one of the major fungal diseases of wheat, he reconsidered the offer, and changed his mind.

The success of Borlaug's methods can be gauged by looking at any wheat field around the world today.

In July 1944, he took up the position to lead the wheat research program near Texcoco, a city about 18 miles (30 km) to the northeast of Mexico City.

CORN AND WHEAT

The agricultural research station in Mexico was originally the idea of Henry Wallace, who had visited the country in 1940 when he was US Secretary of Agriculture in President Franklin D. Roosevelt's government and saw for himself the poverty and shortages of food that existed there at that time. On becoming vice president in the following year, and with the support of the Mexican president Manuel Ávila Camacho, he persuaded the Rockefeller Foundation to fund a project to set up research in Mexico aimed at improving

PLANT BREEDER
Norman Borlaug in 1970 on a trial plot of wheat in Mexico, holding an example of one of the varieties he developed.

the production of corn and wheat. There was a certain amount of self-interest behind the decision. Many of the fungal diseases afflicting American agricultural crops, including wheat rust, had spread north from Mexico and there were worries about civil unrest in the country turning into a communist revolution if steps were not taken to relieve the chronic shortage of food. The US government had no desire to see a communist regime on its southern border and the Rockefeller family had considerable holdings in the country, so they were not keen on that idea either.

RESISTANCE TO RUST

Borlaug was hired to set up research into the control of wheat rust in Mexican crops and to train Mexican agricultural scientists in methods of selective breeding. These had been developed in America to increase the natural immunity of wheat to fungal disease by crossing different varieties of the crop. He began the laborious process of cross-breeding and then planting out the resulting seeds in trial plots to see which, if any, showed the best resistance to rust. After a few years of slow progress he discovered a way of speeding up the research by growing two crops a year in the different climates of central Mexico and the Yaqui Valley of the Pacific northwest of the country.

By 1948, Borlaug had produced wheat that not only showed resistance

Borlaug agreed that the technologies he created gave the world a breathing space to find a more permanent solution.

WHEAT FIELD
Short-strawed, high-yielding varieties of wheat based on the ones developed by Borlaug can now be seen around the world.

to rust, but produced a much heavier crop of grain. Over the next few years Borlaug's new varieties were taken up by farmers all over Mexico and by the mid 1950s the country was producing enough wheat for its own needs and exporting some as well. Borlaug kept breeding improved varieties, crossing the rust-resistant plants with Japanese dwarf varieties to prevent the new heavier cropping plants from falling over due to the amount of grain in their ears. The success of this project can be gauged by looking at any wheat field around the world today, where, almost without exception, short-strawed, high-yielding varieties are now grown.

THE GREEN REVOLUTION

The rapid turnaround in the fortunes of Mexican agriculture did not go unnoticed in other parts of the world. Of particular concern was India, where farming was increasingly unable to feed the rapidly rising population. In 1961, the Indian government asked Borlaug to introduce his methods into their agricultural research stations. The transformation took longer but by 1970 the Indian wheat harvest had doubled and by 1974 the country was self-sufficient in the commodity. A similar breeding program with rice to develop short-strawed, high-yielding varieties led to increased yields in the Indian subcontinent and other parts of Asia.

Since the Green Revolution, as the transformation of Indian farming has come to be called, numerous criticisms of the methods used to achieve it have been made. This is mainly because high-yielding varieties of wheat and rice require the application of relatively high quantities of fertilizers (chemicals added to the soil to increase its fertility) and pesticides (chemicals that protect plants from weeds and insects). Tractors and other machinery are also required.

As well as having environmental consequences, some of which have been severe, the Green Revolution package favors large farmers over small ones because of the investment required to adopt the technology. In the developing world where farming has mostly been done on a small scale, this can create large numbers of landless poor people who are forced to move to cities in search of work. Some environmentalists have even questioned the increase in yields, saying it has come as a result of more land being cultivated rather than the introduction of new methods, although the evidence does not support this.

Later in life, Borlaug, who died at the age of ninety-five in 2009, traveled around the world in an effort to increase awareness of agricultural research and how it can find solutions to the problem of feeding ever-increasing populations.

As the population of the world has continued to grow, agricultural capacity has managed to keep up. The agricultural system has the potential to feed all these people in the future, but it is a sobering thought that, today, there are about a billion people in the world who regularly don't have enough food to eat. Norman Borlaug and his colleagues made a start in addressing the pressing issue of food shortages in the developing world, and he certainly deserved the Nobel Peace Prize for his efforts, but there is clearly a great deal more work to be done.

GREEN CONCERNS

At times Borlaug got frustrated with the criticism his methods attracted, suggesting that some of those critics had never experienced the terrible effects of food shortage, as he himself had seen in Depression-era America, Mexico, and many other developing countries. In truth, some critics gave the impression that they would have preferred the Green Revolution never to have happened, even if this had led to the starvation of millions. More rational critics have pointed out that the Green Revolution averted a humanitarian disaster but does not provide a complete solution to alleviating hunger throughout the world, a point of view that Borlaug himself agreed with.

MARSHALL UNVEILS HIS PLAN TO REBUILD EUROPE

1947

Circumstances: The disastrous state of the economy of Western Europe in the aftermath of World War II

Protagonists: US Secretary of State George Marshall and the staff of the US State Department

Consequences: The beginning of recovery and reconstruction

On June 5, 1947, a little more than two years after the end of World War II, US Secretary of State George Marshall made a speech in which he introduced a change in American foreign policy whereby a massive program of aid would be made available to European countries to reconstruct buildings and facilities destroyed in the war and to kick-start economic recovery.

Marshall was well aware that this new policy might well prove unpopular with the American people and receive a hostile reception in Congress. It was why he was publicly introducing it rather than President Harry Truman, because he was widely regarded in America as the architect of the Allied victory. Even so, while Marshall was making the speech, Truman was holding a press conference in which he condemned the role the Soviet Union had played in the communist takeover of Hungary. It was a classic case of a politician deflecting attention away from a difficult subject by making a headline-grabbing announcement on a different issue.

WAR-TORN EUROPE

The European Recovery Program, or Marshall Plan as it became widely known, had been developed over the previous few months by officials in the State Department, principally Dean Acheson, William Clayton, and George Kennedy. It was a direct response to the realization that the entire European economy was in a state of almost complete collapse. All three had visited European countries in 1946 and had seen for themselves the problems faced by those countries devastated by war. They came to the conclusion that the only way Europe was going to recover was if the German economy, once the principal driver of the European economy, was reconstructed and allowed to function properly.

In a series of negotiations held between Marshall and Vyacheslav Molotov, the foreign minister of the Soviet Union, it had become obvious that the Soviets would not agree to any plan that involved rebuilding Germany. As the British government was, in effect, broke, following its war expenditure it

GEORGE MARSHALL
As US Secretary of State in 1947, Marshall was responsible for the change in American foreign policy in postwar Europe.

quickly became apparent that if anything was going to be done, America had to take the lead. Marshall's decision was to instruct his officials to find a solution to refinancing the European economy. They then, in the first half of 1946, made a series of decisions that led to a radical change in US government policy concerning postwar Germany.

THE MORGENTHAU PLAN

Toward the end of World War II, after an Allied victory seemed inevitable and particularly after the successful invasion of Normandy in June 1944, President Roosevelt turned his mind on what to do with Germany once it had finally surrendered. The resulting plan was named after the Secretary of the Treasury at the time, Henry Morgenthau, and mostly written by Harry Dexter White, an economist in that department. Its principal aim was to restrict the development of postwar Germany to prevent the country from returning to its former dominant economic position so that it would not be able to start any more wars. The way this was to be achieved was to divide the country into two states and give some of its territory to neighboring countries. The coal-mining region of Upper Silesia was given to Poland and the industrial area of the Saar valley to France, while the Ruhr valley, the industrial heartland of Germany, would become a part of an internationally administered zone. In this way, Germany would be deindustrialized, becoming instead an agricultural nation that did not have the capacity to threaten anybody else.

The Morgenthau Plan was presented to the British government in September 1944 and, after initially being very reluctant to accept it, Winston Churchill had his arm twisted by President Roosevelt and eventually relented. Churchill described the plan as being the "pastoralization" of Germany, and cited the disastrous consequences of the Treaty of Versailles adopted at the end of World War I. The harsh measures taken against Germany in the form of an enormous amount of reparations

> **The Morgenthau Plan's main aim was to restrict the development of postwar Germany and to stop it from starting any more wars.**

SOVIET LINKS

Fears of a possible communist uprising in postwar Germany were given some credibility when it later emerged that during the war the chief government economist Harry Dexter White had been regarded by Soviet intelligence as an asset in the American government. Specific evidence against White has never been presented, but it seems that he persuaded Morgenthau of the merits of the plan to deindustrialize the German economy because he thought that communists would be able to take advantage of the ensuing chaos it would cause not only in Germany, but more widely in Western Europe.

(repayments) that would cripple the German economy for many years were among the driving forces behind the rise of Adolf Hitler and the Nazi Party in the 1920s and 1930s. But the British economy was reliant on American finance at the time and Roosevelt either dangled the carrot of further multibillion-dollar loans or made a veiled threat of withholding them until Churchill agreed.

THE MARSHALL PLAN

After the final surrender on May 7, 1945, the Morgenthau Plan was implemented by the Allies in occupied Germany. Among other things, it involved the demolition of those factories in the Ruhr valley that had not already been bombed flat during the war. However, it quickly became apparent that this approach was having disastrous consequences. With no factories, there were no jobs and no wages, so the German economy effectively ceased to function. People were beginning to starve and they had become reliant on American aid to survive. Rising civil unrest led to US fears of a possible communist uprising, a common enough reaction in America at the time.

The Americans also began to realize that continuing with the Morgenthau Plan meant they would have to support the German economy, which no doubt led the State Department to begin work on what would become the Marshall Plan. The scale of the problem was enormous: by the end of the war, some five million houses had been destroyed in Europe and there were twelve million displaced persons. Getting Germany back on its feet again would require a huge amount of money and, after the Marshall Plan had been approved by the US Congress, a multibillion-dollar package was made available.

EUROPE REBUILT

The money, in the form of loans and grants, was offered to many other European countries as well as Germany, including the Soviet Union and those of Eastern Europe. After extensive negotiations with the European countries that would be taking part in the plan, the Organisation for European Economic Co-operation (OEEC) was established

Allied bombing had destroyed the center of numerous German cities, Berlin, Hamburg, Frankfurt, and Cologne included, together with much of its transport and industry.

POSTWAR EUROPE
Many European cities lay in ruins after the end of World War II.

takeover in any Western European country receded.

The relaxation of trade barriers between countries required by the plan can also be seen as part of the process of European integration, even if the European Union of today has its roots in the European Coal and Steel Community, formed in 1951 by six European countries, including Germany, rather than through the Marshall Plan and the OEEC.

TRIUMPH OF US POLICY

By the end of 1951, the Marshall Plan had been replaced by a new policy. Critics have since suggested that the plan enabled Americans to further their own imperialistic and anti-communist aims and that the German economic miracle of the 1960s and 1970s was a result of the policies followed by the German Minister for Economics from 1949 to 1963. But if the Marshall Plan is compared to the disastrous Morgenthau Plan and to the Treaty of Versailles of 1919, it must be regarded as a triumph of American foreign policy, making the decisions taken to implement it among the greatest made in US postwar history.

to administer it and to allocate financial packages to particular countries. Over the course of the next three years, a total of $13 billion was divided among the seventeen European countries taking part in the plan, of which Germany received around $2.2 billion.

The transformation in the European economy began almost immediately. The period between 1948 to 1952 saw an overall increase in GDP (the total value of goods produced in a year) of 35 percent, the fastest growth rate in European history. While this could not be entirely put down to the Marshall Plan, there can be little doubt that it played an important role in stimulating economic activity. Agricultural production also began to rise rapidly and, with the potential food crisis averted, the threat of a communist

ROSA PARKS REFUSES TO STAND UP

1955

Circumstances: A woman takes a seat on a bus in Montgomery, Alabama

Protagonists: Rosa Parks, Martin Luther King Jr., and other activists of the civil rights movement in America

Consequences: The end of segregation on the buses in Montgomery and Martin Luther King Jr. rises in prominence

In 2001 the Missouri state legislature lost a seven-year legal battle to prevent the white supremacist group the Ku Klux Klan from joining its Adopt-a-Highway clean-up program, in which any group that collected litter from the side of a stretch of road was allowed to put up a sign saying that they had sponsored it. In response, the state decided to rename the stretch of Interstate 55 in St. Louis County allocated to the KKK as the Rosa Parks Highway. The KKK did not fulfill their commitment to clean up the highway, depriving the rest of us of an opportunity to enjoy a good laugh at their expense. But the name of the road remains as one of many tributes found all over America to Rosa Parks, who died in 2005 at the age of ninety-two.

On December 1, 1955, in Montgomery, Alabama, Rosa Parks refused to vacate her seat on a segregated bus for a white passenger. She was arrested, which sparked a protest in the city that became an important milestone in the struggle for civil rights in America. Her decision to commit what was, on the ace of it, a relatively minor act of civil disobedience had enormous repercussions. It would eventually result in that famous line from the US Declaration of Independence of 1776 that "all men are created equal" finally ringing true, even if it would probably read better if it said that "all men and women are created equal."

"There comes a time when people get tired. We are here this evening to say to those who have mistreated us for so long that we are tired, tired of being segregated and humiliated, tired of being kicked about by the brutal feet of oppression."

—From a speech given by Martin Luther King Jr. on December 5, 1955, the first day of the Montgomery Bus Boycott

SEGREGATION

By all accounts Rosa Parks was a respectable, soft-spoken woman with strong religious convictions. As she would reveal through her actions, however, she also had a deep sense of injustice about the repression of black people in Alabama and an inner determination to do something about it. The Jim Crow laws legislating for the segregation of the races had been in force in the southern states of America since the 1870s and were supposedly intended to create conditions that were "separate but equal" even if in practice the actual purpose was to enforce the social and economic disadvantages faced by black people. A Montgomery city ordinance dating to 1900 specified the segregation of public transport, and by the 1950s bus companies in the city reserved the front rows of seats on any bus for white people. The law did not specify any requirement for a black person to stand up if a white person did not have a seat, but this had become customary. This meant that when the white section of the bus was full and a white person was having to stand, the bus driver would extend the white section farther back, telling any black people sitting in the row immediately behind the white section to move back or, if there was no room, to stand up.

As if this was not petty enough, black people were also not allowed to walk through the white section to get to the black section if there were any white people on board, but were expected to get on the bus at the front to pay their fare to the driver, then get off and get on again through the back doors. As Rosa Parks had experienced herself, this sometimes resulted in bus drivers, who were all white men, taking a fare from a black person and then driving off before they had the chance to get back on the bus.

ROSA PARKS
A photograph of Parks from December 1955, taken during the Montgomery Bus Boycott, with Martin Luther King Jr. in the background.

POLICE REPORT
The bus boycott ended in
victory in December 1956. The
city authority told black people
that from then on they could sit
wherever they chose.

*People always say that I didn't
give up my seat because I was
tired, but that isn't true. I was not
tired physically, or no more tired
than I usually was at the end of
a working day. I was not old,
although some people have an
image of me as being old then.
I was forty-two. No, the only tired
I was, was tired of giving in.*

NO. 2857

In the early evening of December 1,
1955, Rosa Parks got on the No. 2857
Cleveland Avenue bus in downtown
Montgomery, where she worked as a
seamstress in a department store, and sat
down in the first row of seats allocated
to black people. The bus began to fill up
until there were no seats left in either the
black or white sections, leaving a white
man standing. As black and white people
were not supposed to sit in the same row,
the bus driver told the four men and
women in the first row allocated to black
people to stand up so the white man
could sit down and, after some initial
reluctance, three of the four got up. The
fourth, Rosa Parks, remained seated and,
on being told again to move by the bus
driver, refused to get up, saying, she
would later recall, after he threatened to
call the police, "You may do that." More
than thirty years afterward she wrote:

The police duly arrived
and arrested Parks, who was
taken to a police station where
she was formally charged with breaking
the segregation law, then transferred to
the city jail.

CIVIL DISOBEDIENCE

After about two hours in the jail, Rosa
Parks was bailed out by Edgar Nixon,
the president of the local chapter of the
NAACP (National Association for
the Advancement of Colored People).
Nixon had been looking for a case that
could be used to test the constitutional
legality of the segregation laws in
Montgomery. If Parks agreed to take
part in a lawsuit that could have
dangerous consequences for both herself
and her family, he had now been
presented with the perfect opportunity.

Parks was the secretary of the
Montgomery NAACP and a few months
before had attended a summer school
with classes on such subjects as the civil
disobedience of Mahatma Gandhi in

India, leading to some suggestion that her own actions had been premeditated. She would later say that, while the injustice of segregation had been on her mind, her action was not planned.

BUS BOYCOTT

Parks decided to go ahead with the lawsuit. On Monday, December 5, the day of her court appearance, a boycott of the public bus services was organized by the black community and it was observed by almost everybody. At the trial, which lasted all of five minutes, Parks was found guilty of violating the city ordinance on segregation and fined a total of $10 and $4 costs. That evening at a meeting of community leaders the decision was made to extend the bus boycott and to form an organization, to be called the Montgomery Improvement

I HAVE A DREAM

Prior to being elected as president of the Montgomery Improvement Association, Martin Luther King Jr. had moved to the city where he electrified meetings of the NAACP with his remarkable gift for public speaking. The case of Rosa Parks put King into a prominent position in the civil rights movement, where he came to international attention because of his adoption of nonviolent civil disobedience. The spellbinding power of his oratory is most famously demonstrated in the "I Have a Dream" speech delivered on August 28, 1963, as a part of the March on Washington protest.

Association. A vote was taken to elect a president of the new association and was won by a twenty-six-year-old Baptist minister from Atlanta, Georgia, Martin Luther King Jr.

The bus boycott lasted for 381 days and inspired many other protests and acts of disobedience in the name of civil rights in other states in America. It lasted until the US Supreme Court ruled in the case of another woman from Montgomery, Aurelia Browder, who had experienced much the same treatment as Rosa Parks had done. It found that the segregation of buses was unconstitutional and forced the city and the state of Alabama to integrate its transport system with no segregation. It was one of a series of cases heard by the Supreme Court that challenged the remaining Jim Crow laws.

CIVIL RIGHTS ACT

In the following year, the Civil Rights Act became law, making discrimination of any sort illegal. That was followed in 1965 by the Voting Rights Act, which outlawed all practices aimed at preventing people from any background from registering to vote. By that time, Rosa Parks was living in Detroit, where she worked for the US Congressional Representative for Michigan John Conyers until she retired in 1988. After her death in 2005, her body lay in state for two days in the US Capitol building in Washington, where a bust of Martin Luther King Jr., assassinated in 1968, also stands. The bus she was traveling on that day in Montgomery is now in the Henry Ford Museum in Detroit, where, in April 2012, it was visited by Barack Obama, the first black president of America.

KENNEDY RESOLVES THE CUBAN MISSILE CRISIS

1962

Circumstances: America faces the threat of nuclear warheads on its doorstep

Protagonists: President John F. Kennedy and First Secretary Nikita Khrushchev

Consequences: A nuclear war is averted

The Cuban Missile Crisis lasted for only thirteen days, from October 16 to October 28, 1962, but during that short time America and the Soviet Union came closer to nuclear war than at any other moment in the forty-six-year history of the Cold War, which began at the end of World War II and came to a close in 1991 with the collapse of the Soviet Union.

At the time of the crisis, the forty-five-year-old President John F. Kennedy had been in the White House for just sixteen months, but despite his relative youth and inexperience he made a series of decisions that brought America back from the brink of war. The most important of these was his decision not to take direct military action against Cuba, going against the advice of his senior military commanders. Instead he imposed a naval blockade on the island to prevent Soviet ships carrying missiles from reaching it. But perhaps his greatest contribution to averting a nuclear war and the devastating consequences it would entail was to take a course of action that at no time closed off the

SOVIET SUPPORT
After the failure of the Bay of Pigs invasion of Cuba in 1961, Soviet leader Nikita Krushchev (right) was emboldened to support Fidel Castro with arms.

possibility of finding a diplomatic solution to the crisis. Both he and Nikita Khrushchev, the leader of the Soviet Union, were well aware that the use of military force by either side had the potential to escalate into the use of nuclear weapons.

In the end, Kennedy's strength of character and his ability to make decisions under the most extreme pressure were two of the main reasons why Khrushchev decided to back down.

BERLIN WALL

One of the key points of contention between America and the Soviet Union in the late 1950s and early 1960s was over the future of Berlin, which had been split between western and eastern zones since the end of World War II. Khrushchev wanted Berlin to be reunited and to become part of East Germany. When, in the summer of 1961, it became clear that this solution was not going to be accepted by America or its Western allies, the Soviet Union and East Germany began the construction of what would become the Berlin Wall.

A number of incidents in October at the crossing point between the Berlin zones known as Checkpoint Charlie, in which US officials were prevented from crossing into the eastern zone, resulted in a stand-off between Soviet and American tanks. At that point Kennedy decided to accept the presence of the Berlin Wall rather than risk any further escalation of the crisis.

CASTRO'S CUBA

The lack of resolve shown by Kennedy over Berlin reinforced the impression Khrushchev had developed of him as weak and indecisive after the Bay of Pigs fiasco earlier in the year. A force of Cuban exiles, backed and trained by the CIA, the US intelligence agency, had mounted an invasion of Cuba in April 1961, landing at the Bay of Pigs. It had been comprehensively defeated by Fidel Castro's Cuban army, partly as a result of the lack of support it had received due to Kennedy's decision not to allow the American navy or air force to provide cover. The consequence of this failure was both to increase support for Castro in Cuba and more widely in Latin America and for him to pursue closer ties with the Soviet Union, declaring that the overthrow of the American-backed dictator Batista in 1959 had been a communist revolution. Castro was also concerned about the possibility of a full-scale American invasion of Cuba, leading him to accept Soviet military assistance to challenge that threat, which included the use of defensive surface-to-air missiles.

After initial reluctance to agree to such an aggressive move, Castro also

> "This Government, as promised, has maintained the closest surveillance of the Soviet military buildup on the island of Cuba. Within the past week, unmistakable evidence has established the fact that a series of offensive missile sites is now in preparation on that imprisoned island. The purpose of these bases can be none other than to provide a nuclear strike capability against the Western Hemisphere."
>
> —From a television address to the American people given by President John F. Kennedy on October 22, 1962

SUMMIT MEETING
The low opinion Khrushchev formed of
Kennedy at a summit in Vienna in June
1961 contributed to him underestimating
the president.

finally agreed to the Soviet plan of
secretly installing missiles in Cuba,
which would be capable of carrying
nuclear warheads to locations
throughout America.

NUCLEAR CAPABILITY
Khrushchev had more than Cuban
security in mind when he discussed the
plan with Castro. American intelligence
reports suggested that the Soviet Union
had a greater capability in long-range
nuclear missiles, which could strike the
American mainland from sites within
the Soviet Union. The truth was that
they actually had far fewer than the
Americans. The guidance systems in use
by the Soviets were also not sophisticated
enough to hit targets in America with
any degree of accuracy. Cuba, on the
other hand, was only 90 miles (130 km)
off the coast of Florida, so shorter-range
and more accurate missiles could pose a
much greater threat. The US already had
intermediate-range missiles stationed in
Italy and, in April 1962, the Turkish

government agreed to the installation
of similar US missiles on its territory,
from where they could target Moscow.
So the Cuban missiles would act as a
countermeasure to the American threat.

Khrushchev also thought that, once
the missiles had been installed in Cuba,
Kennedy would prove himself to be a
weak leader again and either accept their
presence rather than risk a war with the
Soviet Union or come to a negotiated
settlement in which, in exchange for the
removal of the missiles from Cuba, he
would agree to the Soviet demand to
take over all of Berlin.

CRISIS MOUNTS
For all of September 1962 and for
the first two weeks of October, the
Americans suspended flights of their
U-2 spy planes over Cuba because of the
presence of Soviet surface-to-air missiles
on the island similar to the type used in
April 1960 to shoot down an American
U-2 spy plane over Russia. But, after
evidence of an increase in Soviet military
activity was uncovered and rumors of
the Soviets' intention to build platforms
for missiles began to circulate, on
October 14 a plane was sent out to fly
over Cuba despite the risks. It took
pictures of a construction site in western
Cuba; these were interpreted by the CIA
the following day as providing certain
evidence of the presence of intermediate-
range missiles on the island.

**Kennedy and his advisers
considered the various possible
US responses. These ranged from
a full-scale American invasion of
Cuba to doing nothing at all.**

UN MEETING

Locations of Cuban missile sites are shown using aerial photographs at a United Nations meeting on October 25, 1962.

President Kennedy was informed the next morning, October 16, and convened a meeting of government ministers and key advisers to discuss the American response. As well as Kennedy himself, the committee, which would become known as ExComm (Executive Committee of the National Security Council), included Vice President Lyndon Johnson, Secretary of State Dean Rusk, Secretary of Defense Robert McNamara, and Kennedy's younger brother Robert, the Attorney General, as well as specialist advisers such as General Maxwell Taylor, the chairman of the Joint Chiefs of Staff, and John McCone, the director of the CIA.

Kennedy continued to perform the public duties in his schedule, not wanting to appear indecisive by announcing the crisis before he knew what he was going to do about it, while in private the members of ExComm went through the various possible responses available to America. These ranged from a full-scale American invasion of Cuba to doing nothing at all. At meetings of ExComm on October 18 and 19 these options were discussed and the military advisers, including General Taylor, stated that their favored option was an invasion. It became apparent that this would take months to organize, by which time it would be too late, so they next advised bombing the missile sites.

Kennedy decided that it would not be possible to guarantee that all the missile sites would be put out of action by bombing and that, in doing so, it was certain to provoke an armed response from the Soviet Union that could lead to nuclear war. The idea of doing nothing was also ruled out for more political reasons: Kennedy had made a promise to the American people only the month before to act if Cuba came into possession of the means to attack the US and by doing nothing he would be breaking that promise and would look as weak as he had over the Bay of Pigs fiasco.

LAUNCH SITE

An aerial reconnaissance photograph taken by a US spy plane, clearly showing a Soviet missile launch site near San Cristóbal, western Cuba.

"QUARANTINE"

By October 22, Kennedy had reached his decision and made a television broadcast to the American people that set out the situation in straightforward language (quoted at the beginning of the chapter). He went on to explain what he intended to do about it, saying:

> To halt this offensive buildup, a strict quarantine on all offensive military equipment under shipment to Cuba is being initiated. All ships of any kind bound for Cuba, from whatever nation or port, will, if found to contain cargoes of offensive weapons, be turned back.

What he was announcing was, in effect, a blockade of Cuba, but he had chosen to describe it as a "quarantine" because under international law blockades were considered to be acts of war.

I NOVEMBER 1962
MRBM LAUNCH SITE 2
SAN CRISTOBAL

MISSILE-READY TENT

FUEL TRAILERS

FORMER LAUNCH POSITION

FORMER LOCATION OF MISSILE-READY TENTS

HIGH ALERT

Khrushchev replied with a broadcast of his own, describing the blockade as a "pirate action" that would lead to war. Kennedy raised the US alert level to DEFCON 2, one level below actual war, and put all US military forces on standby for immediate action. While the world teetered on the edge of a nuclear war, a secret diplomatic channel had been opened between the Americans and Soviets. On October 26, Khrushchev sent Kennedy a telegram offering what had the potential to lead to a peaceful solution to the crisis. Khrushchev said he would remove the missiles from Cuba in exchange for a public commitment from Kennedy not to invade and an end to the blockade of Cuba.

The next day, another communication was received from Khrushchev that was not so conciliatory as the first. It contained a demand for the removal of US missiles from Italy and Turkey. Kennedy decided to respond to the first message publicly, accepting the proposals to lift the blockade and making a commitment not to invade Cuba. He then informed Khrushchev via the diplomatic back-channel that he would also remove the missiles from Italy and Turkey in secret within the next six months. This was not actually a huge concession because, unknown to the Soviets, these missiles were due to be replaced anyway with Polaris missiles launched from submarines.

READY TO FIRE

Years later it would emerge that during the thirteen days of the Cuban Missile Crisis the captain of a nuclear-armed Soviet submarine, which had been detected by the US Navy, had ordered a nuclear missile to be made ready to fire. The action was only stopped by the intervention of a junior officer. The world really had been teetering on the brink of nuclear war, which could have been sparked by a single incident.

END OF CRISIS

Khrushchev agreed, bringing the crisis to an abrupt and successful end on October 28, after which the Soviets immediately began dismantling the Cuban missile sites. By November 20 the missiles had been dispatched back to the Soviet Union. As the agreement to remove US missiles from Italy and Turkey remained secret, the public was given the impression that Khrushchev had settled for a solution that favored America, diminishing his own reputation for hard bargaining, while enhancing Kennedy's.

In the meantime, Berlin stayed divided until the fall of the Berlin Wall in 1989, and Cuba remained a thorn in America's side for a further five decades until relations finally began to thaw in 2015.

The crisis came to an abrupt and successful end on October 28, 1962, after which the Soviets immediately began dismantling the Cuban missile sites.

GEORGE MARTIN SIGNS THE BEATLES

1962

Circumstances: A record producer listens to a band that has been turned down by every other record company

Protagonists: John, Paul, George, and Ringo, along with Brian Epstein and George Martin

Consequences: The emergence of the most popular and biggest-selling band in the history of popular music

On New Year's Day, 1962, The Beatles attended their first proper audition for a record company, recording a demo tape of fifteen songs over an hour in the Decca Records recording studio in West Hampstead, London. The demo consisted of three songs written by John Lennon and Paul McCartney, the rest being cover versions of songs the band regularly played live, which, at least according to their manager Brian Epstein, would better show off the range of their musical skills.

By that time, the band were playing regularly in Liverpool, most famously at the Cavern Club, and had been to Hamburg in Germany on two occasions, each time playing three-month long residencies in clubs where they could end up playing all day and half the night as well. The experience had brought them together as a band musically, even if John, Paul, and the lead guitarist George Harrison did not always see eye to eye with their drummer, Pete Best. After the audition, the band went back to Liverpool and waited for the outcome.

It took a month for Decca to make up their minds and, when they finally did, they made what is now considered to be the worst decision in the history of popular music by turning The Beatles down. A record producer from Decca phoned Brian Epstein to give him the

"There was an unusual quality of sound, a certain roughness that I had not encountered before. There was also the fact that more than one person was singing, which in itself was unusual. There was something tangible that made me want to hear more, meet and see what they could do."

—George Martin, *All You Need is Ears*

CAVERN CLUB
The Beatles with Pete Best on drums playing the Cavern Club in Liverpool on December 8, 1961, shortly before their failed audition with Decca Records.

bad news. He is reported to have said, "Guitar groups are on the way out, Mr. Epstein," and had then gone on to suggest that, as Epstein was already running a very successful record shop in Liverpool, perhaps it would be better if he stuck to the business he knew best.

TURNED DOWN
To be fair to Decca, they may have been the first record company to turn down The Beatles, but they were by no means the last. Over the course of the next few months, Epstein approached all the major British record companies and was turned down by, among others, Pye, Columbia, and HMV. Three of the four record producers employed by EMI listened to the demo tape, which, it would later emerge, Epstein had paid the Decca record producer to make, and each of them said no. The fourth one was on vacation at the time, so he did not get a chance to listen for himself.

GEORGE MARTIN
In April the band went back to Hamburg for their third residency in a club. In May, while they were still in the city, Epstein made what he considered at the time to be one final effort to get them signed to a record company. He took the demo tape to London and, through a friend who worked in HMV's flagship record store on Oxford Street, managed to get it passed on to George Martin, the

fourth EMI record producer who had yet to hear it and who primarily worked for the record company's Parlophone label.

Martin heard something in the recording that he liked, although he would later struggle to say exactly what that something was. But, whatever it had been, it was enough for him to want to meet the band in person and to hear them play live. On June 6, after they had finished their contract in Hamburg, The Beatles auditioned for Martin at EMI's Abbey Road studios in St. John's Wood, London. As before, they played a few of their own songs, but mostly the covers they played in their normal live set. Once they had finished, Martin said it had been very nice and that he would let them know. If they were expecting to be signed on the spot, then they left the recording studios disappointed.

Back in Liverpool, they played more gigs at the Cavern and at various other venues around the city without hearing anything from Martin, until he finally telephoned Brian Epstein and offered them a recording contract. It was the standard one-year deal EMI offered to new artists, with an option to extend beyond the single year if EMI was happy with the outcome of the recording sessions, and it paid a royalty to the band of one penny for every single sold.

The Beatles are by far and away the most successful recording artists of all time. Worldwide sales in all formats have been estimated at more than one billion.

FIRST SINGLE

In September 1962, The Beatles made their first record with George Martin at Abbey Road studios. By that time, Pete Best had been sacked from the band, just when it was about to become enormously successful, and replaced by Ringo Starr, who had been playing with the Liverpool-based band Rory Storm and the Hurricanes. Martin had not been happy with Best's drumming, but the decision to fire him rested with John, Paul, and George, even if they actually got Brian Epstein to break the news. After the first recording, Martin was not overly impressed with Ringo either and booked a session drummer to rerecord the band's first single, "Love Me Do," with Ringo only playing maracas. It was released the following month and, by Christmas, had sold seventeen thousand copies, making each member of the band all of £17 in royalties, and had reached No. 17 in the charts.

BEATLEMANIA

The band recorded again on November 26 and this time Martin was much happier with Ringo and with the overall outcome of the session, saying to the band over the intercom from the control room as they finished playing, "Gentlemen, you've just recorded your first number one record." He was not wrong. After its release in January, "Please Please Me" went to No. 1 and stayed there for thirty weeks. The album of the same name, featuring eight Lennon and McCartney compositions and six covers, also went to No. 1 in the album chart. The next single, "From Me to You," came out in April and went to No. 1 as well. Then the fourth single, "She Loves You," sold a million copies after it came out in August, holding the record as the highest-selling UK single in Britain until it was finally beaten in 1977 by Paul McCartney's song "Mull of Kintyre."

Live performances on TV followed and, what with the moptop haircuts, the suits, and the band's irreverent sense of humor, Beatlemania was born. In the first three years with EMI, The Beatles sold nine million singles in Britain alone and toward the end of their recording career in 1969, the band accounted for 20 percent of the record company's entire sales. By one estimate, worldwide sales figures in all formats have now surpassed the one billion mark, making The Beatles the most successful recording artists of all time. So, if Decca's decision to turn down The Beatles was the worst one made in pop music history, then surely it is equally true to say that George Martin's decision to sign the band for EMI was the best one, not least for the phenomenal sales they have achieved, but also because of the sheer pleasure their songs have given the world.

YELLOW SUBMARINE

A US stamp of 1999 commemorates The Beatles' famous song "Yellow Submarine."

NELSON MANDELA REFUSES TO GIVE IN

1985

Circumstances: The long fight against apartheid in South Africa

Protagonists: Nelson Mandela and President P. W. Botha

Consequences: The creation of a new South Africa

On January 31, 1985, the president of South Africa, P. W. Botha, announced in parliament that he was prepared to release Nelson Mandela from prison if he "unconditionally rejected violence as a political weapon." It was not the first time Botha had made such an offer, except on previous occasions a further condition had been attached that Mandela go into voluntary exile in the Transkei, one of the territories known as Bantustans set up by Botha's government as "homelands" for the black inhabitants of the country.

On February 10, Mandela released a statement, read out by his daughter Zindzi at a mass meeting in Jabulani Stadium, Soweto, in which he said, "I am surprised at the conditions that the government wants to impose on me. I am not a violent man." He then spoke directly of Botha, saying:

Let him renounce violence. Let him say that he will dismantle apartheid. Let him unban the people's organization, the African National Congress. Let him free all who have been imprisoned, banished, or exiled for their opposition to apartheid. Let him guarantee free political activity so that people may decide who will govern them.

He went on to say, "Only free men can negotiate. Prisoners cannot enter into contracts," and stated his position in words that nobody could misinterpret: "I cannot and will not give any undertaking at a time when I and you, the people, are not free."

By the time Mandela made this statement he had served twenty-two years of the life sentence he had received in 1964 for sabotage, the first eighteen of which had involved hard labor in the lime quarry of the notorious prison on Robben Island. In such circumstances it would have been understandable, to say the least, if he had decided that he had done his bit for the cause of ending apartheid in South Africa and agreed to the terms of Botha's offer, particularly considering that he had long since embraced the Gandhian philosophy of civil disobedience and nonviolent protest.

In rejecting the offer and also refusing to enter into any dealings with Botha he both retained the moral high ground and refocused the attention of the rest of the world on the situation in South Africa. Mandela had been committed to the anti-apartheid cause since the 1950s, and had long ago made up his mind to

FIRE PROTEST
In 1950s South Africa, non-white citizens had to carry a pass that prevented them going into "whites only" zones. Nelson Mandela defied the law by publicly burning his pass.

member of his family to go to school, where he was given the English name of Nelson. The first sign of political activism came in 1938 when he was attending the University of Fort Hare, where he met Oliver Tambo, the future president of the African National Congress (ANC). After his first year he was forced to leave the university because of his activism. He then moved to Johannesburg, initially as a means of avoiding a marriage his family had arranged for him. He found a job as a clerk in a law firm and completed the degree he had started at Fort Hare by correspondence course before going on to study law at the University of Witwatersrand.

By this time Mandela had become friends with Walter Sisulu, a member of the ANC, who would become something

help end apartheid or die in the attempt. Nevertheless, whatever his convictions had been in the past, when faced with the choice of immediate release after twenty-two years in prison or continuing with a struggle that at the time seemed unlikely to have a successful outcome, it must have required an extraordinary level of fortitude and inner strength to make the decision to carry on.

ROLIHLAHLA MANDELA

Rolihlahla Mandela was born in 1918 in the Transkei region of the Eastern Cape Province. His father, who died when Mandela was nine, was the chief of his village and came from a branch of the Thembu royal family. He was the first

"I am surprised at the conditions that the government wants to impose on me. I am not a violent man."

of a mentor to him. They would later spend many years imprisoned together on Robben Island. In 1944, Mandela, Sisulu, and Tambo were instrumental in setting up the Youth League of the ANC, created to pursue a more active role in resisting repression.

APARTHEID

By the end of the 1940s, all three men had become prominent in the ANC and had stepped up their activism as a consequence of the 1948 general election in which only white people, who made up about 20 percent of the population, had been allowed to vote. It was won by the Afrikaner-dominated National Party, which immediately began to introduce a raft of legislation implementing its policy of apartheid, an Afrikaans word that means "apart." Under this policy, people were classified as belonging to one of four racial groups: "white," "native" (black African), "Indian," and "colored," which included people of mixed race and anybody else who did not fit into any of the other categories. The laws kept these groups apart and, like other racist legislation, the official line was that each group would be "separate but equal." In practice, of course, the laws maintained the privileged position of white people, who were assigned the best hospitals and schools, while those who were what was considered the lowest class, the black Africans who made up over 70 percent of the population, faced constant discrimination in almost every aspect of their lives.

The introduction of the apartheid laws also led to constant police violence and harassment against members of the ANC, including Mandela.

In 1955, the ANC produced a charter setting out its principles of opposition to apartheid and its campaign for a fully democratic and nonracial South Africa. The government declared it to be treasonous, leading to Mandela and one hundred and fifty other members of the ANC being arrested.

TRIAL

The subsequent trial for treason ended with all the defendants being acquitted. Mandela cemented his reputation with the ANC at this time and, in 1961, became the leader of *Umkhonto we Sizwe* (the Spear of the Nation), the armed wing of the ANC formed in response to the Sharpeville massacre of the previous year in which white South African policemen had killed sixty-nine black anti-apartheid protestors. Up until this point, Mandela had used nonviolent protest, but, as all means of nonviolent protest had been outlawed, he concluded that the only course of action remaining was to begin a campaign of sabotage against government-owned property.

PRISON

On August 5, 1962, after eighteen months of the sabotage campaign, Mandela was arrested. He was initially charged with inciting workers to strike, for which he received a five-year sentence, and then, after the arrest of other ANC members, including Walter Sisulu, he was charged with nine others for over two hundred acts of sabotage. The Rivonia Trial, as it became known, after the suburb where the arrests were made, was widely condemned around the world as a sham. Eight of the ten accused, including Mandela and Sisulu, were found guilty, sentenced to life imprisonment, and sent to Robben Island.

MANDELA'S CELL
The cell at Robben Island where Nelson Mandela was imprisoned has been preserved as a museum.

By the 1980s, Mandela had become famous around the world and was the focus of numerous campaigns aimed at putting pressure on the South African government. Against this backdrop of international condemnation, Botha made the offer to release him under condition that he reject violence.

In 1988, Mandela was moved to a low-security prison in the Western Cape, a sign that the government was considering releasing him. Botha suffered a stroke in the following year and was maneuvered out of office, to make way for F. W. de Clerk to become president.

ROBBEN ISLAND
Conditions at Robben Island were harsh, particularly for black inmates, and Mandela and Sisulu were held there until 1982, when both were transferred to Pollsmoor Maximum Security Prison in Cape Town. The government would later say this was done so that contact between Mandela and P. W. Botha could be established, but a more likely explanation is that he was moved to stop the influence he was having on younger ANC activists who had also been imprisoned on Robben Island in what had become known as the Mandela University.

FROM PRISONER TO PRESIDENT
By then the president of South Africa
following his release from prison,
Nelson Mandela acknowledges the
applause of the crowd at an event
at the United States' Library of
Congress, in October 1994.

FREEDOM

Almost as soon as he entered office in
September 1989, de Clerk announced
that the ban on the ANC, which had been
in force since the 1950s, was to be lifted
and he began the process of dismantling
the apartheid system. On February 2,
1990, he announced that Mandela was
finally to be released and, nine days later
and in front of the world's media,
Mandela walked out of Victor Verster
Prison (where he had been moved in
1988), a free man for the first time in
twenty-seven years.

After being released, Mandela was
elected president of the African National
Congress and entered into negotiations
with the government to establish the
country's first fully democratic elections.
The process was marred by violent
confrontations between anti-apartheid
factions, along with the murder of the
ANC leader Chris Hani in 1993 by a
white man, leading to fears that a more
widespread conflict might develop based
on racial differences.

At the general election of April 27,
1994, the ANC won a landslide victory
and Nelson Mandela became the first
black president of South Africa. The date
symbolically marked the end of the
apartheid era and has become known as
Freedom Day in South Africa. In 1993,
the Nobel Peace Prize was awarded
jointly to Mandela and F. W. de Clerk.

Mandela retired from politics at the
age of eighty, having served one term
as president and in the knowledge that
his life's work had been successfully
completed, even if the process of

reconciliation that he began still has a long way to go. He died on December 5, 2013, at the age of ninety-five, and South Africa's President Zuma proclaimed a national mourning period of ten days.

Nelson Mandela's birthday, July 18, has been declared Mandela Day by the United Nations.

GORBACHEV INSTITUTES PERESTROIKA

1986

Circumstances: The disastrous economic situation of the Soviet Union in the 1980s

Protagonists: Mikhail Gorbachev and the people of Eastern Europe and the Soviet Union

Consequences: The collapse of the Soviet Union, the end of the Cold War, and the beginnings of democracy in Eastern Europe

At the twenty-seventh Congress of the Communist Party of the Soviet Union, held in Moscow in February 1986, Mikhail Gorbachev, who had become general secretary of the party in March of the previous year, made a speech in which he set out his intention to revive the Soviet economy. In doing so he used two words, *perestroika* and *glasnost*, which were picked up by the Western media and came to represent a sea change in both the method of government employed within the Soviet Union and how it was perceived by the outside world.

Perestroika means "restructuring" and referred to the changes Gorbachev was in the process of implementing in the political and economic structures of the Soviet Union. Glasnost is usually translated into English as "openness" and, in the sense in which it was being used, referred to a policy of transparency in the workings of government and a willingness to discuss the failures of the past publicly by allowing more freedom for the press and the individual to express their opinions.

NEED FOR REFORM

Two other words he used in the same speech that did not find such wide acceptance outside the Soviet Union but were equally important were *demokratizatsiya* (democratization) and *uskoreniye*, which means "acceleration" and was used by Gorbachev to highlight the urgency of the need for change and to express his desire to take the necessary measures as quickly as possible. What the speech did not contain was any detail about what these changes would actually entail or how he intended to go about implementing them. It is generally

---

Perestroika means "restructuring" and referred to the changes Gorbachev was in the process of implementing in the Soviet Union.

POLITICAL RIVALS
Mikhail Gorbachev and Boris Yeltsin shake
hands after the failure of an attempted
coup against Gorbachev in August 1991.

accepted now that he probably did not know himself at the time. But the decisions made by Gorbachev had consequences far beyond what he had envisaged, and the eventual outcome was almost exactly the opposite of what had been intended. They not only transformed the Soviet Union, but led to its dissolution, and even played a part in the reunification of Germany, the revolutions throughout Eastern Europe, and the end of the Cold War.

THE SOVIET ECONOMY

The situation Gorbachev inherited on becoming general secretary was both politically and economically dire. The policy of Leonid Brezhnev, the Soviet leader from 1966 to 1982, had been to build up the military capability of the USSR in order to compete with the Americans, but in doing so he had starved the domestic economy of investment and it had stagnated.

Over the course of his premiership, the government hierarchy had become stuffed with aging party officials, leading to high levels of corruption and a resistance to change in any form. At the same time, the Soviet Union and the Warsaw Pact countries of Eastern Europe had been kept together by the threat of military force, much as they had been during the Stalinist era of the past. Productivity rates in industry and agriculture had been falling for decades, and the state had attempted to conceal the disastrous nature of the economic decline from the people of the Soviet Union by suppressing free speech. At the same time as the economy was falling apart, Gorbachev also had to deal with the continuing war in Afghanistan, which the Soviet Union had started in 1978 in support of the failing communist regime there and which showed no sign of ending. From April 1986, he also had to contend with the Chernobyl nuclear disaster, the worst ever accident to occur in a nuclear power station.

GORBACHEV

Gorbachev had risen through the ranks of the Communist Party to gain, in 1979, a position in the Politburo, the party's central committee and governing body, and had come to prominence under the leadership of Yuri Andropov after he became general secretary on the death of Brezhnev. Andropov died at the age of seventy after only fifteen months in charge and was succeeded by an even older man, Konstantin Chernenko, who was also in ill health and died in March 1985. It had become obvious that the next general secretary would have to be a younger and healthier man and, as Gorbachev was the youngest member of the Politburo at fifty-four and was not tarnished by association with his predecessors, he became the obvious choice for the position.

Once Gorbachev gave the Soviet media the freedom to criticize the party, they went much further than he anticipated.

GLASNOST

Gorbachev immediately attempted to begin the process of change that was essential for the future of the Soviet Union. But he quickly came to realize that the only way he could bring about reform in the face of resistance from the old guard in the party was to be open about the disastrous state of the economy and the mistakes of the past. This was to be made known to the people of the country, who had previously only been kept informed by party propaganda (controlled information that portrayed the government in a favorable light).

Gorbachev's idea of democratization had been limited to introducing elections to appoint party members to positions within the Communist Party. He had no intention of extending this to include free elections involving other types of political parties. But once he had allowed

> "He had no grand plan and no predetermined policies; but if Gorbachev had not been Party General Secretary, the decisions of summer 1986 would have been different. The USSR's long-lasting order would have endured for many more years, and almost certainly the eventual collapse of the order would have been much bloodier than it was to be in 1991. The irony was that Gorbachev, in trying to prevent the descent of the system into general crisis, proved instrumental in bringing forward that crisis and destroying the USSR."
>
> —Robert Service, *A History of Twentieth-Century Russia*

BERLIN WALL

Mass protests in communist East Germany led to the fall of the Berlin Wall in 1989 and the reunification of Germany.

people freely to express their opinions, they not only began to demand full democracy, but the republics making up the Soviet Union, with the exception of Russia, saw it as an opportunity to demand independence.

END OF COMMUNISM

Much the same happened in the communist countries of Eastern Europe and when it became apparent that Gorbachev was not going to use military force to prevent them from breaking away, as previous Soviet regimes had done, the movement toward democracy gained momentum. In 1989, a wave of revolutions swept through Eastern Europe and by 1991 the communist regimes had fallen in Hungary, Poland, Czechoslovakia, Bulgaria, Romania, and East Germany.

At the same time, the Soviet republics were agitating for independence and once the first one, Lithuania, had declared itself independent without Russian interference, most of the others immediately followed suit.

THE SOVIET UNION BREAKS UP

In August 1991, hardliners in the communist regime attempted to stage a coup against Gorbachev. He was held under house arrest for two days, until a popular uprising led by his political opponent Boris Yeltsin overcame the coup and Gorbachev was released. In December the remaining members of the Soviet Union, now only made up of Russia, Ukraine, and Belarus, agreed on a formal dissolution. Gorbachev resigned and, after the first democratic election ever to be held in Russia, Yeltsin was voted in as its new president.

Gorbachev hardly had the chance to begin the process of perestroika before the entire communist state came crashing down, so in this sense his decision to transform the Soviet Union could be seen as a total failure. But unintended as it may have been, Gorbachev achieved a peaceful transition to a more democratic form of government, and instigated the collapse of communism throughout Europe and the break-up of the Soviet Union itself.

AUNG SAN SUU KYI RETURNS TO BURMA

1988

Circumstances: A Burmese expatriate returns home to look after her sick mother

Protagonists: Aung San Suu Kyi, her family, and the pro-democracy campaigners of Burma

Consequences: A slim chance that Burma is heading slowly toward democracy

Before returning to Burma (also known as the Republic of the Union of Myanmar) in April 1988, Aung San Suu Kyi described herself as being an Oxford housewife. She was married to Michael Avis, an academic specializing in Tibetan literature and culture, and had two teenage sons, so in some respects it was an accurate description. But she was also the daughter of Aung San, the man revered in Burma as "the father of the country" who in, 1947, had been instrumental in negotiating Burmese independence from Britain. He had been set to become its first prime minister when he and other members of his government-in-waiting had been assassinated by their political rivals.

Suu Kyi was only two years old at the time of her father's assassination and at the age of fifteen had left Burma when her mother was appointed as the Burmese ambassador to India. After studying in India and then earning a degree in philosophy, politics, and economics at St. Hugh's College, Oxford, she worked at the headquarters of the United Nations in New York for three years. After her marriage to Avis, she studied in India and at the School of African and Oriental Studies in London. It was hardly the normal background of an Oxford housewife and, as Michael Avis would later write, after she had received a telephone call from Burma early in April 1988 to inform her that her seventy-six-year-old mother had suffered a stroke, he instantly knew that their lives of comfortable domesticity would never be the same again.

THE RETURN

The decision to go to Burma had initially been made so Suu Kyi could look after her mother, who was in hospital in Rangoon (now known as Yangon). When she was well enough, she was

> Suu Kyi was a well-known figure in the country because of the reputation of her father.

moved back to the family home, a colonial-era house situated on Inya Lake on the outskirts of the city. Suu Kyi was forty-two years old and had not lived in Burma for any length of time since leaving the country at fifteen, only returning occasionally for short visits to see her family. Her visit on this occasion coincided with a tumultuous period in the post-independence history of Burma, which had been under military rule since a coup in 1962 ousted the democratically elected civilian government. The coup had been led by General Ne Min and he and his military government attempted to impose a Soviet-style system on the country with disastrous results.

Through a combination of ineptitude and corruption, Burma had become one of the most impoverished in the world, despite being rich in natural

resources, and in the summer of 1988 dissatisfaction with the military government boiled over into mass protests. Ne Min unexpectedly announced his resignation on July 23, warning that if the protests continued the army would open fire and would not be shooting into the air.

8888 UPRISING

On August 8, 1988, a date that led to the protests becoming known as the 8888 Uprising, a general strike was called, together with marches and demonstrations across the country. The government responded in the way Ne Min had said it

SUU KYI
Aung San Suu Kyi campaigning in a by-election for the Burmese parliament in March 2012, which she went on to win.

would, with a show of force in which soldiers fired into unarmed crowds, killing many hundreds of people.

SECOND STRUGGLE

Up until this point, Suu Kyi had not become actively involved in the protests. She remained at home with her mother, but had been visited there over the previous few months by a number of activists in the pro-democracy movement. Even though she had not lived in Burma for almost thirty years, she was a well-known figure in the country because of the reputation of her father. Following the terrible loss of life inflicted on unarmed civilians by the Burmese army, which had been founded by her father, she felt compelled to become involved in the protests.

After giving a speech to a small number of people in the hospital where her mother was being treated, her first ever public oratory, on August 26 she addressed a huge crowd, estimated at being at least half a million strong, gathered at the Shwedagon Pagoda in central Rangoon. It was the place where her father had given speeches himself in the fight for independence from the British more than forty years previously and after his assassination he had been buried near the pagoda. In choosing this spot, Suu Kyi was associating herself with his memory and, as well as calling for free and fair multiparty elections in the country, she also described the uprising as the "second struggle for national independence."

CRACKDOWN ON PROTESTS

On September 18, and with the popular protests in the streets continuing, General Saw Maung assumed control of the government in what was effectively another coup and began an even harsher crackdown on the protest movement. In the expectation of all opposition political parties being banned by the new military government, Suu Kyi and a number of other prominent pro-democracy campaigners formed their own party, the National League for Democracy, of which she became general secretary.

Maung announced that his government would only be in place until elections could be organized, which were to take place in May 1990. In July of 1989, Suu Kyi and other members of the National League for Democracy were put under house arrest, where they would remain throughout the run-up to the election. Despite these restrictions, Suu Kyi's party gained more than 50 percent of the vote in the election, which translated into 392 of the 492 seats available in the Burmese parliament.

At first Maung said that he would only remain in power while a new constitution was being written, but two months later the military government declared the result of the election invalid.

HOUSE ARREST

Suu Kyi was known in Burma before the pro-democracy protests began, but she became internationally recognized for the role she played in them and in 1991 was awarded the Nobel Peace Prize. Over the next twenty years, she would spend a total of fifteen years confined to her house on Inya Lake with only short visits allowed from her family. In 1997 Michael Avis was diagnosed with terminal cancer and was refused permission to enter the country to visit his wife for one last time. The military government offered to allow Suu Kyi to travel to Britain, but

ICON OF DEMOCRACY
Supporters hold a banner displaying the
portraits of President Htin Kyaw and Aung
San Suu Kyi in April 2016.

she was aware that she might not be
allowed to come back again, so she
stayed under house arrest. Finally, she
was released in November 2010 as part
of what appeared to be a thaw in the
authoritarian military government. She
was permitted to travel abroad, where she
was showered with accolades and treated
as if she were a visiting head of state.

DEMOCRATIC ELECTION

Elections were then held in Burma,
although the government reserved the
majority of the seats for the military. In
May 2012, Suu Kyi won a by-election
and took up her seat in the lower house
in July of that year. In the 2015 elections
her party won a landslide victory, gaining
enough seats to form a government. The

constitution prohibited Suu Kyi from
becoming the president as she was a
widow and the mother of foreign
children (a clause written in 2008 to
exclude her from the position). Htin Kyaw
was sworn in as president in April 2016,
with Suu Kyi as state counselor, although
she has maintained that she effectively
runs the government.

The victory marks the first democratic
election of the ruling party through
fair and free polls and Htin Kyaw has
become the first non-military leader
of Burma. Nonetheless the Burmese
military still retains a considerable
amount of power in government and is
heavily involved in brutal ethnic fighting
in regions along Burma's borders over
which the elected leaders have little
control. It is still very much early days
for democracy in Burma.

> **Suu Kyi spent a total of fifteen years
> confined to her house on Inya Lake
> with only short visits allowed
> from her family.**

TIM BERNERS-LEE INVENTS THE WORLD WIDE WEB

1990

Circumstances: A software engineer attempts to find the solution to the problem of how to share information between scientists in a large research institution

Protagonists: Tim Berners-Lee and his fellow workers at CERN

Consequences: The development of the most widely used application on the internet

In the late 1980s, Tim Berners-Lee was working as a software engineer at CERN, the European Organization for Nuclear Research, in Geneva. Over ten thousand scientists were working for CERN either directly or affiliated to it from universities and research institutions around the world. The only way these people could stay in touch was by email and through file sharing, which was time-consuming and not a particularly efficient way of keeping everybody informed about what everybody else was doing.

Berners-Lee had briefly worked for CERN previously, for six months in 1980. There he had developed a prototype of an information-sharing system that he called ENQUIRE. It used hypertext (highlighted words in a piece of text that can be used to link to other texts) as a way of managing large amounts of data. While this research did not actually lead anywhere and appears to have been lost after Berners-Lee first left CERN, the need for a convenient way of managing information remained when he returned some years later.

WORLD WIDE WEB

Between his two stints at CERN, Berners-Lee had been working for a British software firm on developing uses of the internet. In 1989, he decided to try combining the old research he had done on hypertext with the internet in an attempt to produce a system for sharing information between CERN scientists, wherever they happened to be in the world.

In a typically self-deprecating manner, Berners-Lee would later write

"This is for everybody."

—Tweet sent by Tim Berners-Lee while participating in the opening ceremony of the London 2012 Olympic Games

WEB PIONEER
Tim Berners-Lee talks about the web at a conference in Florida in 2012. He is still the director of the World Wide Web Consortium.

INFO.CERN.CH
By the end of 1990, Berners-Lee and Cailliau had developed a web server and connected a Hypertext Transfer Protocol (HTTP) to it over the internet. By August of the following year, they had put up the first website with the address, info.cern. ch, which contained the first webpage, http://info.cern.ch/hypertext/WWW/TheProject.html, giving details about the project at CERN and instructions on how to use the World Wide Web.

Over the next few years, more servers began to appear in other scientific institutions around the world, including the National Center for Supercomputing Applications in Illinois, where the Mosaic web browser was developed. As well as allowing images to be placed within text pages for the first

of how he achieved this: "I just had to take the hypertext idea and connect it to the Transmission Control Protocol and domain name system ideas [on the internet] and—ta-da!—the World Wide Web." Needless to say, it was actually a little more complicated than that, but over the following year, and in collaboration with Robert Cailliau, a computer scientist from Belgium also working at CERN, he designed the first web browser.

Then, while the two of them were chatting in the cafeteria about possible names for what they had developed, he suggested it be called the World Wide Web, having realized by then that it had a much wider application than simply as a means for CERN scientists to stay in touch with each other.

> **"I just had to take the hypertext idea and connect it to the Transmission Control Protocol and domain name system ideas [on the internet] and—ta-da!—the World Wide Web."**

time, it was simple to install, easy to use, and worked on PCs and Macs, opening up the web to a much wider number of users among the general public as well as scientists. It set the standard that has been followed by almost all subsequent web browsers such as Internet Explorer, Mozilla Firefox, and Google Chrome.

ANOTHER DECISION

As if making one great decision was not enough, Berners-Lee, together with the management at CERN, then went on to make another one. In 1993, all the software written by Berners-Lee concerning the World Wide Web was placed in the public domain, enabling anybody who wanted to use it for any purpose they had in mind to do so without paying royalties to either

Berners-Lee or CERN. In a statement, CERN said:

> *CERN relinquishes all intellectual property rights to this code, both source and binary form, and permission is granted for anybody to use, duplicate, modify, or redistribute it.*

The statement also explained that CERN was making the code freely available to "further compatibility, common practices, and standards in networking and computer supported collaboration." Berners-Lee later wrote of this decision:

> *CERN's decision to make the Web foundations and protocols available on a royalty-free basis, and without additional impediments, was crucial to the Web's existence. Without this commitment, the enormous individual and corporate investment in Web technology simply would never have happened, and we wouldn't have the Web today.*

Berners-Lee was again being extremely modest about his own role in the decision and failed to mention that if commercial companies had been forced to pay royalties for using his code, he could potentially have become a very rich man indeed. But it was this act of selfless generosity, together with the development of the Mosaic browser, which really allowed the Web to flourish.

FREE TO EVERYBODY

In October 1994, Berners-Lee left CERN to found the World Wide Web Consortium (W3C) at the Massachusetts Institute of Technology to set industry standards for the further development of the Web and to ensure that access to it

FREEDOM OF THE CITY
Berners-Lee is awarded the honorary Freedom of the City of London in September 2014.

NeXT COMPUTER
Berners-Lee used a computer terminal like this one made by NeXT when developing the World Wide Web.

The contribution Berners-Lee has made to the development and spread of the internet through his invention of the World Wide Web has been extensively recognized over the years. In 2004, he was knighted for "services to the global development of the Internet" and he also took part in the opening ceremony of the London Olympics 2012. In a moment of calm during the excitement of the ceremony, Berners-Lee was seated at a NeXT computer terminal like the one he used to invent the World Wide Web.

As he was working for a European organization at the time, located in Switzerland and France, had a Belgian collaborator, and was using computer equipment made in America by the company set up by Steve Jobs after he left Apple in 1985, it is debatable just how much the World Wide Web can be considered a British contribution to international culture.

stays free to everybody. He remains the director of W3C and in 2009 also set up the World Wide Web Foundation, which describes itself as being "a nonprofit organization devoted to achieving a world in which all people can use the Web to communicate, collaborate, and innovate freely, building bridges across the divides that threaten our shared future."

One of the recent projects of the foundation is the development of the Web Index, which measures the growth of the Web in countries around the world and ranks them according to how open and inclusive they are in allowing free access to information.

But, minor quibbles aside, the decisions that led to the development of the World Wide Web and making it freely available to everybody must surely be among the greatest made in the history of information technology, on a level with the inventions of writing and the printing press. The potential of the internet is still being explored, but there can be little doubt that the work done by Tim Berners-Lee will continue to play a part in its future development, which, if he has anything to do with it, will no doubt be made freely available to us all.

The software written by Berners-Lee concerning the World Wide Web was made freely available to everyone. This act of selfless generosity allowed the Web to flourish.

APPLE RE-EMPLOYS STEVE JOBS

1996

Circumstances: After being forced out of the company he founded, Steve Jobs is offered an opportunity to return

Protagonists: Steve Jobs and other past and present employees of Apple

Consequences: The struggling computer company was transformed into the market leader in consumer electronics

Steve Jobs, who died in October 2011 aged fifty-six after suffering from pancreatic cancer for a number of years, set up Apple in his garage at the age of twenty-one along with his old school friend Steve Wozniak, and Ronald Wayne. Wayne was twenty years older than Jobs and described his role in the fledgling company as being one of "adult supervision." Wayne sold his 10 percent share in the company for $800 shortly after it was incorporated, which, with the benefit of hindsight, was not the best business deal he had ever made. In 2012, Apple's market capitalization (the value of one share multiplied by the number of shares issued) was $625 billion, making it the most valuable publicly traded company in the world and worth more than two and a half times the value of Microsoft.

The phenomenal success of the company can mostly be attributed to the diversification of its business. Apple had begun by concentrating solely on computers and software but broadened to producing innovative consumer electronics such as the iPod, iPhone, and, more recently, the Apple Watch. Its marketing strategy is also a key factor, making its products the must-have accessories even though,

> *"Jobs, exuding confidence, style, and sheer magnetism, was the antithesis of the fumbling Amelio [the CEO of Apple at the time] as he strode onstage. The return of Elvis would not have provoked a bigger sensation."*
>
> **—From a report on Macworld 1997, Steve Jobs's first public appearance after returning to Apple, by Jim Carlton of the *Wall Street Journal***

or perhaps because, they have often been more expensive than their competitors.

Much of the credit for this success goes to Jobs, who from the start was not heavily involved in the technical side of product development, but demonstrated an extraordinary ability to spot the commercial potential of new technology and recognize the importance of design.

STEVE JOBS

Jobs was described as inspirational and mercurial by some and abrasive and impossible to work with by others.

STEVE LEAVES...

The fortunes of Apple have not always been so bright, particularly in the mid 1980s when, despite having what was widely regarded as a superior product, the company began to fall behind Microsoft in the lucrative and expanding market in personal computers. In 1983, Jobs had hired John Sculley as chairman and chief executive of Apple, persuading him to move from Pepsi. Jobs remained in his role as operations director for the Macintosh division of the company, with a management style that could be inspirational at one moment and

> **The enthusiasm Steve Jobs brought to Apple's much publicized product launches was a key reason for the turnaround of the company.**

abusive at another. The working relationship between Jobs and Sculley broke down over the pricing policy of a new Macintosh model and was not helped by Jobs frequently describing Sculley behind his back as a "bozo" who was wrecking the company.

Tensions came to a head at a board meeting in May 1985 at which Jobs attempted to regain control of the company, but was outvoted and removed from his managerial position. He resigned a few weeks later and took five other disillusioned employees with him to start NeXT, which specialized in producing personal computer workstations for universities and research institutions and supplied the computer used by Tim Berners-Lee at CERN to invent the World Wide Web.

... AND COMES BACK AGAIN

In the early 1990s, the performance of Apple dipped badly as a result of the launch of a number of unsuccessful products. By 1994, Martin Spindler had replaced John Sculley as CEO of the company and had identified the outdated nature of the Macintosh platform and its operating system as being the main cause of the company's problems. He attempted to rectify this situation by effectively buying in new technology rather than developing it themselves, but his efforts yielded few results.

In February 1996, Spindler was replaced by Gil Amelio, who did not get

iPAD
Jobs launches the iPad, a personal tablet, in 2010. The product sold three hundred thousand units on its first day.

along very well with Jobs, but nevertheless was aware that the best solution to the problems at Apple, which had begun to lose significant amounts of money, was to

perhaps the changing circumstances of his personal life had made him less abrasive and, as the founder of Apple, he appears to have wanted the opportunity to revitalize the struggling company. A deal was struck between Amelio and Jobs in which Apple paid $427 million in shares for NeXT and Jobs was given a seat on the board of directors. It would prove to be a brilliant decision for Apple as a company, but not so great for Amelio personally because Jobs soon replaced him as CEO.

LEVI'S AND BLACK SWEATER

The iMac range of desktop computers was released in 1998 and sold well, marking the beginning of a change in fortunes that continued with other "i" products launched by Jobs himself in a series of highly publicized events at which he was always seen wearing his trademark pair of Levi's and black turtleneck sweater. The enthusiasm he brought to these demonstrations was certainly a key reason for the turnaround of the company, but what really did the trick was making things that a huge number of people wanted to buy. The company is riding high and as of 2016, is still the world's largest information technology company.

use the operating system that had been developed by NeXT. By the time Amelio made Jobs an offer to buy NeXT, Jobs was in his forties and married with children. The animation company Pixar, which he had bought in 1985, had also just had a major success with the movie *Toy Story*. He remained as driven and inspirational as he had ever been, but

THE GOOD FRIDAY AGREEMENT

1998

Circumstances: The long and difficult peace process in Northern Ireland

Protagonists: David Trimble, John Hume, Ian Paisley, Martin McGuinness, Gerry Adams, together with many political leaders from Britain, the Republic of Ireland, and America, and the long-suffering people of Northern Ireland

Consequences: The chance of peace

The signing of the agreement in Belfast on Good Friday, April 10, 1998, by representatives of the British and Irish governments, together with those from most of the main political parties of Northern Ireland, was a major milestone in a long and tortuous peace process. It was not actually a peace treaty because there was never any declaration of war in the first place, but it provided a framework through which it was hoped that the armed conflict, or the "Troubles" as it was commonly called, would finally come to an end.

One of the provisions set out in the final document was for a referendum vote for the people of Northern Ireland to accept or reject the terms set out in the agreement and a separate referendum for the Republic of Ireland to vote on the required amendments to the Irish constitution. Both were held on May 22 of that year and both results were strong endorsements of the agreement: in Northern Ireland 71 percent of those taking part voted in favor of accepting the agreement, while in the Republic an emphatic 94 percent voted to change the constitution, giving up the Republic's claim on the territory of Northern Ireland and extending the right to Irish citizenship to include the whole of Ireland.

The implementation of the Good Friday Agreement, then, was not only the result of decisions made by politicians in Britain, the Republic of Ireland, and Northern Ireland, but was also a collective decision made throughout Ireland, North and South, to, in the words of John Lennon, "give peace a chance."

THE TROUBLES

The conflict is often said to have begun in 1969, when serious rioting occurred in a number of cities in Northern Ireland resulting in the deployment of the British Army, and came to an end with the signing of the Good Friday Agreement. But the roots of the Troubles can be

BELFAST 1970
A loyalist banner
on a street off the
Shankill Road, scene
of numerous acts
of violence during
the thirty years
of the Troubles.

PARTITION

The direct cause of the Troubles was the everyday discrimination faced by the Catholic minority of Northern Ireland after the partition of Ireland in 1922, when the twenty-six counties of the mainly Catholic South became the Irish Free State and subsequently, in 1937, the Republic of Ireland. The six counties of the North, where Protestants made up about two-thirds of the population, remained part of Britain.

The purpose of this partition was to avoid a civil war threatened by armed volunteer forces loyal to the British Crown, who thought that, in a united Ireland, the Protestants of the North would face discrimination from the Catholic-dominated government in Dublin. The government of Northern Ireland allowed discriminatory practices to occur in the province and took measures to ensure that the Protestant majority would continue to dominate the political process. There were no actual laws in place to enforce the discrimination, but the inbuilt bias in the political system and in the police force led to a deep sense of resentment in the Catholic community.

traced back all the way to the sixteenth and seventeenth centuries, when Protestant immigrants from England and Scotland were given land formerly belonging to Irish Catholics in a process known as the Irish plantations.

While the Troubles may be formally over, the peace process is an ongoing one, occasionally interrupted by acts of violence, even if most of the paramilitary organizations on both sides have declared an end to the conflict. The British Army operation in the province was drastically scaled down after the Good Friday Agreement was signed and, in August 2007, also formally came to an end.

The Good Friday Agreement provided a framework through which it was hoped that the Troubles would finally come to an end.

THE OPPOSING SIDES

The array of political parties and paramilitary groups in Northern Ireland throughout the period of the Troubles makes an already complex situation even more confusing.

In a nutshell, the Protestant majority are described as unionists and loyalists because of their desire to remain part of the union of Britain and their loyalty to the British Crown. The two main unionist political parties involved in the peace process were the Ulster Unionist Party, led by David Trimble, and the Democratic Unionist Party, led by Ian Paisley, both of whom, prior to the peace process, had been fiercely against any dealings with anybody from the opposite side.

The republicans, almost exclusively made up of Catholics who wanted a united Ireland, leading to them also being known as nationalists, were represented by the moderate Social Democratic and Labour Party, under the leadership of the highly respected John Hume, and Sinn Féin. This was the political wing of the Provisional Irish Republican Army, originally a splinter group of the IRA, which had fought against the British in the struggle for Irish independence. It became the most effective of the numerous paramilitary organizations in the province. The two key figures in Sinn Féin were Martin McGuinness and Gerry Adams, both of whom, it has been alleged, had at one time held senior positions in the IRA.

THE PROCESS

The peace process gradually emerged out of secret meetings held between representatives of the British government and Sinn Féin, beginning in the late 1980s, together with a growing perception on both sides that there could be no military solution to the Troubles. Over the years, these talks developed into a wider set of negotiations that included the Irish government as well and in which John Hume and David Trimble played significant roles. President Bill Clinton was also involved in getting the process underway, inviting Gerry Adams for what was considered a controversial visit to America in January 1994. The month before Adams's visit to America, the British prime minister, John Major, and Irish taoiseach (prime minister), Albert Reynolds, issued the joint Downing Street Declaration, which contained much of what would later form the Good Friday Agreement, in which both recognized the right of the people of Northern Ireland to self-determination (choose its own government) and the British government stated that it had "no selfish strategic or economic interest in Northern Ireland."

DIFFICULT NEGOTIATIONS

In April 1994, the IRA announced a three-day ceasefire, followed five months later by a "cessation of military operations," taken by most people, but not all, to mean a permanent ceasefire.

John Hume and David Trimble played significant roles in the negotiations, receiving in 1998 the joint award of the Nobel Peace Prize.

PEACE MAKERS
Former Irish taoiseach (prime minister)
Bertie Ahern and former British prime
minister Tony Blair, who helped to push
through the Good Friday Agreement.

This was followed by a ceasefire
announcement from the main loyalist
paramilitary organizations. A bitter
argument developed between the
politicians from both sides concerning
the withdrawal (decommissioning) of
arms by various paramilitaries, with
parties boycotting negotiations and
Ian Paisley regularly refusing to have
anything to do with just about everybody
else. The logjam was in part broken by
Clinton in appointing Senator George
Mitchell as the US Special Envoy, who
developed a set of principles to get the
peace process moving and to negotiate
the withdrawal of weapons. Clinton also
visited the province in November 1995
and spoke at a mass rally in Belfast in
which he described terrorists of both
sides as being "yesterday's men."

George Mitchell went on to chair the
formal peace negotiations and his great
patience and good sense were two of the
main reasons for the eventual success
of the talks. He had, for instance, to deal
with the apparently insurmountable
obstacle of some loyalist politicians,
including Paisley, refusing to join
negotiations before the IRA had
withdrawn its arms, while the IRA
refused to give up its weapons until the
talks had begun. Somehow Mitchell
managed to find a way through this
minefield and even continued with
the talks after the IRA returned to its
campaign of violence in 1996, setting off
huge bombs in the City of London and
the center of Manchester. The ceasefire
was reestablished in July 1997 and the
peace process was pushed along by
newly elected prime minister Tony Blair.

START OF PEACE

After two years of interrupted talks,
the Good Friday Agreement was finally
signed and, as well as setting out the
position of the British and Irish
governments, it contained clauses
concerning weapons decommissioning
and the setting up of a local assembly
in Northern Ireland.

At the first session of the assembly,
Ian Paisley was sworn in as first minister
with Martin McGuinness as his deputy,
while Tony Blair watched from the
gallery, apparently sitting a few seats
away from the senior leadership of
the IRA. In what must be the most
remarkable turnaround in the history of
Northern Irish politics, the eighty-one-
year-old Paisley not only embraced the
peace process, but got along very well
with his former archenemy McGuinness.
As Paisley put it, if he could put the past
behind him and look toward a brighter
future, then surely there was hope that
the hard-won peace could last.

FURTHER READING

Allen, Charles. *Ashoka: The Search for India's Lost Emperor*. Little Brown, 2012.

Ambrose, Stephen E. *Eisenhower: Soldier and President*. Simon and Schuster, 1990.

Armitage, David. *The Declaration of Independence: A Global History*. Harvard University Press, 2007.

Armstrong, Karen. *Buddha*. Weidenfeld and Nicolson, 2000.

Aughton, Peter. *Newton's Apple: Isaac Newton and the English Scientific Renaissance*. Weidenfeld and Nicolson, 2003.

Barker, Graeme. *The Agricultural Revolution in Prehistory: Why did Foragers become Farmers?* OUP, 2006.

Berners-Lee, Tim. *Weaving the Web: The Past, Present and Future of the World Wide Web by its Inventor*. Orion Business, 1999.

Brinkley, Douglas, and David R. Facey-Crowther. *The Atlantic Charter*. Palgrave Macmillan, 1994.

Brinkley, Douglas. *Mine Eyes Have Seen the Glory: The Life of Rosa Parks*. Weidenfeld and Nicolson, 2000.

Bryce, Trevor. *The Kingdom of the Hittites*. OUP, 2005.

Caesar, Julius. *The Civil War*. Penguin, 1967.

Columbus, Christopher. *The Four Voyages*. Penguin, 1969

Crackcraft, James. *The Revolution of Peter the Great*. Harvard University Press, 2003.

Cunningham, Noble E. *The Presidency of James Monroe*. University of Kansas, 1996.

Danziger, Danny, and John Gillingham. *1215: The Year of the Magna Carta*. Hodder and Stoughton, 2003.

Darwin, Charles. *The Voyage of the Beagle*. Penguin Books, 1989.

Davies, Hunter. *The Beatles: The Authorised Biography*. Heinemann, 1968.

Finkel, Caroline, *Osman's Dream: The Story of the Ottoman Empire 1300–1923*. John Murray, 2005.

Fischer, Louis. *The Life of Mahatma Gandhi*. Cape, 1951.

Freeman, Charles. *A New History of Early Christianity*. Yale University Press, 2009.

Fursenko, Aleksandr, and Timothy Naftali. *One Hell of a Gamble: Khrushchev, Castro, Kennedy and the Cuban Missile Crisis 1958–1964*. John Murray, 1997.

Gilbert, Martin. *Churchill: A Life*. William Heinemann, 1999.

Glassner, Jean-Jaques. *The Invention of Cuneiform: Writing in Sumer*. Johns Hopkins University Press, 2003.

Goldsworthy, Adrian. *Caesar: The Life of a Colossus*. Weidenfeld and Nicolson, 2006.

Goodwin, Doris Kearns. *Team of Rivals: The Political Genius of Abraham Lincoln*. Simon and Schuster, 2005.

Grayling, A. C. *Descartes: The Life of Réne Descartes and Its Place in His Times*. The Free Press, 2005.

Hibbert, Christopher. *The French Revolution*. Allen Lane, 1980.

Hobsbawm, Eric. *The Age of Revolution: Europe 1789–1848*. Weidenfeld and Nicolson, 1962.

Hogan, Michael J. *The Marshall Plan: America, Britain, and the Reconstruction of Western Europe, 1947–1952*. CUP, 1987.

Isaacson, Walter. *Steve Jobs*. Little Brown, 2011.

Jardine, Lisa. *Worldly Goods*. Macmillan, 1996

Johnson, R. W. *South Africa's Brave New World: The Beloved Country Since the End of Apartheid*. Allen Lane, 2009.

Keane, John. *The Life and Death of Democracy*. Simon and Schuster, 2009.

Kukla, Jon. *A Wilderness So Immense: The Louisiana Purchase and the Destiny of America*. Alfred A. Knopf, 2003.

Leuchtenburg, William E. *Franklin D. Roosevelt and the New Deal*. Harper and Row, 1963.

Man, John. *The Gutenberg Revolution: The Story of a Genius and an Invention that Changed the World*. Review, 2002.

Mandela, Nelson. *Long Walk to Freedom: The Autobiography of Nelson Mandela*. Little Brown, 1994.

Popham, Peter. *The Lady and the Peacock: The Life of Aung San Suu Kyi*. Rider, 2011.

Powell, Jonathan. *Great Hatred, Little Room: Making Peace in Northern Ireland*. The Bodley Head, 2008.

Roberts, Alice. *The Incredible Human Journey*. Bloomsbury, 2009.

Sale, Kirkpatrick. *The Conquest of Paradise: Christopher Columbus and the Columbian Legacy*. Hodder and Stoughton, 1991.

Scarre, Chris, ed. *The Human Past: World Prehistory and the Development of Human Societies*. Thames and Hudson, 2009.

Schickel, Richard. *D. W. Griffith*. Pavilion Books, 1984.

Shaw, Ian. *The Oxford History of Ancient Egypt*. OUP, 2000.

Sobel, Dava. *A More Perfect Heaven: How Copernicus Revolutionised the Cosmos*. Bloomsbury, 2011.

Stephenson, Paul. *Constantine: Unconquered Emperor, Christian Victor*. Quercus, 2009.

Strathern, Paul. *The Medici: Godfathers of the Renaissance*. Jonathan Cape, 2003.

Stringer, Chris, and Peter Andrews. *The Complete World of Human Evolution*. Thames and Hudson, 2005.

Tobin, James. *First to Fly: The Unlikely Triumph of Wilbur and Orville Wright*. John Murray, 2003.

Wald, Elijah. *Escaping the Delta: Robert Johnson and the Invention of the Blues*. Amistad, 2004.

Zamoyski, Adam. *Rites of Passage: The Fall of Napoleon and the Congress of Vienna*. HarperPress, 2007.

INDEX

PICTURE CREDITS

Key: t=top, b=bottom, l=left, r=right, c=center